أحمـ

Parties and Party Systems in the New Germany

Parties and Party Systems in the New Germany

Edited by
STEPHEN PADGETT
University of Essex

Dartmouth
Aldershot • Brookfield USA • Hong Kong • Singapore • Sydney

Published by
Dartmouth Publishing Company Limited
Gower House
Croft Road
Aldershot
Hants GU11 3HR
England

Dartmouth Publishing Company
Old Post Road
Brookfield
Vermont 05036
USA

A CIP catalogue record for this book is available from the British Library

Library of Congress Cataloging-in-Publication Data
Padgett, Stephen, 1951–
    Parties and party systems in the new Germany / Stephen Padgett.
       p. cm.
    ISBN 1-85521-237-4 : £30.00 ($55.95 (est.))
    1. Political parties–Germany.   2. Germany–Politics and
government–1990–   I. Title.
JN3972.A979P22   1993
324.243–dc20   93-2710
                                                       CIP

ISBN 1 85521 237 4

Printed and bound in Great Britain by
Hartnolls Limited, Bodmin, Cornwall

Contents

List of Figures

List of Tables

List of Abbreviations

AFA	Arbeitsgemeinschaft für Arbeitnehmerfragen
	Working Group for Employee Affairs
AL	Alternative Liste
	Alternative List
ASF	Arbeitsgemeinschaft Sozialdemokratischer Frauen
	Working Group of Socialist Women
BU90	Bündis 90
	Alliance 90
BFD	Bund Freier Demokraten
	Association of Free Democrats
CDU	Christlich-Demokratischen Union Deutschlands
	Christian Democratic Union of Germany
CSU	Christlich-Soziale Union
	Christian Social Union
DA	Demokratischer Aufbruch
	Democratic Awakening
DBD	Demokratische Bauernpartei Deutschlands
	Democratic Farmers' Party of Germany
DFB	Deutscher Frauen Bund
	German Womens' Federation (of the former GDR)
DFP	Deutsche Forumspartei
	German Forum Party
DGB	Deutscher Gewerkschaftsbund
	Federation of German Trade Unions
DJ	Demokratie Jetzt
	Democracy Now
DSU	Deutsche Soziale Union
	German Social Union
DVU	Deutsche Volksunion
	German People's Union
EWA	Erster weiblicher Aufruf
	First Women's Appeal

FDGB   Freier Deutscher Gewerkschaftsbund
                Confederation of Free German Trade Unions
FDP   Freie Demokratische Partei
                Free Democratic Party
FDJ   Freie Deutsche Jugend
                Free German Youth Organisation (of the former GDR)
FRG   Federal Republic of Germany
GAL   Grüne Alternative Liste
                Green Alternative List
GDR   German Democratic Republic
IFM   Initiative Frieden und Menschenrechte
                Initiative for Peace and Human Rights
IMF   International Monetary Fund
JUSO   Jungsozialisten
                Young Socialists
LDPD   Liberal-Demokratische Partei Deutschlands
                Liberal Democratic Party of Germany
LDP   Liberal-Demokratische Partei
                Liberal Democratic Party
NF   Neues Forum
                New Forum
NDPD   National-Demokratishe Partei Deutschlands
                National Democratic Party of Germany
PDS   Partei des Demokratischen Sozialismus
                Party of Democratic Socialism
SDP   Sozialdemokratische Partei in der DDR
                Social Democratic Party in the GDR
SED   Sozialistische Einheitspartei Deutschlands
                Socialist Unity Party of Germany
SPD   Sozialdemokratische Partei Deutschlands
                Social Democratic Party of Germany
SSW   Südschleswigschen Wählerverbandes
                South Schleswig Union of Voters
Stasi   Ministerium für Staatssicherheit
                Ministry for State Security
UFV   Unabhangiger Frauen Verband
                Independent Women's Association

Notes on Contributors

William M. Chandler is Professor of Political Science at McMaster University. He has published widely on political parties in Germany and Canada, party system transformation, public policy, and federalism.

Mike Dennis is Senior Lecturer in the School of Humanities and Social Sciences, University of Wolverhampton. He is the author of *German Democratic Republic: Politics, Economics and Society* (1988), and of a forthcoming book *Socio-economic Modernisation in East Germany: From Honecker to Kohl*. He has written extensively on East Germany and has edited a special GDR issue of the journal *East Central Europe*.

Eva Kolinsky is Professor and Director of the Centre for Modern German Studies at Keele University. She has published extensively on contemporary German politics, political culture, and women in politics and society. Her books include *Parties, Opposition and Society in West Germany* (1984), *Women in West Germany: Life Work and Politics* (1989), and (as editor) *Opposition in West Germany* (1987), *The Greens in West Germany* (1989), *Political Culture in France and West Germany* (1991) and *The Federal Republic of Germany: End of an Era* (1991). She is co-editor of *German Politics*, editor of the Berg series, *German Studies*.

Stephen Padgett is Jean Monnet Lecturer in European Politics, University of Essex. He has written widely on the German Social Democratic Party and on political economy and policy-making in the Federal Republic. He is the co-author of *Political Parties and Elections in West Germany* (1986), and *A History of Social Democracy in Post War Europe* (1991), and co-editor of *Developments in German Politics* (1992). He is also co-editor of the journal *German Politics*.

Geoffrey K. Roberts is Reader in Government, University of Manchester. He is the author of various books and articles on political parties and elections in Germany, and on the unification process. He has written extensively on the Free Democratic Party. Formerly Chairman of the Association for the Study of German Politics, he is currently a member of an international research group on 'Stability and Democracy in Eastern Europe'.

Stephen J. Silvia is Assistant Professor at the American University, Washington DC. In 1993 he was a Visiting Scholar at the Free University of Berlin. His recent publications include articles on the German Social Democratic Party in Eastern Germany (*West European Politics*, and the labour movement and social democracy in Germany (*International Journal of Political Economy.*

Gordon Smith is Professor of Government, London School of Economics. He has written extensively on both comparative European and German politics. His publications include *Politics in Western Europe* (1989), *Democracy in Western Germany* (1986), and (as co-editor) *Developments in German Politics* (1992) He is co-editor of two journals, *West European Politics*, and *German Politics.*

Roland Sturm is Professor of Political Science, Tübingen University. He has published a wide range of books and articles on German and European politics. Among his most recent publications are *Haushaltspolitik in westlichen Demokratien* (1989), *Großbritannien* (1991), *Die Industriepolitik der Bundesländer und die Europäische Integration* (1991) and *Staatsverschuldung* (1992),

Hans-Joachim Veen is Director of Political Consultation and Research at the Konrad-Adenauer-Stiftung, Sankt Augustin, and Lecturer at Mainz University. He is the author of numerous books and articles on political parties and electoral behaviour. His recent publications include (as editor) *From Brezhnev to Gorbachev: Domestic Affairs and Soviet Foreign Policy* (1987), (as co-author) *Wählerverhalten im Wandel: Bestimmungsgründe, gesellschaftliche Trends, Forschungsanwendungen am Beispiel der Bundestagswahl 1987* (1987), and (as co-author) *Die Grünen zu Beginn der neunziger Jahre, Profil und Defizite einer fast etablierten Partei* (1992).

Series Foreword

The Association for the Study of German Politics (ASGP) was established to encourage teaching and research in the politics and society of the German-speaking countries. Since its formation in 1974, the ASGP has brought together academics from a variety of disciplines – politics, languages, history, economics and other social sciences – who, along with others with practical and personal interests, are concerned with contemporary developments in these countries. Through its conferences, research seminars, and its journal *German Politics*, the ASGP has proved itself to be an invaluable forum for discussion and research. This series represents a significant extension of ASGP activities. The Association believes that its wide range of expertise will ensure that the series will be of value to teachers, students, and those involved in policy and research, providing them with readily accessible material on current issues.

Preface

This book is the third in the ASGP series of studies of key aspects of German politics. It contains the work of some of the leading members of the Association, alongside contributions by eminent colleagues in Germany and North America. The Association has always placed great value on its international connections and looks forward to further collaboration in the future.

Although unification has not brought about a major upheaval in the structure of the German party system, none of the parties has escaped its effects. The objective of the book is to evaluate the impact of unification both on the parties and on the dynamics of the party system. The underlying question, outlined in the Introduction, concerns the capacity of 'party democracy' for contributing to the political integration of the two parts of Germany and the consolidation of the new German polity.

In view of the rapid political change in Germany since unification, it has inevitably been necessary to call upon contributors to update their material during the preparation of this volume. As editor, I would like to thank them for their patient cooperation in the face of my requests.

Stephen Padgett
Department of Government
University of Essex

Introduction: Party Democracy in the New Germany

Stephen Padgett

Political parties have been so closely identified with liberal democracy that it is almost impossible to conceive of the one without the other. The emergence and development of party democracy is entwined with that of the liberal democratic order to such an extent that the centrality of the party in liberal democracy is more or less taken for granted. Parties have also been seen as key actors in the formation of new polities, and the consolidation of the new German polity may thus be seen as conditional upon the vitality of the parties, and the cohesion and stability of the party system. It is to these questions that the present volume is addressed.

In recent years, however, conceptions of party democracy have been subject to a re-evaluation. In the context of post-industrial society, it has been argued, political parties demonstrate a much reduced capacity to fulfil the functions ascribed to them in the classical models of party democracy. Indeed, they have been seen to relinquish some of those roles to other political forms. The vocation of parties in liberal democracies has thus become steadily less compelling. An assessment of the capacity of party formations for contributing to the consolidation of the new German polity should therefore begin with a review of the changing role of parties in liberal democracies.

The Classical Model of Party Democracy

The primary role of parties as agents of *political integration* was emphasized in the seminal work of Lipset and Rokkan (1967). Modern party systems in Western Europe derived from patterns of social cleavages – economic religious, cultural, regional, linguistic – which dated back to their origins. Party formations sprang from these cleavages, subsequently

1

serving to manage and resolve the conflicts which they generated. Their capacity to do so stemmed from bonds of identification between parties and collective groups of citizens, enabling them to integrate social groups into the broader community or nation. Although these social groups progressively lost their sharpness of definition, (especially in the post-war era) the party systems to which they gave rise proved remarkably persistent (Rose and Urwin, 1970: 295). This has been explained in terms of enduring patterns of psychological partisanship at the individual level, which offset the weakening of group-based party loyalties. Thus parties continued to mobilize and structure the electorate in relatively stable blocs, transforming potential social conflict into electoral competition, and providing governments with a secure foundation of support.

Closely related to the integration function of political parties was a second role; providing *democratic mediation between state and society.*

> Parties reflected the public will and provided the crucial linkage between the citizenry and the state. They did so as mass organisations, for it was as mass organisations that they belonged to the society from which they emanated. (Mair, 1990: 2)

Indeed they may be said to have played an important role in the formation of the political will of the people, a role ascribed to the parties in the Basic Law of the Federal Republic. Their ability to fulfil this role depended on the organic relationship between parties and society which stemmed from their representative character. Parties represented, or at least reflected (Sartori, 1968: 1–25), the broad group formations which constituted society.

The group-based character of parties enabled them to fulfil a third function: *the articulation and ordering of interests.* Parties expressed the interests of the groups which they represented, but they also served to mediate and reconcile competing group demands.

> Parties have an expressive function; they develop a rhetoric for the translation of contrasts in the social and the cultural structure into demands and pressures for action or inaction. But they also have instrumental and representative functions: they force the spokesmen for the many contrasting interests and outlooks to strike bargains, to stagger demands, and to aggregate pressures. (Lipset and Rokkan, 1967: 5)

An essential element in the function of interest articulation was its indirectness. Parties were not simply systems for the imposition of group demands upon government. Rather, they served to filter the demands arising in society, shaping them into an overarching 'national interest'. In the filtering process, demands were frequently moderated to render them mutually compatible and reconcilable with the limited capacity of the state to deliver. Parties thus performed an important 'buffer function' between interest-related or popular demands, on the one hand, and government and the state on the other.

A fourth role of parties in liberal democracies, closely related to the above, was that of *policy formulation*. The demands arising in society were formulated into party programmes and election manifestoes, which in the classical model of party democracy, set the agenda for the party in government. Whilst satisfying party-related interests, programmes had to be sufficiently broad to command wide electoral support, an imperative which militates against the 'egotism' of narrow group interests.

Fifth, parties serve to *coordinate relations between executive and legislature*. 'Parties emerged as *the* institutions capable of asserting coordination and control over the authoritative decision-making process in modern mass democracies' (Flanagan and Dalton, 1984: 14–15). *Elite recruitment* is the sixth function of political parties in the classical model of party democracy. It is from the ranks of political parties that national leaders and elected office-holders are usually drawn.

The Decline of Party Democracy

The apex of party democracy is encapsulated in Neumann's concept of the mass party, or the *party of social integration*. Parties of individual representation, he argued, had given way to parties representing broad social formations, 'assuring the individual's share in society and incorporating him into the community' (Neumann, 1956: 405). This new type of party made very extensive claims on the loyalty of its adherents, exerting an increasing influence over the individual's daily life. Parties of social integration had steadily enlarged their scope and power within the political community.

> The party in modern mass democracies has generally taken on an ever increasing area of commitments and responsibilities. This is ... but the natural consequence of the extension of the public domain and the constantly changing governmental functions in a reintegrated twentieth century. (Neumann, 1956: 405)

Neumann's models for the modern mass party were the European Socialist and Christian Democratic parties which were based on the social ties of class or religion.

The decline of these social collectivities in the post-war era led Kirchheimer to develop his very influential concept of the *Volkspartei* (Kirchheimer, 1966: 177–200). Ideologically eclectic and socially diverse, the evolution of the *Volkspartei* was geared to electoral rather than social integration. Kirchheimer took a sanguine view of the potential of the *Volkspartei* for the electoral integration of diverse social groups, believing that it would be possible to reconcile diverse interests or to transcend social diversity in an appeal to overarching national interests (Kirchheimer, 1966: 186). On the other hand, he argued that the remoteness of these parties from society had progressively reduced the capacity of the parties to perform their social functions: '… the political party's role in Western industrial society today is more limited than would appear from its position of formal pre-eminence' (Kirchheimer, 1966: 200).

Contemporaneous with Kirchheimer's concept of the *Volkspartei* was the social theory of Mancur Olsen, which emphasized the individualization and atomization of politics in modern society. Olsen argued that the pursuit of individual interest had progressively replaced collective action as the dominant form of political behaviour. He pointed to the incompatibility between the individualist orientation towards personal achievement and welfare and the ethos of collective action out of which mass parties had grown.

> If the members of a large group rationally seek to maximise their personal welfare they will not act to advance their common or group objectives. (Olsen, 1965: 2)

Olsen's theory of the breakdown of collective social action contributes to an explanation of the transformation from mass party to *Volkspartei*. However, it also indicates a potential weakness of the latter, since the proliferation of competing interests inevitably strains the capacity of the *Volkspartei* for representation.

The *Volkspartei* model was an ideal type, to which no party fully corresponded, yet it captured a general trend in the evolution of large parties in Western European democracies. Generally these parties vindicated Kirchheimer's confidence in their capacity for structuring the electorate and maintaining a stable partisan base. From the 1970s, however, the electoral dominance of *Volksparteien*, and their role as pillars of party systems was challenged on a number of fronts. Increasing levels of electoral volatility (Pedersen, 1979), indications of electoral dealignment (Dalton, Flanagan and Beck, 1984), declining levels of partisan identification (Crewe, 1985) and party system fragmentation (Wolinetz 1979) led to a more sceptical assessment of the capacity of the *Volkspartei* for electoral integration.

As Kirchheimer predicted, the severance of the parties from their social origins has appeared to prejudice their capacity for performing some of the other functions ascribed to parties in the classical models of party democracy (Flanagan and Dalton, 1984). Amorphous in composition, professionalized in terms of leadership and organization, parties are now much less clearly representative of recognizable social formations. The organic ties between parties and society have been displaced by the client relationship, weakening their capacity for mediating between society and the state, and for managing social conflict. Social change, and changes in the issue environment have also contributed to the loss of party control over social conflict. Increasingly differentiated patterns of social stratification mean that the 'old' issues of economic distribution are more diffuse and complex. Moreover, distributional issues are now overlaid by a new issue dimension relating to the quality of life and personal fulfilment. These conflicts are difficult to order on the traditional left–right axis within which *Volksparteien*, despite their social and ideological openness, continued to operate.

The function of interest articulation is one which parties have increasingly come to share with interest organizations in the corporatist domain. The intensification of corporatist relations has led to the increasing reliance of organized interests upon quasi-institutional or informal relations with government, marginalizing the party as a focal point of interest group activity. Moreover, alternative forms of interest articulation – citizens' initiative groups and new social movements – have proved very difficult for the parties to incorporate. In policy formulation, too, the role of parties has declined. The social and political diversity of party electorates and the complexity of the issue environment militiate increasingly against the projection of sharply defined policy programmes. With the decline of the programmatic party, a steady process of policy convergence can be detected, with policy profiles becoming less distinctive. Research has given grounds for a profound scepticism over the agenda-setting function or impact of party programmes on government policy. With the increasing scope and intensity of government intervention, and the corresponding technical complexity of its activities, the focus of policy-making has shifted towards the technocratic–bureaucratic sphere. These tendencies have also reduced the capacity of parties for coordination or control between executive and legislature. Of the functions of the party in the classical model of liberal democracy only that of élite recruitment has remained untouched.

Parties in the New German Polity

It is against the background of these degenerative trends in party democracy that the performance of the party system in the Federal Republic will now be evaluated. This will provide the basis for a consideration of the impact which unification has had upon the parties and party system, and an assessment of the potential of the parties for the consolidation of the new German polity. The evaluation of party performance will take as its yardstick the functions ascribed to parties in the classical models of party democracy.

Social and Political Integration

Social cleavages have been less pronounced in the Federal Republic than in other Western European countries. Traditional class networks were undermined by the social revolution which accompanied National Socialism and were eroded further by demographic movements associated with the postwar influx of refugees from the East. Moreover, the intensity of economic development in West Germany accelerated the dissolution of the bonds that linked individuals to group and community networks (Dalton, 1989: 101). Thus, although residual social groups remained bound to the sociocultural milieux of class and religion, society as a whole displayed a marked homogeneity. Social cohesion and consensus were the hallmarks of West German society, and this was reflected in the dynamics of a party system geared to the politics of centrality (Smith, 1976: 387–407).

Whilst eroding traditional social formations, however, the forces of socioeconomic modernity have created new patterns of social diversity, characteristic of post-industrial society. A number of dimensions of societal diversification have been identified in the German context: different levels of educational attainment and correspondingly divergent career trajectories (Alber, 1991: 33–4); generational differentiation (Baker *et al.*, 1981); differences in access to welfare resources (Offe, 1991: 124–46); and the diversification of lifestyles (Beck, 1987: 340–55). In short, whilst technological and economic change has created new opportunities for some sections of society, other sections have become economically marginalized, or socially and culturally disoriented. (Betz, 1991: 17). Thus post-industrial society is marked by a tendency towards social differentiation which might have been expected to produce fragmentation in politics and the party system.

There is general agreement that the social cleavages associated with post-industrial society have failed to produce new political alignments, and that their impact upon the structure of the party system has been rather limited. Indeed it has been argued that, in the German context, the trend towards post-industrialization has been weak, and that society continues to reflect the classical industrial axis. 'Generally...the nexus of family, market, and welfare state remains within the logic of the traditional industrial order' (Esping-Andersen, 1991: 164).

Nevertheless, from the early 1980s the Federal Republic displayed quite pronounced patterns of electoral dealignment, reflecting a weakening in the social foundations of electoral behaviour and a decline in the strength of party affiliation amongst voters. As Padgett shows in Chapter 1 of this volume, these tendencies resulted in an increase in electoral volatility, falling levels of voter participation, and a decline in the *Volkspartei* share of the electorate. The effects of electoral dealignment have been a loosening up of the party system and an elongation of the spectrum of parties in the system to include the New Left and the radical Right.

Against this evidence of party system change, however, there is countervailing evidence of stability. Smith argues in Chapter 3 that the core of the party system remains intact, and that destabilizing change is confined to the margins of the system. Although in the German context the erosion of the cleavage structures identified by Lipset and Rokkan was particularly pronounced, the core parties in the system have successfully maintained their hold upon the electorate. Smith accounts for this paradox with reference to the 'organizational resources' of the parties. In particular, it is their access to state finance, and their capacity for strategic flexibility which has enabled them to maintain their dominance in the face of social change and despite the upheavals associated with unification.

The impact of social change, and the balance between persistence and change in the German party system, has preoccupied scholars for a decade, but the debate has yet to provide a definitive answer. The conclusion offered by this volume is that whilst the core composition of the party system remains but little altered, the capacity of the *Volksparteien* for electoral mobilization and integration has been eroded. Moreover, whilst unification has not radically reshaped the party system, it will test the cohesion of the system and tax further the integrative capacity of the parties. These themes are taken up by Chandler, Roberts and Silvia in Part Two.

Post-unification Germany contains new dimensions of social differentiation. The first and most obvious dimension is between the 'haves' in the West and the 'have nots' East of the Elbe. In terms of wage levels, employment, labour-market skills, welfare entitlements and socio-cultural sophistication, a vast gulf separates the two parts of Germany. Granted political citizenship in the Federal Republic, East Germans are nevertheless excluded from the 'economic democracy of consumers' which they perceive in the West. Second, East German society itself contains the potential for acute social differentiation. Under state socialism, the GDR resembled a

declassed society in which the means of economic advancement was proximity to the ruling party. With its dissolution, the social structure here is in
a state of flux. Some observers have pointed to a syndrome of 'lifeboat
economics' in which 'everyone is looking for an individual way to escape'
from the economic insecurity of the new German *Länder*. The individualization and atomization of society, they argue, militates against the logic of
institutionalized collective action upon which party democracy rests (Offe,
1992). Third, the influx of migrants from the new German *Länder*,
(*Ubersiedler*), along with ethnic Germans from Eastern Europe (*Aussiedler*),
has created new social cleavages in the West. These are intensified by the
economic pressures arising out of the costs of unification.

Composed largely of parties with their origins and foundations in the
West, the party system in the new *Länder* lacks organic social roots. Parties
do not 'belong' to society in the sense in which they do in the classical
model of party democracy. The alien relationship between party system and
society is reflected in the social composition of party support in the East.
There is little discernible resemblance between patterns of party support
and the historic cleavages identified in the Lipset and Rokkan model. In
short, the organic relationship between social structures and party formations is absent in the new German *Länder*. As Veen argues in Chapter 2, the
capacity of the party system for social and political integration will depend
on the consolidation of those patterns of partisanship which emerged in the
elections of 1990.

Mediation Between Society and the State

In the aftermath of the Third Reich, parties were ascribed a privileged
status in the Federal Republic. The promotion of party democracy was a
central preoccupation in the framing of the Basic Law and the role of the
parties as intermediaries between society and the state is formally set out in
Article 21: 'The political parties shall participate in the forming of the
political will of the people'. Parties were identified as the special instrument of democracy and were granted powers of patronage which enabled
them to penetrate state institutions (Dyson, 1973: 84). State financing subsequently served to consolidate the relationship between parties and the
state. The intensity of the relationship led some observers to refer to 'the
party state'.

The party state is manifested most strikingly in the axis between the
parties and the bureaucracy. The relationship is symbiotic. Party affiliates
colonize public administration; conversely, civil servants constitute a considerably overproportional fraction of party membership (Paterson and
Southern, 1991: 222–3), and the strength of their numbers increases sharply

amongst elected representatives in the federal and state parliaments. Party life is pervaded by an administrative culture which places a premium on objectivity and expertise, especially in the context of Bundestag and Landtag committees. The participation here of civil servants from government ministries tightens the nexus between parties and the bureaucracy, giving 'a kind of institutional logic to party politics'. De-emphasizing ideology and partisanship, parties become involved as specialist actors in the policy process (Bulmer, 1989: 34–5). The result has been a depoliticization of the interface between party and state.

The corollary of the institutionalization of party–state relations in the Federal Republic is a rather distant, and essentially inorganic, relationship between the parties and society. Of all the Western European parties, the CDU–CSU and SPD distanced themselves furthest from the traditional form of the mass party and came closest to Kirchheimer's ideal type. Indeed, they consciously shunned the 'tribal politics' of the traditional mass party. To be sure, both *Volksparteien* had roots in the traditional sociocultural milieux, but almost from the outset of the Federal Republic, both downplayed the social legacy of their origins. In adopting the *Volkspartei* mode, they conformed to Kirchheimer's characteriziation of quasi-official structures, relatively remote from society.

The relatively weak social foundations of the *Volksparteien* were buttressed, however, by their identification with a pervasive consensus with which broad sections of society could identify. The most enduring themes of this overarching consensus were the unconditional identification of the Federal Republic with the West, the social market economy, monetary stability, and anti-communism. The *Volksparteien* were very successful in articulating these themes, and in reaffirming consensus values in the face of challenges from the radical Right and the new Left. They represented the focal point of a consensus which became synonymous with the success of the institutional and socioeconomic order of the Federal Republic. It was no accident that the steady rise of the *Volkspartei* vote coincided with the consolidation, and perfection, of *Modell Deutschland*.

The close identification of the *Volksparteien* with the political consensus of the West German model served to offset the effects of their remoteness from society in other respects. Although both major parties had a membership approaching one million, they were dominated by narrow élites controlling large bureaucratic machines. Members had only very limited opportunities to participate in internal party life. This participation deficit was compounded by a 'representation gap'. Dominated by civil servants and interest group functionaries, the composition of the major parties diverged very markedly from the social profile of the population. Reflecting both the institutionalization of the party politics in the state apparatus, and the pronounced *Volkspartei* character of the parties, these effects led some observers to point to a 'legitimation crisis' in the party system (Habermas, 1975; Dittberner and Ebbighausen, 1973).

Although this critique was at odds with the high level of *Volkspartei* support in the 1970s, it received some retrospective corroboration in the following decade. The limited opportunities for participation in the established parties led to the growth of political activity outside the parties in the form of *Bürgerinitiativen* (citizens' initiative groups). Small in size, uncoordinated and diverse in character, these groups represented the antithesis of *Volkspartei* politics and were the forerunners of the Green Party which broke into the previously frozen federal party system in 1983.

This challenge to the organizational form of the *Volkspartei* coincided with the erosion of the consensus around *Modell Deutschland*. The fissure between the Old Politics represented by the established parties and the New Politics orientation of the Greens, was compounded by a questioning of the orthodoxies of the social market formula. The *Wendepolitik* of the incoming Kohl government in 1982 was in large part rhetorical, but it was emblematic of a breach with the previous Social Liberal era. It also introduced a policy agenda with some potential for social conflict. The subsequent failure of the Kohl government to meet the policy challenges which it had set itself, and the inability of the opposition Social Democrats to offer constructive alternatives led to an ill-defined sense of disillusionment with the established parties. For parties with shallow social roots, the erosion of a supportive consensus and perceptions of policy failure inevitably have far-reaching implications. As will become apparent from the chapters by Chandler, Roberts and Silvia in Part Two, all the major parties have suffered from a loss of dynamism and internal cohesion.

Volkspartei malaise was manifested in an ossification of internal party life, falling membership, declining electoral performance and a weakening in partisan identification. Survey data shows that whereas in 1972 55 per cent of the electorate reported very strong or strong party affiliations, by 1991 the level of strong partisanship had declined to 35 per cent (Dalton, 1992: 73). The erosion of partisanship was compounded by the fall-out from a series of scandals concerning irregular practices in the financing and conduct of the parties. Widespread perceptions of a decline in the ethical and moral standards of party politics were reflected in a syndrome of *Parteienentfremdung* (alienation from the parties). Germans now express less confidence in their political parties than in any other democratic institutions (Stöss, 1990).

In the Eastern *Länder*, the parties stand in a peculiarly inorganic relationship to society. As Dennis shows in Chapter 8, there was relatively little continuity between the forces which led the democratic revolution in the

GDR and the parties which comprised the party system after the election of 1990. The only strands of continuity are the organizational foundations of the CDU and FDP in the block parties of the old regime, and the legacy of Social Democracy in Eastern Germany before 1933. Neither of these relationships provides a formula for 'organic bonding' between the parties and society. On the one hand the association of the centre right parties with the GDR has very strong negative connotations. On the other, it was clear from the pattern of SPD support in the elections of 1990 that after half a century of suppression, the cultural roots of Social Democracy in Eastern Germany have withered.

The capacity of the parties for forging new bonds with citizens in the East is reduced by the location of their centres of gravity in the West. Since the merger of sister parties in the two parts of Germany in 1990, indigenous party activity is confined to the local and *Land* levels. The federal system provides a focus for high-profile party activity in the East. However, the five new *Land* parties are heavily reliant on the organizational and leadership resources of their Western counterparts. Three out of five *Land* premiers are Westerners, as are a substantial number of cabinet members and members of *Land* parliaments. Ironically, as Sturm shows in Chapter 4, Western candidates in the *Land* elections of October 1990 were generally better known (and respected) than indigenous aspirants. The prominence of Westerners in the parties of the new *Länder* is likely to inhibit the bonding process.

If the level of participation is taken to be an indication of the strength of bonds between party and society, then early indications are inauspicious. Although political participation was a major theme of opposition groups under the GDR regime, the participatory impetus has declined since unification. The relapse into the passivity and the retreat into the private sphere is characteristic of the political culture of the totalitarian regime. It reflects also the disappointed expectations of those who identified democracy with affluence. As Kolinsky shows in Chapter 9, the cultural underpinnings of party democracy are missing in the East. The fragility of the relationship between parties and society is evident from the steady decline of party membership after the initial influx. It is reflected also in an unusually low level of party identification in the new *Länder*.

Interest Articulation

The Federal Republic possesses a very highly developed system of organized interests which spans the private economic sectors, the social arena and the public policy sphere. Interest representation extends rather further than in most liberal democratic countries. Interest groups perceive themselves as participants in the formulation of public policy, and the state frequently recognizes their participation as legitimate. It is not uncommon for public functions to be delegated by the state to private interest organizations. Political parties are closely bound to these interlocking networks of interest representation through repeated interaction in the policy process and through formal or informal ties between the parties and 'related' interests. At the macro-level, corporatist relations are relatively weak, due to the decentralized structure of the peak organizations of both business and labour. It is at the sectoral level where the networks of democratic corporatism are at their most dense, and their operation here provides an insight into the dynamics of party–state relations outlined in the previous section.

The articulation of interests in the policy process is structured upon a triple axis between ministerial bureaucracy, organized interests and the parties. First, a close relationship of consultation and representation normally exists between a ministry and those organized interests relevant to its policy sector. Ministers, state secretaries and officials are normally sympathetic to sectoral interests, sometimes to the point of acting as their advocates. Second, the party–state axis is mediated by the minister, and runs between ministry officials (often party affiliates) and party policy experts. The third line in the triangle runs between policy experts and sectoral interest representatives in the parties, and interest group officials. This pattern of interaction is fostered by the character of the Federal Parliament. Legislation is shaped by highly influential committees which bring together the three sets of actors: civil servants, sectoral representatives and party policy specialists. Parties are not pivotal in this triangular relationship. The predominant axis may be said to be that between ministerial officials and sectoral interests. However, parties have not been marginalized in the networks of democratic corporatism.

Relations between parties and organized interests are too extensive and complex to elaborate fully here. Nevertheless it is possible to draw some general conclusions and point to some particular examples. In general, the *Volkspartei* character of the German parties means that the fit between parties and economic interests is not as close as in some other countries (Paterson and Southern, 1991: 242). *Volksparteien* must bundle together and reconcile the interests of a broad spectrum of voters. For example, the Christian Democrats' electoral constituency in the Catholic working class serves to offset its affinities to industry and business. The labour wing of the CDU is institutionalized in the form of the social committees, which vie for intraparty influence with the *Wirtschaftsrat* representing industry and business. The relationship between the Social Democrats and organized labour is an ambiguous one. Although there are no formal ties, informal relations are strong, but even these can be subordinated to wider political considerations. Thus although relations between parties and economic interests are pervasive, they are generally rather diffuse.

There are, however, some striking examples of the colonization of parties by sectoral interests. The Deutsche Bauenverband (German Farmers Union) has been able to exploit the electoral potential of the farmers' lobby to secure its influence in both the CDU–CSU and the FDP. The party axis reinforces the client relationship between the Farmers' Union and the Ministry of Agriculture, and is reflected in the very successful defence of farmers' interests within the Common Agricultural Policy of the European Community. The FDP represents the independent professions, and is sometimes referred to as the party of the three As – *Ärtze* (doctors); *Änwalte* (lawyers) and *Äpotheker* (pharmacists). Its influence was evident in the reform of health care provision and financing in the 1980s. Small and medium-sized business is also very influential in the FDP, reflected in the generous subsidization of those sectors where small business predominates. The FDP's almost institutionalized role in coalition governments make it a very attractive magnet for interest group activity.

The prevalence of coalition government in the Federal Republic means that the range of interests with access to decision-making through the parties is very broad. Policy formulation through government is often characterized by intense bargaining between parties and intraparty factions with ties to a multiplicity of interests. Whilst this reinforces the consensual orientation of German policy-making, it can lead to policy stalemates and second-best solutions. The experience of a variety of sectors in the 1980s shows how coalitions of vested interests can block radical policy re-orientation or modernizing change (Webber, 1992). The intensity of electoral competition in the Federal Republic also makes parties reluctant to jeopardize the support of key blocks of voters by overriding group interests. Moreover, the imperative of maintaining coalition or internal party equilibrium also militates against radical change. Thus the same characteristics which make the German party system efficient at articulating and aggregating sectional interests may tend to produce sub-optimal policy outcomes.

The dense network of organizational activity comprising civil society is missing from the new German *Länder*. Under the GDR regime virtually all forms of socioeconomic organization were state subordinates. Only the churches were autonomous and even they were compromised by the terms of their coexistence with the state. The precondition for democratization is therefore the emergence of a democratic civil society. 'The democratisation of a society implies its collectivisation; virtually all interests that are in any way represented are put forward by formally organised structures for collective action' (Offe, 1992). The prevailing ethos of 'lifeboat economics', however, is antithetic to the logic of collective action, and organized interest articulation is only weakly developed in the new *Länder*.

Its most extensive development is to be found in the labour movement, but the organizational apparatus is that of the West German trade unions. Recruitment was exceptionally strong, and by December 1990 East German trade union membership stood at around four million. However, membership motivations tend to be instrumental, and there is already evidence of a tension between the high expectations of economic improvement amongst the membership, and the limited capacity of the unions to deliver (Fichter, 1991: 31–3). The resultant frustrations overspill institutional channels, giving rise to direct action in the form, for example, of demonstrations against the privatization policy of the *Treuhandanstalt* (Trustee Authority responsible for the privatization of the East German economy).

The capacity of the parties in the new *Länder* to articulate specifically Eastern interests is inhibited by their subordination to the Bonn party system. Most distributional issues precipitate a cleavage in East–West interests which an all-German party system can only articulate at the cost of intraparty conflict. From the beginning of the unification process, the articulation of demands in the East has deviated sharply from the liberal democratic model. Unmediated by organized interests or parties, insistent populist demands have been brought to bear upon government – for the acceleration of unification, for favourable exchange rates in currency unon, for transfer payments to support labour markets and welfare provisions, and for wage convergence. Political logic and the threat of East–West migration has induced the government to grant the legitimacy of these demands.

In the west the intensification of distributional conflict which accompanied unification places the institutional and normative foundations of democratic corporatism under strain. The social market economy – the solvent in which conflict is normally dissolved – is now in question as trade unions, churches and private economic interests place their own interpretations on its precepts. This situation is mirrored in the party system, with interparty conflict over the balance between privatization and interventionism in the East and over the distribution of tax burdens and subsidy cuts in the West.

Policy Formulation

The role of political parties in the Federal Republic in formulating policy and putting the central themes of their programmes into practice is constrained by the characteristics of the policy-making environment. The formulation of policy is confined within relatively tightly drawn boundaries. Domestic policy formulation has been circumscribed within parameters defined by the social market economy, while foreign and security policy has been subject to the constraints of geopolitics, the Federal Republic's semi-sovereign status, and its dependency on the West for security. Consequently party policy is characterized by a rather high degree of cross-party agreement. Supra-partisanship is also a product of characteristics of the party system discussed above: the centre orientation of the *Volksparteien*, the broad (and overlapping) spectrum of interests which these parties represent, and the predominance of coalition governments.

The realization of party policy objectives is inhibited by a further set of constraints arising out of the institutional fragmentation of government and public administration. The constitutional and political foundation of federal government gives rise to a syndrome of ministerial autonomy, militating against the coordinated pursuit of a political mission. A diffuse distribution of powers and responsibilities across the federal system operates against party-driven policy. Moreover, parties may be crowded out of the policy arena by a range of institutional actors such as the Bundesbank and Federal Constitutional Court over which the parties have no control.

This combination of transnational and specifically German factors places the parties in a paradoxical position. On the one hand it limits the capacity of individual parties to realize their own policy agenda, dampening the policy effects of changes in party government – clearly evident in the experience of both the Social Liberal governments of 1969–82 and of Helmut Kohl's Christian Liberal government since 1982. On the other hand, institutional fragmentation creates the need for coordination which the parties are strategically placed to supply.

> The real links coordinating decision-making are the organized parties, thus giving to party government and its leaders the dominant position within the organization of power. (Wildenmann, 1987: 83; cited Roberts, 1989: 51)

Thus parties are influential in the policy process, but on terms which are often outside their own control.

With the multiplication of issues in modern society, the terms on which the parties participate in the policy process are even less subject to their control. The range of issues has widened to include the New Politics agenda, the incorporation of which into the policy profile of the *Volksparteien* has proved problematical. Moreover, the globalization and liberalization of the international economy has forced the Federal Republic to re-evaluate some aspects of social market orthodoxy. Demographic change has led to a reassessment of the state's capacity to fulfil its social responsibilities, and has placed the structural reform of health care and pensions on the agenda.

Unification has had a seismic effect upon the policy agenda, raising a miasma of economic and social dilemmas: financing the costs of unity without undermining monetary stability; social equalization between East and West; the allocation of economic burdens in the West; and controlling wage pressures in both parts of Germany. These dilemmas are compounded by the emotive issue of immigration, which dominated state elections in 1991–92. The realization of national unity raises questions about the identity of the German nation and its role in the world. In short, although unification took place on the basis of the established socioeconomic and constitutional order of the Federal Republic, some of the orthodoxies of that order have been challenged. The renegotiation of these orthodoxies, within a policy-making environment characterized by institutional fragmentation, accentuates the coordinating role of the parties. Unification thus reinforces the centrality of parties in the policy process, but their capacity to fulfil this functional role depends upon the cohesion of the party system.

Coordinating Executive and Legislature

The legislative process in the Federal Republic is characterized by a high degree of interdependence between executive and legislative branches of government, with the parties playing a pivotal role between the two. Interdependence stems, first, from the requirements of coalition government which effectively draws the parties into the legislative process. To ensure the support of all coalition parties, legislative measures are often negotiated between the respective parliamentary *Fraktionen*. Indeed, the *Fraktionen* are normally represented at the outset of the parliament in negotiations over the government programme. Second, executive–legislature relations are conditioned by the logic of the federal system. Federal government cannot control the legislative process merely by virtue of a Bundestag majority, since opposition parties invariably exercise a government role in some of the *Länder*, and participate in the legislation through the Bundesrat. Third, the highly developed Bundestag committee system gives the parliamentary parties a role in shaping legislation, and the fact that most bills are passed by majorities greater than the government majority reflects the level of participation of opposition parties in the legislative process (Paterson and Southern, 1991: 123). These features of the legislative process militate against the polarity of government and opposition parties, which buttresses executive domination in some parliamentary arenas.

The centrality of parties in relations between the executive and the legislature is reflected in the pervasive role of the *Fraktionen* in the Bundestag. Highly structured and disciplined, they exercise control over all aspects of the parliamentary procedure and agenda. The office of *Fraktion*

Chairman is the fulcrum of government–party relations and is occupied by a figure of national prestige. Governments rely very heavily on *Fraktion* leaders to manage the parliamentary party, and those who lead government parties regularly participate in Cabinet meetings. The input of the *Fraktionen* in the legislative process is enhanced by the existence of party working groups (*Arbeitskreise*) which formulate policy positions to be taken up in committee. Generally, party *Fraktionen* have discharged their mediation role between the executive and parliament with a high degree of success, maintaining their own authority in the legislature without precipitating government instability. Whether they can continue to do so in the new German polity, however, is more open to question.

Unification has not formally changed the organization of either the parties or the Bundestag itself. Deputies drawn from the new *Länder* (123 out of a total of 662) have been absorbed into the existing *Fraktionen*. No new parliamentary committee or working group has been established in consequence of the enlargement of the Federal Republic. On the other hand, since the 1990 federal election the capacity of the government parties for maintaining coalition stability has declined. Indicative of this is the increasing tension between the coalition parties which reached a peak in spring 1992 with the *imbroglio* over the appointment of a Foreign Minister to succeed Hans-Dietrich Genscher. Not only did Chancellor Kohl feel obliged to concede the decision to the junior coalition partner, but the FDP leadership's nomination was subsequently overturned by the parliamentary party.

Furthermore, since unification the relationship between the executive and legislature has altered as a result of the changing balance of the party system in the *Länder*. The erosion of CDU support in *Land* elections has deprived the federal government parties of a Bundesrat majority, making them reliant on the opposition SPD for legislation requiring the assent of the upper house. The split-majority syndrome – reminiscent of the 1970s when the CDU–CSU commanded the Bundesrat against the Social Liberal coalition – has led to the emergence of the Bundestag–Bundesrat Mediation Committee as a focal point of interparty bargaining. This situation accentuates the centrality of the parties in the legislative process. With a political agenda laden with constitutional and fiscal measures requiring Bundesrat approval, effective government depends increasingly on the capacity of the parties for consensus-building. The changing political landscape of the new German federal system is examined by Sturm in Chapter 4.

Elite Recruitment

As in all major Western democracies, apart from the United States, the German parties retain their hold over recruitment to political office – a process heavily influenced by the territorial infrastructure of the federal system (Smith, 1989: 61). The structure of the parties mirrors that of the federal system, with key organizational centres located at sub-national level. Regional and *Land* party organizations therefore exercise a large measure of autonomy from the party in Bonn and include amongst their functions the selection of candidates for Bundestag elections. Thus, *Land* parliaments and governments are an important recruiting ground for the political élite in Bonn, reflected in the fact that since the Adenauer era, all Federal Chancellors have first risen to prominence in *Land* government. In the long term, this pattern of recruitment to office through the party structure in the *Länder* will ensure the incorporation of Easterners in the all-German political élite. In the short and medium term, however, party élites continue to be dominated by Westerners.

The formation of a democratic party élite in Eastern Germany began from *tabula rasa*. Virtually all holders of public office in the GDR were tainted by their association with the communist regime, but, in the absence of the requisite organizational and political skills elsewhere in society, the parties have had to draw on these elements. However, the fall-out rate of resignations from office at all levels, following revelations of Stasi connections, has been quite high.

The CDU and FDP in the East are composed of three elements; the remnants of the old GDR block parties: indigenous elements newly recruited to party activity (the so-called 'renewers') and leadership personnel 'parachuted' in from the West. The SPD also contains the latter category, augmenting indigenous elements from the left of the democratic revolution (*Neues Forum*) and from the Protestant churches. All three of the major parties have elected Easterners as deputy chairmen; Angela Merkl (CDU), Wolfgang Thierse (SPD) and Uwe-Berndt Lühr (FDP). Little more than symbolic gestures, these appointments were largely the result of Western patronage. Party élites remain very heavily dominated by Westerners and will remain so for the foreseeable future.

Conclusion

The foregoing analysis is broadly indicative of the resilience of parties and party system in the Federal Republic, but it is still possible to identify some of the tendencies associated with the 'decline of party democracy' hypothesis. Having largely relinquished the traditional mass party function of social integration, the *Volksparteien* were quite successful in retaining their capacity for integration at the electoral level. Indeed, the rejection of 'tribal politics' gave these parties the strategic flexibility to respond effectively to social change. Despite the emergence of new patterns of social stratification, there has been no fundamental realignment of electoral relations. However, whilst the core composition of the party system remains unchanged, there is evidence, since the 1980s, of a tendency towards electoral dealignment and a weakening of the integrative capacity of the *Volksparteien*. The reduced capacity of the parties for structuring the electorate leaves both government and opposition vulnerable both to fluctuations in the political climate and to the clamour of populist demands.

The experience of the Federal Republic does not support the argument that parties have become marginalized in the political process – a central element in the 'decline of party democracy' hypothesis. Four factors can be adduced to demonstrate the continuing relevance of parties in the German context: the institutionalization of parties within the state apparatus; their entrenchment in the network of organized interest representation; their strategic location within the diffuse and fragmented environment of policy-making; and their coordinating role between executive and legislature. The centrality of parties in the German polity marks them out for a key role in the realization of national unity.

The capacity of the parties to fulfil these functional roles depended largely upon the subordination of partisanship to consensus. However, unification has undermined some of the social and economic orthodoxies on which this consensus rested, intensifying social and distributional conflict. The renegotiation of these orthodoxies against the background of increased social conflict places additional strain upon intraparty cohesion and interparty cooperation. The broad range of interests encompassed within the parties, and their susceptibility to 'capture' by party-related interests, may prejudice their capacity for the management of socioeconomic conflict, especially where the interests of key voting groups are at stake. Electoral instability and the 'loosening-up' of the party system in the *Länder* provides an unfavourable environment for conflict management.

The corollary of the quasi-institutional role of the German parties, moreover, is a remoteness in relations between parties and society. A prerequisite for the successful containment of conflict within the confines of intraparty and interparty bargaining is the recognition that parties represent or reflect society. The relatively shallow social roots of the parties (especially in the East) may prejudice their capacity for the resolution of conflict. It has been argued above that party democracy in Germany is relatively robust; a central question addressed by this volume is whether it is strong enough to withstand the intensification of social conflict in the new German polity.

References

Alber, J. (1991), 'Continuity and Change in German Social Structure: Why Bonn is Not Weimar' in U. Hoffmann-Lange (ed.), *Social and Political Structures in West Germany: from Authoritarianism to Postindustrial Democracy*, Boulder Col.: Westview Press, pp. 15–41.
Baker, K., Dalton, R. J. and Hildebrant, K. (1981), *Germany Transformed: Political Culture and the New Politics*, Cambridge Mass.: Harvard University Press.
Beck, U. (1987), 'Beyond Status and Class: Will There be an Individualized Class Society?' in V. Meja, D. Misgeld and N. Stehr (eds), *Modern German Sociology*, New York: Columbia University Press, pp. 340–55.
Betz, H-G. (1991), *Postmodern Politics in Germany: the Politics Resentment*, Basingstoke: Macmillan.
Bulmer, S. (1989), 'Unity, Diversity and Stability: The Efficient Secrets Behind West German Public Policy' in S. Bulmer (ed.), *The Changing Agenda of West German Public Policy*, Aldershot: Dartmouth, pp. 13–39.
Crewe, I. (1985), 'Introduction: Electoral Change in Western Democracies: a Framework for Analysis' in I. Crewe and D. Denver (eds), *Electoral Change in Western Democracies: Patterns and Sources of Electoral Volatility*, London and Sydney: Croom Helm.
Dalton, R. J., Flanagan, S. C. and Beck, P. A. (1984), *Electoral Change in Advanced Industrial Democracies: Realignment or Dealignment?*, Princeton, NJ: Princeton University Press.
Dalton, R. J. (1989), 'The German Voter' in G. Smith, W. E. Paterson and P. H. Merkl (eds), *Developments in West German Politics*, Basingstoke: Macmillan, pp. 99–121.
Dalton, R. J. (1992), 'Two German Electorates?' in G. Smith, W. Paterson, P. Merkl and S. Padgett, *Developments in German Politics*, Basingstoke: Macmillan, pp. 52–76.
Dittberner, J. and Ebbighausen, R. (eds) (1973), *Parteiensystem in der Legitimationskrise*, Opladen: Westdeutscher Verlag.
Dyson, K. (1973), *Party, State and Bureaucracy in Western Germany*, London: Sage.
Esping-Andersen, G. (1991), 'Postindustrial Cleavage Structures: A Comparison of Evolving Patterns of Social Stratification in Germany, Sweden and the United States' in F. F. Piven, *Labour Parties in Post-industrial Societies*, Cambridge: Polity Press, pp. 147–68.
Fichter, T. (1991), 'From Transmission Belt to Social Partnership? The Case of Organized Labor in Eastern Germany' *German Politics and Society*, 23, Summer, pp. 21–39.
Flanagan, S. C. and Dalton, R. J. (1984), 'Parties Under Stress: Realignment and Dealignment in Advanced Industrial Societies', *West European Politics*, 7, (1), pp. 7–23.
Habermas, J. (1975), *Legitimation Crisis*, Boston: Beacon Press.
Kirchheimer, O. (1966), 'The Transformation of the Western European Party Systems' in J. La Polombara and M. Weiner, *Political Parties and Political Development*, Princeton, NJ: Princeton University Press, pp. 177–200.

Lipset, S. M. and Rokkan, S. (1967), 'Cleavage Structures, Party Systems and Voter Alignments' in S. M. Lipset, and S. Rokkan (eds), *Party Systems and Voter Alignments: Cross National Perspectives*, New York: Free Press, pp. 1–64.

Mair, P. (1990), 'Introduction' in P. Mair (ed.), *The West European Party System*, Oxford: Oxford University Press, pp. 1–22.

Neumann, S. (1956), 'Towards a Comparative Study of Political Parties' in S. Neumann (ed.), *Modern Political Parties*, Chicago: University of Chicago Press, pp. 395–421.

Offe, C. (1991), 'Smooth Consolidation in the West German Welfare State: Structural Change, Fiscal Policies and Populist Politics' in F. F. Piven (ed.), *Labour Parties in Post-industrial Societies*, Oxford: Polity Press, pp. 124–46.

Offe, C. (1992), 'German Reunification as a Natural Experiment', *German Politics*, **1**, (1), pp. 1–12.

Olsen, M. (1965), *The Logic of Collective Action: Public Goods and the Theory of Groups*, Cambridge Mass.: Harvard University Press.

Paterson, W. E. and Southern, D. (1991), *Governing Germany*, Oxford: Blackwell.

Pedersen, M. (1979), 'The Dybnamics of European Party Systems: Changing Patterns of Electoral Volatility', *European Journal of Political Research*, **7**, (1), pp. 1-26.

Roberts, G. (1989), 'Political Parties and Public Policy' in S. Bulmer (ed.), *The Changing Agenda of West German Public Policy*, Aldershot: Dartmouth, pp. 40–56.

Rose, R. and Urwin, D. W. (1970), 'Persistence and Change in Western European Party Systems since 1945', *Political Studies*, **18**, (3), 287–319.

Sartori, G. (1968), 'The Sociology of Parties: a Critical Review' in O. Stammer (ed.), *Party Systems, Party Organisations and the Politics of the New Masses*, Berlin: Free University of Berlin.

Smith, G. (1976), 'West Germany and the Politics of Centrality', *Government and Opposition*, **11** (4), pp. 437–55.

Smith, G. (1989), 'Political Leadership' in G. Smith, W. E. Paterson and P. Merkl (eds), *Developments in West German Politics*, Basingstoke: Macmillan, pp. 60–76.

Stöss, R. (1990), 'Parteikritik und Parteienverdrossenheit' *Aus Politik und Zeitgeschichte; Beilage zur Wochenzeitung Das Parlament*, B21/90, Bonn, pp. 15–24.

Webber, D. (1992), 'Kohl's *Wendepolitik* after a Decade', *German Politics*, **1**, (2).

Wildenmann, R. (1987), 'The Party Government of the Federal Republic of Germany: Form and Experience' in R. S. Katz (ed.), *Party Governments: European and American Experiences*, Berlin and New York: de Gruyter.

Wolinetz, S. (1979), 'The Transformation of the Western European Party Systems Revisited', *West European Politics*, **2**, (1), pp. 4–28.

Part One
Party System Dimensions

1   The New German Electorate

Stephen Padgett

A study of parties and party systems must begin with an analysis of their electoral foundations. Party systems reflect the structure of the electorate and patterns of electoral behaviour. Party strategies and programmes, interparty and inner-party relations are all shaped in some way by the electoral landscape. This chapter will examine the structure of the electorate and trends in voting behaviour in both parts of Germany. It will be argued that the evidence of the late 1980s and early 1990s indicates an erosion of the stable bedrock of the electorate in the old Federal Republic and a corresponding increase in electoral volatility. The incorporation of the new *Länder* into the German electorate exacerbates these tendencies, adding to the potential for party system change in the new Germany.

Until the 1980s, the Federal Republic of Germany appeared to be a counter-example to the trends towards partisan dealignment and party system change which had been identified in the UK and USA. Hyperstability in the party system and a marked stability in the party share of the vote suggested an underlying persistence in patterns of electoral behaviour. High and rising levels of electoral participation and the *Volkspartei* share of the vote led to the conclusion that the major parties were actually strengthening their grip over the electorate (Crewe, 1985, 6). An increase in electoral volatility in the 1980s, however, led to a review of these findings.

Some observers continued to emphasize traditional socioeconomic and confessional cleavages and the persistence of established patterns of voting behaviour, at least in certain sections of the electorate. Thus whilst recognizing the erosion of traditional social networks in advanced industrial society, (Pappi, 1977), it was nevertheless maintained that social cleavages continued to form the basis of electoral stability.

> The German polity is characterised by very stable social cleavages.... . The very phenomenon of the group anchored character of voting behaviour is an important cause of the continuity of the cleavage system. (Pappi and Terwey, 1982: 183)

In common with Pappi, Klingemann addressed the social structural under-pinnings of electoral behaviour, identifying certain social groups as stabil-izing forces, and others where volatility prevails (Klingemann, 1985: 249). However, whilst agreeing with Pappi that stability is the dominant charac-teristic of the German electorate, Klingemann underlines the fragile quality of that stability.

> While old cleavage structures may be very stable, the group anchored character of the voting behaviour of these strata is becoming less and less a guarantee for the continuity of stable, social-group politics. (Klingemann, 1985: 252)

Placing a stronger emphasis upon change, Baker *et al.* (1981) identified 'a long term decline in the determining force of social characteristics as a guide for political behaviour' concluding that 'on the whole German parti-sanship reflects a social base less and less' (Baker *et al.*, 1981: 193). Paral-lel to this decline in the social structural dimension of electoral behaviour they identified an increasing orientation in the electorate towards issues. This tendency was related to generational turnover in the electorate, with a progressively more pronounced issue or value orientation evident in each successive generational cohort of voters.

This chapter will review the balance between stability and change in the new German electorate. Although the party share of the vote remained relatively constant in the West over the late 1980s and early 1990s there are indications of an underlying volatility: an increase in the incidence of change voting; a progressive decline in the *Volkspartei* share of the vote; and a declining rate of electoral turnout, particularly among young voters. In parallel with these trends, there has been a continuing erosion of patterns of group-based voting, particularly in the 'hard core' of the manual working-class electorate. The evidence also points to a progressive decline in parti-san identification, reflected in increasingly wide fluctuations of party sup-port indicated by opinion polls.

The social composition of party support in the new German *Länder* is, in some respects, an inversion of the pattern in the former Federal Republic. Thus the social profile of the all-German electorate is further eroded. Lacking a firm basis for stable partisan alignments, the electorate in the East appears to rely very heavily on issue judgements as a basis for elec-toral choice. In an unstable socioeconomic environment, those judgements may prove to be transitory, increasing the potential for volatility in the new German electorate.

Electoral Volatility in the West

Electoral volatility can be measured using the Pedersen Index of aggregate, or net change in the party share of the vote between one election and another. The Index is derived from the addition of the percentage point inter-election change in each party's share of the vote, which is then divided by two. This method of assessing volatility does not, however, show the full scale of individual vote change, since it fails to detect self-cancelling voter exchange between the parties. Gross change – the total number of individual voters switching from one party to another – is a more comprehensive measure of volatility, but is notoriously difficult to quantify, since it relies upon survey data which is inevitably fallible, especially in relation to an individual's recall of a previous vote.

In post-war West Germany, electoral change on the Pedersen Index declined with the concentration of the party system in the early years of the Federal Republic, arriving at a low plateau in the 1970s. After a sharp increase in the 'realigning election' of 1983, net volatility reverted to its previous low levels in the elections of 1987 and 1990. Behind this appearance of stability, however, there is considerable evidence of underlying electoral change.

Whilst net change in the two most recent Bundestag elections has been relatively limited, inter-election change between Landtag elections has increased in scale. Electoral change at this level has been particularly marked in the Landtag elections since December 1990 (see Table 1.2). Patterns of change between Landtag elections also display a marked heterogeneity from one *Land* to another. This may be taken as an indication of the impact of local factors in *Land* elections, and/or of fluctuations in the wider political climate. However, the sensitivity of the electorate to either of these effects is itself evidence of volatility. Moreover, in other national contexts the increasing heterogeneity of patterns of electoral change between regions has been taken as an aspect of increasing volatility (Curtice and Steed, 1980; 1984; cited Crewe, 1985a: 13).

The magnitude of changes in the party share of the vote between a Bundestag election and the preceding Landtag election gives a measure of intra-election, as opposed to inter-election, change: that is, a measure of partisan change within the timescale of Federal elections (see Table 1.3). On the Pedersen Index, intra-election change between a Bundestag election and the preceding Landtag election is well in excess of inter-election change between either Bundestag or Landtag elections. This may be taken to indicate 'soft' change, with partisanship weakening in Landtag elections but reasserting itself in the subsequent Bundestag election. In short, the evidence suggests that although the Bundestag election of 1983 stands out

Table 1.1 Bundestag Elections, 1949–90

	1949	1953	1957	1961	1965	1969	1972	1976	1980	1983	1987	1990*
Participation	78.5	85.8	87.8	87.7	86.8	86.7	91.1	90.7	88.6	89.1	84.3	78.5
CDU–CSU	31.4	45.2	50.2	45.3	47.6	46.1	44.9	48.6	44.5	48.8	44.3	44.2
SPD	29.2	28.8	31.8	36.2	39.3	42.7	45.8	42.6	42.9	38.2	37.0	35.9
FDP	11.9	9.5	7.7	12.8	9.5	5.8	8.4	7.9	10.6	7.0	9.1	10.6
Greens	–	–	–	–	–	–	–	–	1.5	5.6	8.3	4.7
Volkspartei vote	60.6	74.0	82.0	81.5	86.9	88.8	90.7	91.2	87.4	87.0	81.3	80.1
Pedersen* Index	–	14.2	8.0	9.5	5.4	5.4	5.7	3.7	4.5	8.4	5.7	4.9

* Calculated from +/– party share of vote for CDU–CSU, SPD, FDP, Greens (from 1980) and a residual category, 'others'.
** 1990 figures relate to the former Federal Republic excluding Berlin.

Table 1.2   Change in Party Shares of Vote Between Landtag Elections, 1975–92 (Pedersen Index)

	1975–79	1979–83	1983–87	1987–90	1990–92
Schleswig–Holstein	4.0	3.9	3.9	11.2	8.6
Hamburg	9.1	8.6	9.6	5.0	6.5
Niedersachsen	3.9	6.3	6.4	3.9	–
Bremen	7.2	6.2	11.3	10.6	12.2
Nordrhein–Westfalen	2.0	6.3	6.7	2.5	–
Hessen	3.1	6.0	8.2	6.4	2.9
Rheinland–Pfalz	4.6	6.3	6.3	7.6	6.8
Baden–Württemberg	5.4	5.8	2.7	4.7	12.0
Bayern	4.2	3.8	6.9	3.5	–
Saarland	5.3	6.5	7.1	8.7	–
AVERAGE	4.9	6.0	6.9	6.4	8.2

Table 1.3   Change in Party Shares of Vote Between Bundestag Election and Previous Landtag Election, 1980–90 (Pedersen Index)

	LTW–BTW 1980	LTW–BTW 1983	LTW–BTW 1987	LTW–BTW 1990
Schleswig–Holstein	11.9	3.4	11.5	18.3
Hamburg	9.2	5.1	5.5	9.1
Niedersachsen	11.7	5.9	3.5	6.8
Bremen	7.3	5.4	13.3	10.3
Nordrhein–Westfalen	6.0	5.6	9.0	9.6
Hessen	6.1	4.5	7.5	6.8
Rheinland–Pfalz	5.3	3.5	9.4	4.6
Baden–Württemberg	8.5	2.2	8.4	7.6
Bayern	3.0	3.9	4.4	4.8
Saarland	3.8	2.7	8.9	5.1
AVERAGE	7.3	4.2	8.1	8.3

as a milestone of change, it does not signify a realignment followed by a reversion to relative stability, but rather the beginning of an extended period of electoral change.

Although there exists no authoritative quantification of gross volatility in the German context, there is general agreement that the 1980s witnessed a considerable increase, with the election of 1983 representing a watershed. (Forschungsgruppe Wahlen Mannheim, 1983: 24–5; Infas, 1983). Conradt identifies a secular trend towards change voting, dating from the 1960s but steepening from 1969 and reaching a peak of around 24 per cent in 1983 (Conradt, 1986). According to his data, vote-switching in the early 1980s was twice its level in the 1960s. The election of 1990 saw a continuation of this trend, with 'very heavy' change voting (Forschungsgruppe Wahlen Mannheim, 1990c: 52).

Table 1.4 is calculated from estimates of voter exchange between parties based on survey poll data (Infas, 1980, 1987; Forschungsgruppe Wahlen 1990c). It shows the stability in the party vote (voters who cast their vote for the same party as in the previous election) as a percentage of the vote and of the total electorate. Although fallibility of the survey data on which the calculations are based means that the results can only be taken as an approximation of gross volatility, they do give a broad measure of trends from one election to another.

Table 1.4   Electoral Stability Between Bundestag Elections, 1980–90

	Stable vote as % of total vote*	Stable vote as % of electorate	Non-voters as % of electorate	Instability as % of electorate
1980	75.7	67.9	11.3	21.6
1987	75.8	63.9	15.7	20.4
1990**	71.1	55.9	21.5	22.6

* % voting for same party as in previous election.
** Including Berlin: election for House of Representatives 1989; Bundestag election 1990.

Sources:
Infas, *Infas-Report Wahlen*; *Wahl zum 9 Deutschen Bundestag*, Bonn-Bad Godesberg, January 1980.
Infas, *Infas-Report Wahlen*; *Wahl zum 11 Deutschen Bundestag*, Bonn-Bad Godesberg, January 1987.
Forschungsgruppe Wahlen Mannheim, *Bundestagswahl 1990: eine Analyse der Ersten Gesamtdeutschen Bundestagswahl am 2 Dezember 1990*, Mannheim, December 1990.

Although the fall in the stable party vote as a percentage of the total vote between 1980 and 1990 is relatively modest, it is much more pronounced as a percentage of the electorate as a whole. Over this decade the stable core of the electorate declined by more than 10 percentage points. In the election of 1990, stable partisan voters made up little over half of the total electorate, against two-thirds in 1980. The sharp decline in stable partisan voting reflects the considerable increase in non-voting in the elections of 1987 and 1990. In the German context, it has been shown that non-voting is a very significant dimension of voter exchange between parties (Laemmerhold, 1983) and an indicator of electoral volatility and dealignment (von Beyme, 1985; 298).

Electoral Volatility in the East

Some caution is required in drawing conclusions from the elections in the five new *Länder* in 1990. The GDR *Volkskammer* election of March, the Landtag elections of October and the Bundestag election in December took place during a period of acute political change. The emerging party system was in a state of flux with parties forming and disintegrating with great rapidity, and interparty alliances shifting from one election to another. Interpreting election results in the five new *Länder* is thus problematical, and requires some contextual background. In the *Volkskammerwahl* in March the CDU headed the *Allianz für Deutschland* (Alliance for Germany) along with the *Demokratischer Aufbruch* (Democratic Awakening) and the *Deutsche Soziale Union* (German Social Union). Thereafter, with the introduction of a 5 per cent clause into the electoral law, the DA merged with the CDU, which also absorbed most of the electorate of the DSU. A similar process of concentration took place among the Liberal parties which had contested the *Volkskammer* election. Comparisons of the *Volkskammer* and Bundestag election results must be sensitive to these intervening developments. Table 1.5 gives the Alliance vote in the *Volkskammer* election with the CDU vote in parentheses below. Change in the CDU vote between the *Volkskammer* and Bundestag elections is based on the Alliance vote. Liberal parties are given as the FDP.

The very heavy poll for the Alliance/CDU in the *Volkskammer* election was widely interpreted as a vote for rapid unification and proved unsustainable as the harsh realities of unification progressively dispelled the early euphoria. The decline in the CDU vote also reflected the increase in the vote for the FDP in the Bundestag election, with survey poll data indicating some 10 per cent of CDU voters in the October Landtag election switching to the FDP. The PDS vote, seen as a GDR regime payroll vote,

Table 1.5 The Party Vote in the Five New *Länder*

	Participation	CDU	SPD	FDP	Greens BU 90	PDS	Others
Mecklenburg							
Volkskammer	93.0	39.3* (36.4)	23.9	3.6	4.3	22.4	6.4
Landtag	65.2	38.2	27.0	5.5	6.4	15.7	7.1
Bundestag	71.0	41.2	26.6	9.1	5.9	14.2	2.8
Change Vks–Btg	−22.0	+1.9** (+4.8)	+2.7	+5.5	+1.6	−8.2	−3.6
					Pedersen Index		11.8
Brandenburg							
Volkskammer	93.5	38.5* (34.0)	28.9	4.8	5.4	18.4	4.0
Landtag	67.4	29.4	38.3	6.6	9.2	13.4	3.1
Bundestag	74.0	36.3	32.9	9.7	6.6	11.0	3.5
Change Vks–Btg	−19.5	−2.2** (+2.3)	+4.0	+4.9	+1.2	−7.4	−0.5
					Pedersen Index		10.1
Sachsen Anhalt							
Volkskammer	93.5	47.8* (44.7)	23.6	7.7	4.0	14.0	3.0
Landtag	65.6	39.0	26.0	13.5	5.3	12.0	4.2
Bundestag	72.4	38.6	24.7	19.7	5.3	9.4	2.3
Change Vks–Btg	−21.1	−9.2** (−6.1)	+1.1	+12.0	+1.3	−4.6	−0.7
					Pedersen Index		14.5
Sachsen							
Volkskammer	93.7	57.7* (43.6)	15.1	5.7	4.7	13.3	3.5
Landtag	73.5	53.8	19.1	5.3	5.6	10.2	6.0
Bundestag	76.4	49.5	18.2	12.4	5.9	9.0	5.0
Change Vks–Btg	−16.3	−8.2** (+5.9)	+3.1	+6.7	+1.2	−4.3	+1.5
					Pedersen Index		12.5
Thuringen							
Volkskammer	94.7	60.2* (53.0)	17.4	4.6	4.1	11.2	2.4
Landtag	72.1	45.4	22.8	9.3	6.5	9.7	6.3
Bundestag	76.4	45.2	21.9	14.6	6.1	8.3	3.9
Change Vks–Btg	−18.3	−15.0** (−7.8)	+4.5	+10.0	+2.0	−2.9	+1.5
					Pedersen Index		17.9
Five New Lander							
Volkskammer	93.4	48.0* (40.8)	21.9	5.3	4.9	16.4	3.5
Landtag	69.1	43.6	25.2	7.8	6.9	11.6	4.9
Bundestag	74.7	41.8	24.3	12.9	6.0	11.1	3.9
Change Vks–Btw	−18.7	−6.2** (+1.0)	+2.4	+7.6	+1.1	−5.3	+0.4
					Pedersen Index		11.5

* Alliance vote (i.e. including DA and DSU); CDU vote in parentheses.
** Based on Alliance vote in *Volkskammer* (March) elections: CDU change between *Volkskammer* and Bundestag elections in parentheses.

was eroded broadly in parallel with the increase in the vote for the SPD and the Greens between March and December.

Broken down by *Land*, the Pedersen Index of inter-election change ranged from 10.1 (Brandenburg) to 17.9 (Thuringen) with an aggregate Index for the five new *Länder* as a whole of 11.5. Not unexpectedly, these results indicate a relatively high rate of net electoral change. Net change was concentrated between the *Volkskammer* election in March and the *Landtag* elections in October with an Index for aggregate change across the five new *Länder* of 9.2, as against an Index rating of 5.1 between October and the Bundestag election in December.

The calculation of gross change in Table 1.6 is based on an exit poll of voters in the 1990 Bundestag election in the five new *Länder* and East Berlin (8,131 respondents and the former FRG (17,144 respondents). Results show stable party voting at around 70 per cent in the five new *Länder* between the Landtag elections of October and the Bundestag election of December 1990 – strikingly similar to the level in the West. Given the lower level of participation in the East, however, this translates into a lower level of stability in the electorate as a whole. The stable core of the electorate in the five new *Länder* between October and December 1990 amounted to barely one half.

In the absence of established party alignments in the new *Länder*, and in a period of rapid political change, a high level of electoral volatility is

Table 1.6   Electoral Stability in the West and East, 1990

	Stable vote as % of total vote*	Stable vote as % of electorate	Non-voters as % of electorate	Instability as % of electorate
New Länder	71.0	53.0	25.3	21.7
Former FRG	71.1	55.9	21.5	22.6

* %voting for same party as in previous election.

Former FRG: Bundestag Election 1987 and Bundestag Election 1990.
5 New *Länder*; Landtag Election Oct 1990–Bundestag Election 1990.
E. Berlin; Municipal Election May 1990–Bundestag Election 1990.
W. Berlin; Election to House of Representatives 1989–Bundestag Election 1990.

Source:
Forschungsgruppe Wahlen Mannheim, *Bundestagswahl 1990: eine Analyse der Ersten Gesamtdeutschen Bundestagswahl am 2 Dezember 1990*, Mannheim, December 1990.

unsurprising. The key question, however, is whether the volatility of 1990 is merely a temporary phase in the formation of relatively stable partisan alignments, or whether it will become an endemic feature of the electorate in the East.

Electoral Participation and the *Volkspartei* Vote

The Federal Republic has experienced a particularly sharp decline in participation in the late 1980s and early 1990s. Participation rates have fallen from the 1983 level of 89.1 per cent to 84.3 per cent in the Bundestag election of 1987 and 78.5 per cent in the old Federal Republic in the election of 1990 (see Table 1.1). A common explanation for the low level of participation in the latter two elections has been the predictability of the result (in both elections a clear-cut victory for the CDU–CSU had been confidently expected). However, the trend is also visible in Landtag elections. In 21 Landtag elections between 1984 and 1991, the average fall in participation was 3.6 per cent compared to an average decline of 1.0 per cent for the 20 elections between 1978 and 1983. Declining participation in Landtag elections suggests that the fall in turnout for Bundestag elections has a deeper-rooted cause than merely the predictability of the outcome.

A breakdown of electoral districts for the Bundestag election of 1990 shows that the rate of decline in participation was particularly sharp where participation was already lower than average (Forschungsgruppe Wahlen Mannheim, 1990c: 48). It also shows that these electoral districts are characterized by an above-average decline in the vote for the two major parties (the CDU–CSU and the SPD), pointing to a syndrome of declining participation in parallel with a declining *Volkspartei* share of the vote (Gibowski and Kaase, 1991: 8).

Over the entire period of the Federal Republic the rate of electoral participation has run parallel to the *Volkspartei* share of the vote. Rising levels of participation and *Volkspartei* support in the first three post-war decades culminated in 1972 and 1976, before falling moderately in 1980, stabilizing in 1983 and declining precipitously in 1987 and 1990. The scale of the decline in *Volkspartei* support is seen most dramatically in relation to the total electorate, rather than as a percentage of votes cast. In this way the parallel downward trends in participation and in the *Volkspartei* vote are compounded together. The result shows a 19.3 per cent fall in the *Volkspartei* share of the total electorate in 14 years to 1990, and a 14.8 per cent fall in the seven years to 1990 (see Table 1.7). A perspective on these results is given by comparison with the UK, where the major party share of the vote fell by 16.5 per cent in the 17-year period between the elections of 1966 and 1983. (Crewe, 1985b: 106).

Table 1.7 *Volkspartei* **Vote as a Percentage of Total Electorate, 1972–90**

1972	1976	1980	1983	1987	1990
82.1	82.7	77.4	77.6	68.5	62.9

In the East, the level of electoral participation fluctuated widely between the *Volkskammer* election of March (93.4 per cent), the Landtag elections of October (69.1 per cent) and the Bundestag election of December (74.7 per cent). These fluctuations should be seen against the circumstantial background. The very high turnout for the March election reflected both the historic significance of the first free election in the Eastern part of Germany since 1932 and the fact that it could also be regarded as a plebiscite for unification. The reduced turnout in the October and December elections can be seen as a 'normalization', although participation in the new *Länder* in the Bundestag election was lower than that in the former Federal Republic. The poll for the *Volksparteien* was 66.1 per cent of the vote or 48.6 per cent of the total electorate. These relatively low figures largely reflected the continued existence of the PDS. Even if the PDS vote is discounted, however, the electorate of the East shows a rather higher incidence of minor party voting than in the West.

Electoral participation in the Federal Republic is particularly low among young voters – a tendency dating back to the 1970s, when participation rates among the young lagged some 6–8 per cent below the average. With the emergence of the Greens as a focal point for the young, the gap closed. In the election of 1990, however, the generational participation deficit reasserted itself at a level above the previous high (see Table 1.10, p. 40). In the East the deficit was even more pronounced, with the turnout for the under-30 age groups between 13.6–18.9 per cent below average. Participation rates in the East also show a 'gender effect', with very low turnout – barely 50 per cent – amongst 18–21 year-old women. In both East and West, young voters are less inclined towards *Volkspartei* voting. The vote for the Greens/Bündnis 90, the PDS, and the Republicans is significantly above average among the under-30s, and these trends can be seen as indicative of the alienation of young voters from the established parties. If they

Table 1.8   Participation by Age Group: 1990 Bundestag Election (Deviation from Average)

Age group	All Germany	West	East
18–21	–11.4	–8.8	–17.9
21–25	–13.3	–11.5	–18.9
25–30	–9.9	–8.6	–13.6
30–35	–5.5	–5.0	–6.5
35–40	–0.8	–1.8	+2.5
40–45	+3.5	+3.3	+3.8
45–50	+5.4	+4.7	+7.0
50–60	+7.4	+6.7	+9.8
60–70	+9.7	+8.9	+12.0
70+	+0.2	–0.5	+0.7
Total	77.5	78.5	74.7

Source: Gibowski and Kaase, 1991.

continue, and upcoming generations of voters are not integrated into the party system, the result will inevitably be an escalation of electoral volatility.

The Social Base of the Electorate in the West

The two main social cleavages in the electorate of the former Federal Republic run, first, along the lines of occupational social class and, second, along confessional or religious–secular lines. These two cleavage lines cross-cut one another, and it is not always easy to discern which is stronger. Patterns of group-based voting behaviour rooted in class and religion have proved surprisingly resistant to the post-war trends towards secularization and post-industrialism. However, there has been a gradual long-term weakening of ties which accelerated in the early and mid-1980s among some social strata. Data from the elections of 1987 and 1990, suggests a continuing weakening of group-based voting behaviour on both the class and confessional dimensions.

The most pronounced breakdown in group-based voting behaviour has occurred in the historic alliance between the non-Catholic working class and the SPD. The decline in their support for the SPD in 1990 was heavily disproportionate to the fall in the party's share of the overall vote. By contrast, the SPD share of the middle-class vote remained relatively stable in 1987 and 1990. The erosion of partisanship in the SPD's manual-worker electorate can be set in the context of a progressive trend which first became apparent in 1983. The weakening of manual-worker partisanship has not, however, occurred evenly across different categories of workers, and closer examination of the breakdown of the SPD manual-worker vote from 1983 to 1990 provides a useful insight into the dynamics of partisan change.

The evidence supports the hypothesis that 'the ice begins melting at the edges' (Berger *et al.*, 1984). Early signs of weakness in the voting alliance between the working class and the SPD emerged in 1983, when the party sustained losses at the geographical and social margins of its manual-worker electorate. Geographically, the decline in the SPD's manual-worker electorate was initially concentrated in Baden–Württemberg, an area of small to medium-sized towns and cities set in rural environs, with a relatively prosperous, predominantly light industrial base. In its electoral heartland of the heavy industrial, highly urbanized *Ruhrgebiet*, by contrast, the decline of the party's manual-worker vote was much less pronounced. Socially also, partisan change occurred at the margins of the manual-worker constituency, with SPD partisanship declining sharply among non-trade union members, and especially among Catholics in this category (see Table 1.9). This decline was partially offset by a *strengthening* of partisanship in the hard-core SPD support group of trade union member workers.

In 1987 the picture was reversed, with a dramatically sharp decline in manual-worker partisanship in the SPD's *Stammwählerschaft* of non-Catholic, trade union member workers. This was offset by the consolida-

Table 1.9   Manual-worker Vote by Trade Union Membership and Confession (Former FRG)

	Trade Union Member								Non-Trade Union Member							
	Catholic				Non-Catholic				Catholic				Non-Catholic			
Election	'80	'83	'87	'90	'80	'83	'87	'90	'80	'83	'87	'90	'80	'83	'87	'90
CDU–CSU	49	48	41	41	13	21	17	35	52	66	53	57	22	40	30	37
CDU/ +/– CSU	–4	–1	–7	0	–5	8	–4	18	–9	14	–13	4	–9	18	–10	7
SPD	43	47	52	40	77	79	68	60	41	27	37	32	63	53	56	50
SPD +/–	2	4	5	–12	3	2	–11	–8	4	–14	10	–5	3	–10	3	–6

Source: Gibowski and Kaase, 1991.

tion of SPD support in the weaker SPD partisan group of Catholic workers. Among Catholic trade union members, SPD support exceeded that for the CDU, a phenomenon for which there was no precedent. An explanation for these shifting patterns of manual-worker voting can, perhaps be found in the circumstances of the 1987 election. SPD Chancellor candidate Rau was identified with the traditional manual-worker culture, and his campaign theme of social solidarity, as well as his well known credentials as a practising Christian, may have found an echo in the ethos of social Catholicism. Above all, he had a following in his home state of North-Rhine–Westphalia which extended beyond his own party's electorate, and which won the SPD an increased share of the vote here against the national trend.

The incursion of declining partisanship into the social democratic *Stammwählerschaft* is confirmed by the election of 1990. Although SPD partisanship declined across all categories of manual workers, the decline was most pronounced among trade union members. If the data for 1987 is compounded with that for 1990 a very pronounced decline in the hard core of partisanship is revealed. SPD partisanship among non-Catholic, trade union members fell by 19 per cent between 1983 and 1990, clearly revealing the dynamics of partisan dealignment in the working-class electorate. The erosion of group partisanship began on the social margins of the SPD's manual-worker constituency, but penetrated to its core in the elections of 1987 and 1990.

A weakening in partisanship among the CDU–CSU's Catholic electorate is also discernible, although the evidence is much less decisive and is concentrated on the 1987 election. In this election, CDU support in electoral districts with a high percentage of Catholics (61–93 per cent) fell mildly disproportionately (–5.2 per cent) to the decline in the overall party vote (–4.5 per cent). The decline in the CDU Catholic vote was partially reversed in 1990, but remained unusually low among Catholic, trade union member manual workers, where FDP voting increased sharply. The erosion of CDU–CSU support in this group might, very tentatively, be taken as evidence of dealignment. On the other hand it is not entirely out of line with previous patterns. Whilst the CDU has historically had a pronounced and consistent majority among the non-union member, Catholic working class, its advantage has been less pronounced and consistent where Catholicism is counteracted by trade union membership.

Group-based voting behaviour is particularly weak among the new middle class of white-collar employees and civil servants. The weakness of partisanship in this group is well known, and stems from its ambiguous social position.

... the new middle class finds itself with a position in the social structure and a lifestyle that places it between the working class and the old middle class. As a result its loyalties are divided between these other two strata, and its votes are split between the parties of right and left. (Baker *et al.*, 1981: 172).

Partisanship in this social group is dependent upon the confessional variable and trade union membership. The non-Catholic and trade union member new middle class gives a majority of its votes to the SPD, with Catholics and non-union members favouring the CDU–CSU. However, these majorities have been neither pronounced nor consistent. The new middle class has been the principal source of electoral change in the Federal Republic.

The Inverted Social Profile of the Electorate in the East

Whilst the social structural foundations of the electorate in the former Federal Republic have been steadily eroded over the last two decades, socioeconomic variables remain the dominant determinants of electoral behaviour. The Lipset–Rokkan model of party systems and electoral relations, derived from historic social cleavages frozen in time, retains some explanatory value. In the new *Länder*, the relationship between social structure and electoral behaviour is a radically different one. The party system which emerged in the East in 1990 was simply transposed, for the most past, from the Federal Republic, and was exogenous to GDR society. Although the roots of this party system could be traced back to a common social heritage in the Weimar Republic and beyond, the social revolutions of national socialism and communism destroyed the social foundations of partisanship in the East. The social profile of partisanship which emerged in the elections of 1990 was, in some ways, an inversion of that found in the Federal Republic.

The predominance of the SPD among manual workers which, although weakening, remains a characteristic of the electorate of the former Federal Republic, is reversed in the new *Länder*. However, precise breakdown of the East German electorate by class is hard to determine since class distinctions were not recognized in the old regime, and official GDR census figures were based on sector rather than class. The only available data is based on the self-ascription of social class by respondents in survey polls, using the categories commonly used in the former Federal Republic. However, survey data from different sources is mutually corroborative, and Table 1.10 can be regarded as a broad reflection of the main trends in class voting. It shows that CDU support among manual workers (49.8 per cent) is significantly higher than its share of the overall vote in the East (41.8 per

Table 1.10   Class Voting by Party: West and East

West/East	CDU W	CDU E	SPD W	SPD E	FDP W	FDP E	Greens W	Greens E	PDS W	PDS E
Manuals	39	50	47	25	6	11	3	5	0	5
White-collar employees	43	37	36	25	12	15	5	10	0	10
High-grade wc Employees + civil servants	47	34	32	24	13	19	6	6	0	13
Self-employed	57	50	18	16	18	22	5	5	0	5
Students	32	18	34	23	12	12	17	25	1	16

Source: Gibowski and Kaase, 1991.

cent) and around 13 per cent higher than its support among white-collar employees (37.0 per cent).

The SPD trailed far behind the CDU in the manual-worker electorate with a poll of 24.8 per cent. Even when the SPD's manual-worker support is blocked with that of the PDS, to represent 'the Left', there is still a wide margin of advantage for the CDU. The scale of manual-worker CDU voting is reflected in the relative strengths of the parties across the *Länder* in the Bundestag election. Of the 15 electoral districts in the East where the CDU won its best results, 13 were in the state of Sachsen where some 54.1 per cent of the electorate are engaged in industrial employment. At 60.9 per cent, the CDU share the manual-worker electorate in this state was significantly above average for Eastern Germany. The most favourable SPD results were in Mecklenburg and Brandenburg, the two states with the lowest concentration of industrial workers in the electorate (33.0 and 43.2 per cent respectively). The PDS is also strongest in these two states, giving a combined 'left-wing' party share of the vote exceeding that of the CDU.

In the non-manual electorate, the balance of party support between the CDU and SPD was much more even. Among white-collar employees, (*Angestellte*) CDU support was 37.0 per cent against 25.1 per cent for the SPD, and 35.0 per cent for the SPD and PDS combined, quite close to the party share of the vote in the electorate overall. Support for the SPD showed no appreciable class profile. The Alford Index of class voting (left-wing party share of the manual-worker vote left-wing party share of the middle-class vote) showed a rating of virtually zero.

Table 1.11 Confessional Voting by Party: West and East

	CDU		SPD		FDP		Greens		PDS	
West/East	W	E	W	E	W	E	W	E	W	E
Catholic	56	66	27	12	9	11	5	6	0	2
Protestant	40	53	40	20	13	15	4	6	0	2
No Confession	26	33	45	29	11	13	12	9	1	13

Source: Gibowski and Kaase, 1991.

On the confessional dimension, the electorate in the five new *Länder* conforms more closely to the patterns of the former Federal Republic, with CDU support strongly correlated with affiliation to the Catholic Church. Amongst the small number of Catholics in the East, the CDU is overwhelmingly dominant, with 65.8 per cent against and 11.5 per cent for the SPD. Early expectations that the SPD would benefit from the historic Protestant predominance in Eastern Germany have been unrealized. Unlike in the West, where the major party balance among Protestants is almost exactly even, the CDU in the East is able to claim a clear majority (53.4 per cent) of survey respondents indicating affiliation to the Protestant Church. The scale of Christian Democratic dominance among both confessional groups is particularly telling in view of the surprisingly high percentage of respondents in the new *Länder* indicating a confessional orientation (41.6 per cent) as opposed to 'no confession' (55.2 per cent). Among respondents indicating a secular orientation, although the major party balance is not reversed, Christian Democratic dominance is greatly reduced, and the parties of the Left (SPD, PDS, Greens) come close to a majority. The similarity of confessional voting patterns in East and West means that the confessional profile of the new all-German electorate is virtually unchanged from that of the former Federal Republic (see Table 1.11).

Party Identification and Issue Voting

Relative stability in the electorate of the former FRG in the 1970s, despite the widely recognized erosion of the social structural determinants of voting behaviour, led to the conclusion that traditional group-based voting alliances had been replaced or supplemented by enduring psychological ties between voters and parties. The 'party identification' model of voting behaviour provided an explanation for the persistence of electoral stability against the background of social change in the post-war era. An explanation for the breakdown of electoral stability in the 1980s and 1990s might therefore be sought in the erosion of party identification in the new German electorate.

Until the mid-1980s, survey data showed little conclusive evidence for the long-term weakening of party identification, (Dalton, 1984: 126). However, a sharp fall in the level of party identification appeared in data from the election of 1983, particularly in relation to the two *Volksparteien* where party identification had previously been strongest. Whilst, in 1980, around two-thirds of *Volkspartei* voters had expressed 'strong' identification with their party, three years later the figure had fallen to around 40 per cent for the SPD and 45 per cent for the CDU–CSU. Data from the elections of 1987 and 1990 served to confirm the trend (Forschungsgruppe Wahlen Mannheim, 1987: 9; 1990c, 20).

Parallel to the apparent decline in party identification, it is possible to discern a corresponding increase in the salience of political issues in party preference. The period 1987–90 witnessed a significant increase in the volatility of party preference from the previous inter-election period. In the period 1983–87, support for the CDU–CSU varied within a range of 12 per cent, against a fluctuation range for SPD support of 11 per cent. In the 1987–90 period, the range of fluctuation for both parties increased sharply, to 19.5 and 18.5 per cent respectively (Forschungsgruppe Wahlen Mannheim, 1987: 6; 1990c, 19). During this latter period, party preference is clearly related to issue response.

A steady 12-month decline in support for the CDU–CSU in Landtag elections and survey polls began with the political scandal surrounding the Schleswig–Holstein Landtag election of May 1988, which culminated in the suicide of CDU state premier Rainer Barschel. The 'Barschel Affair' was one of a series of political scandals, which some believe have led to a syndrome of *Parteienentfremdung* or alienation between voters and parties (Stöss, 1990: 15–21). The *Volksparteien* have been particularly afflicted, and a corresponding weakening of party identification is not an implausible hypothesis.

CDU–CSU unpopularity also coincided with a period of mishandled reforms in taxation and health care which called the competence of both the government and the Chancellor into question. At its nadir, in March 1989, Kohl's popularity rating stood at just 20 per cent, with 54 per cent of the electorate expressing disapproval. Thereafter, CDU–CSU support recovered gradually, and the balance of party support in the European parliamentary election of June 1990 was even. From September–October, when the influx of refugees from the GDR first placed the German question on the political agenda, the balance of party support changed repeatedly. Only in June 1990, when the government appeared to have mastered the unification process, and the CDU had succeeded in making the issue its own, did the party reassert its lead in the polls. There is no evidence in the German context in the 1980s and early 1990s to indicate that party support is directly related to economic issues or performance (Kirchgässner, 1989: 175–95). Indeed, the trough of unpopularity experienced by the CDU–CSU during 1988–89 coincided with unprecedented economic success, thereby rendering the decline in government party popularity from 1988–89 particularly striking. This, and the oscillation in the balance of party support in the 1987–90 period, is indicative of an ultra-sensitivity to issues in the German electorate, which is consistent with a decline of party identification.

A further explanation for the weakening of party identification can be found in the impact of New Politics on the party system. Although New Politics value orientations have by no means superseded traditional value structures as the basis of electoral behaviour, they have become superimposed upon the latter. The cross-cutting effect of the conflict between Old and New Politics values has added a new dimension to the new German electorate. The increasing complexity of value cleavages now presents a very difficult environment for strategic party choice. As the established parties have adjusted to the New Politics agenda, the issue images of the parties have lost their clarity. Both the *Volksparteien* have made quite far-reaching concessions to the New Politics agenda, whilst attempting to retain important aspects of their old programmatic profile. The Janus face of the SPD, simultaneously projecting itself to the Old and the New Left, is symptomatic of this syndrome, and accounts in large measure for the decline of manual-worker partisanship. The CDU on the other hand is caught between its conservative old middle-class roots and the *Neue Mitte*. The vulnerability of the CDU–CSU to the radical Right can be seen in these terms.

Partisan identification arises out of issue affinities between parties and voters, which are consolidated over time and support relatively stable patterns of partisanship. With the multiplication and increasing complexity of issues in modern society, and the consequent weakening of the issue profiles of the parties, affinities between voters and parties become less sharply defined. Unification is likely to accelerate this process. The major parties now have to reconcile the competing demands emanating from East and West, attempting to project an appeal simultaneously to voters in two distinct electoral constituencies. This can only weaken their issue profile, with negative effects upon the strength of partisan identification.

Conclusion

The evidence of the late 1980s and early 1990s suggests that the volatility first evident in the election of 1983 is now a permanent condition of the German electorate. Whilst old patterns of partisanship have lost their force, it is difficult to identify sustained and consistent trends leading to the formation of new alignments. Instead, the picture is one of short-term fluctuations in the behaviour of particular social groups, which have tended to cancel each other out in the longer term. Hence the combination of relative *net stability* with *gross change* which has characterized of the electorate of the former Federal Republic since 1983. On the limited evidence available, the electorate in the East contains a similar or greater potential for volatility than that in the West.

The two most striking trends in this period are, first, the decline in participation in the last two Bundestag elections which is also reflected in Landtag polls. This decline is related to a second trend – the decline in the vote for the *Volksparteien* which had previously served as bastions of stable voting patterns and high levels of party identification. Dealignment, in the German context, is clearly related to the weakening hold of these parties over the electorate. In the new *Länder*, the *Volksparteien* command the vote of less than half of the total electorate.

It is, as yet, too early to say with certainty what impact the newly enfranchised electorate in the East will have upon the party system in the Federal Republic. Although the results of the 1990 election were remarkably similar in East and West, the underlying structure of the two electorates is quite different. With their shallow roots, patterns of electoral behaviour which have emerged in the East are likely to be susceptible to a political environment which is still in flux. The new German electorate will, therefore, continue to be characterized by *Wende ohne Ende* – a permanent state of change – in which politics is paramount in determining electoral outcomes.

References

Baker, K. Dalton, R. J. and Hildebrandt, K. (1981), *Germany Transformed. Political Culture and the New Politics*, Cambridge Mass.: Harvard University Press.

Berger, M., Gibowski, W. G., Roth, D. and Schulte, W. (1984), 'Das Eis Schmilzt zuerst an der Randen ... zur Infas These von den stammwählerschaft der SPD', *Zeitschrift für Parlamentsfragen*, June.

Beyme, K. von (1985), *Political Parties in Western Democracies*, Aldershot: Gower.

Conradt, D. (1986), *The German Polity*, London and New York: Longman.

Crewe, I. (1985a), 'Introduction. Electoral Change in Western Democracies: A Framework for Analysis' in I. Crewe and D. Denver (eds), *Electoral Change in Western Democracies: Patterns and Sources of Electoral Volatility*, London and Sydney: Croom Helm.

Crewe, I. (1985b), 'Great Britain' in I. Crewe and D. Denver (eds), *Electoral Change in Western Democracies: Patterns and Sources of Electoral Volatility*, London and Sydney: Croom Helm.

Curtice, J. and Steed, M. (1980), 'The Analysis of the Voting' in D. Butler and D. Kavanagh (eds), *The British General Election of 1979*, London: Macmillan.

Dalton, R. J. (1984), 'The West German Party System between Two Ages' in R. J. Dalton, S. C. Flanagan and P. A. Beck, *Electoral Change in Advanced Industrial Democracies: Realignment or Dealignment?*, Princeton NJ: Princeton University Press.

Forschungsgruppe Wahlen Mannheim (1980), *Bundestagswahl 1980: eine Analyse der Wahl zum 9 Deutschen Bundestag am 5 Oktober 1980*, Mannheim.

Forschungsgruppe Wahlen Mannheim (1983), *Bundestagswahl 1983: eine Analyse der Wahl zum 10 Deutschen Bundestag am 6 März 1983*, Mannheim.

Forschungsgruppe Wahlen Mannheim (1987), *Bundestagswahl 1987: eine Analyse der Wahl zum 11 Deutschen Bundestag am 25 Januar 1987*, Mannheim.

Forschungsgruppe Wahlen Mannheim (1990a), *Wahl in der DDR: eine Dokumentation Volkskammerwahl vom 18 März 1990*, Mannheim 1990.

Forschungsgruppe Wahlen Mannheim, (1990b), *Wahl in den Neuen Bundesländern: eine Analyse der Landtagswahlen vom 14 Oktober 1990*, Mannheim 1980.

Forschungsgruppe Wahlen Mannheim (1990c), *Bundestagswahl 1990: eine Analyse der Ersten Gesamtdeutschen Bundestagswahl am 2 Dezember 1990*, Mannheim.

Gibowski, W. G. and Kaase, M. (1991), 'Auf dem Weg zum Politischen Alltag: eine Analyse der ersten gesamtdeutschen Bundestagswahl', *Aus Politik und Zeitgeschichte: Beilage zur Wochenzeitung Das Parlament*, B 11–12/91, Bonn, pp. 1–20.

Infas (1980), *Infas-Report Wahlen: Wahl zum 9 Deutschen Bundestag am 5 Oktober 1980*, Bonn.

Infas (1983), *Infas-Report Wahlen: Wahl zum 10 Deutschen Bundestag am 6 März 1983*, Bonn.

Infas (1987), *Infas-Report Wahlen: Wahl zum 11 Deutschen Bundestag am 25 Januar 1987*, Bonn.

Kaase, M. and Gibowski, W. G. (1990), 'Deutschland im Übergang; Parteien und Wähler vor der Bundestagswahl 1990', *Aus Politik und Zeitgeschichte: Beilage zur Wochenzeitung Das Parlament*, B 37–38/90, Bonn, pp. 14–26.

Kirchgässner, G. (1989), 'Der Einfluss wirtschaftlicher Variablen auf die Popularität der Parteien' in J. W. Falter, H. Rattinger and K. G. Troitzsch (eds), *Wahlen und Politisches Einstellungen in der Bundesrepublik Deutschland*, Frankfurt am Main: Peter Lang, pp. 175–95.

Klingemann, H-D, (1985), 'West Germany' in I. Crewe and D. Denver (eds), *Electoral Change in Western Democracies: Patterns and sources of Electoral Volatility*, London and Sydney: Croom Helm.

Laemmerhold, C. (1983), 'Auf Biegen und Brechen; die Nichtwähler im. Prokrustesbett der Wanderungsbilanzen' in M. Kasse and H-D. Klingemann (eds), *Wahlen und Politisches System*, Opladen: Westdeutscher Verlag.

Pappi, F-U. (1977), 'Sozialstruktur gesellschaftlicher Wertorientierung und Wahlabsicht, *Politische Vierteljahresschrift*, **18**, pp. 195–229.

Pappi, F-U. and Terwey, M. (1982), 'The German Electorate' in H. Döring and G. Smith (eds), *Party System and Political Culture in Western Germany*, New York: St Martins Press.

Stöss, R. (1990), 'Parteikritik und Parteienverdroßenheit', *Aus Politik und Zeitgeschichte: Beilage zur Wochenzeitung Das Parlament*, B 21/90, Bonn, pp. 15–24.

2 The First All-German Elections

Hans-Joachim Veen

The twelfth election to the German Bundestag was a watershed in the political and social development of the Federal Republic. On 2 December 1990, after more than 40 years of a divided Germany, the first post-war all-German parliament was elected. German unification, consummated under German and international law on 3 October 1990, was democratically legitimated *ex post facto* by the entire German nation. For the citizens of the old Federal Republic, unlike their counterparts in Eastern Germany, this was the first opportunity to express their desire for unity through the ballot box. Nevertheless, the aspiration for unification, reflected in the polls since the Berlin Wall had been breached, had been overwhelming in both West and East (see Figure 2.1). At the beginning of 1990 around 70 per cent in the West and 80 per cent in the East were in favour of a unified state. By September 1990, support for unification had risen to around 90 per cent in both parts of the country (Gibowski and Kaase, 1991: 11).

Nevertheless, opinion polls revealed deep-seated differences between the two parts of Germany in terms of political culture and voter profiles. These differences will strongly determine the lines of future political conflict and will have a manifold impact on the party system as well. Ultimately the parties and the party system as a whole may well be permanently changed, although at present it would be impossible to predict the nature and extent of the realignments.

Attitudes Towards Unification

Although, from the outset, support for unification was high in West Germany, it had to contend with both doubts about the pace of unification and

47

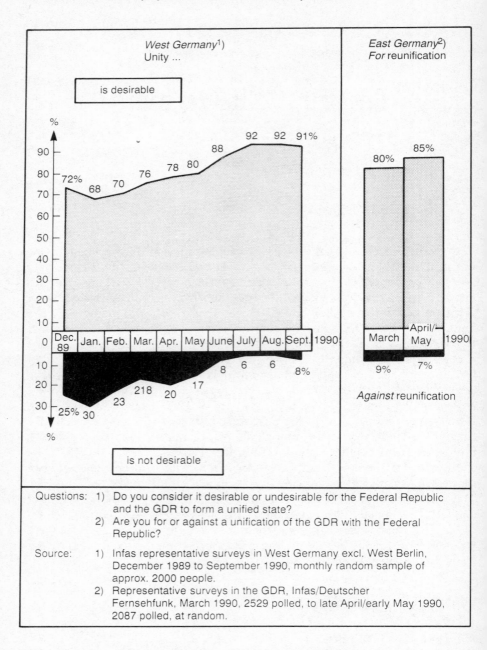

Figure 2.1   Attitudes Towards Unification, 1989–90

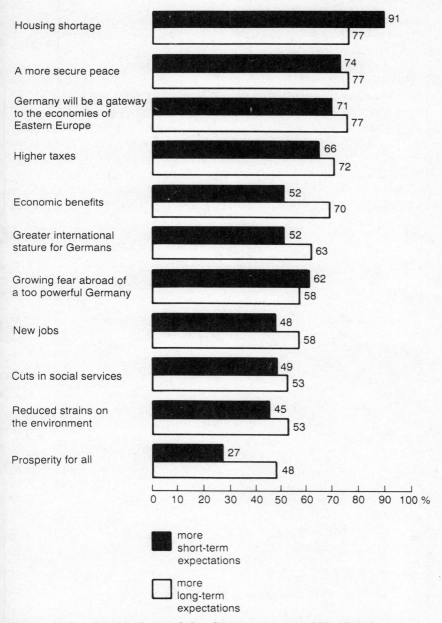

Figure 2.2   Perceptions of the Consequences of Unification

Source: Research Institute of the Konrad Adenauer Foundation, April 1990.

with widespread fears concerning the economic consequences (see Figure 2.2). Beneath the prevailing desire for unification West German opinion vacillated extraordinarily between fear of the economic, financial and social costs and the expectation of long-run economic and general political benefits (Veen, 1990).

Up to about May–June the West Germans who, comprising four-fifths of the total population, would decide the issue, were still very ambivalent and undecided about Chancellor Kohl's determined policy of speedy unification. The race between the governing and opposition parties was still wide open. It was not until June that public opinion swung behind the government's course (see Figure 2.3); optimistic economic forecasts and the conviction among West Germans that the economic problems of unity could be overcome had won the day.

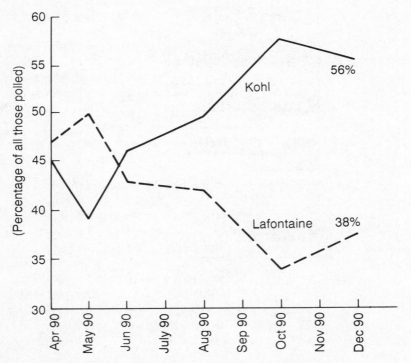

Figure 2.3   Chancellor Preference, April 1990

Source: Politbarometer – monthly survey of 1,000 people representative of those eligible to vote in (West) Germany; all-German figures as of November 1990.
Computation and graphics: Forschungsgruppe Wahlen, Mannheim.

The introduction of the Economic, Monetary and Social Union on 1 July 1990 marked the turning-point in political opinion. From then on, approval of both Kohl's policy on Germany and the governing parties in general steadily increased, while support for the challenger Lafontaine and the SPD declined. As of August 1990, the race for the first all-German election was 'over' for the great majority of Germans, with nearly 90 per cent of the people expecting a victory for the governing parties (Infas, 1991: 120).

This anticipation may have been a factor (though not the only one) in the extraordinarily low voter turnout for the first all-German elections. Of the approximately 60.4 million eligible to vote – some 48.1 million in the former Federal Republic and nearly 12.3 million in the East German *Länder* – just under 47 million cast their ballot, representing a turnout of 77.8 per cent, lower than ever before recorded in Bundestag elections in the old Federal Republic. In the Western electoral districts (excluding Berlin) the 78.6 per cent turnout effectively matched that of the first Bundestag election in 1949, and marked a drop of nearly 6 per cent from the Bundestag election of 1987. In the Eastern electoral districts even fewer participated in the election. At 74.5 per cent the turnout was higher than in the 14 October 1990 elections for *Länder* parliaments, yet was almost 20 per cent lower than in the epoch-making 18 March election to the People's Chamber which saw an extremely high election turnout of 93.4 per cent.

The Election Results

As expected, the twelfth Bundestag election upheld the previous governing parties, the CDU–CSU and FDP, which together received 54.8 per cent of the vote, an increase of 1.4 per cent on the previous Bundestag election. As shown in Table 2.1, the CDU–CSU (43.8 per cent) emerged as by far the strongest political force, extending its margin over the SPD. With 44.3 per cent and 41.8 per cent of the second votes in the old and new electoral regions, the Union showed fairly balanced strength. The SPD attracted just one-third of the vote (33.5 per cent) in this election. The party met with a very different response in East and West. While it won 35.7 per cent of the second votes in the former territory of the Federal Republic, it came up with just 24.3 per cent in the new *Länder*. Table 2.2 gives a breakdown of the election results in the East.

The FDP made the greatest gains in this election, recording, for the first time since 1980, a double-figure percentage of the vote. Its second-ballot vote of 11.0 per cent represented its best showing in a Bundestag election since 1961. In the Western electoral region it scored 10.6 per cent, in the

Table 2.1   Bundestag Election Results, 1990

	Percentage of Second Votes	Number of Seats
CDU	36.7	268
CSU	7.1	51
(CDU–CSU)	(43.8)	(319)
SPD	33.5	239
FDP	11.0	79
PDS/LL[1]	2.4	17
A90/Greens[2]	1.2	8
GREENS	3.8	–
REP	2.1	–
THE GRAYS	0.8	–
ÖDP	0.4	–
NPD	0.3	–
DSU	0.2	–
Other	0.3	–
Total		662

1   In the Eastern electoral region 11.1 per cent.
2   In the Eastern electoral region 6.1 per cent.

Eastern 12.9 per cent, and in the Halle–Altstadt constituency it even won a seat outright with 34.5 per cent of the first ballot.

The poor showing of the Greens was a surprise to many. In the Western electoral region they won just 4.8 per cent of the vote and are no longer represented in the twelfth Bundestag. The fact that there are, nevertheless, Greens representatives sitting in the twelfth Bundestag derives from a peculiarity of the electoral law governing just this one election. In July 1990, on petition of a number of the smaller political parties, the Federal Constitutional Court set aside the original application of the five-per-cent clause to Germany as a whole, on the grounds of equal chances. Accordingly, the five-per-cent barrier was applied separately in West and East Germany, thereby making it possible for the East German combined list of Alliance 90–Greens, who won 6.1 per cent of the vote, to enter the Bundestag. Had the West German Greens joined forces with the Greens in the East prior to election day, together they would have surmounted the five-per-cent hurdle with 5.1 per cent and gained 26 seats from the Western

Table 2.2   Election Results in the East, 1990

	People's Chamber[1] 18 March 1990 %	*Länder* Parliaments[2] 14 October 1990 %	Bundestag 2 December 1990 %
Voter turnout	93.4	69.1	74.5
CDU	40.8	43.6	41.8
DSU	6.3	2.4	1.0
FDP	5.3	7.8	12.9
SPD	21.9	25.2	24.3
Forum/Alliance 90/ Greens	4.9[3]	6.9[4]	6.2[5]
PDS	16.4	11.6	11.1
Other	4.4[6]	2.5[7]	2.8[8]

1 Each voter had just one vote.
2 No Landtag election in East Berlin: the SFK's own calculations.
3 'Alliance 90 = New Forum-Democracy Now – Initiative for Peace and Human Rights'; 'Green Party + Independent Women's League'.
4 New Forum; Alliance 90; New Forum–The Greens–Democracy Now; The Greens; Green List/New Forum; Independent Women's League.
5 Combined list: Alliance 90/Greens–Citizens' Initiative Movements; The Greens.
6 Including The Democratic Farmers' Party of Germany (2.2 per cent) 'Democratic Awakening – social and ecological' (0.9 per cent).
7 Including The Republikaner (0.6 per cent); German Beer-Drinkers' Union (0.4 per cent)
8 Including The Republikaner (1.3 per cent); The Grays initiated by the Seniors' Alliance – Gray Panthers (SSB–GP) (0.8 per cent).

electoral region alone. Under these circumstances, the composition of the Bundestag might have been very different: the Union parties would have failed to gain a structural majority and, at least on paper, other coalition possibilities would have emerged. In the event, Alliance 90–Greens are represented only by the eight seats won in East Germany.

The PDS–Left list also profited from the divided application of the five-per-cent clause. Nevertheless, its nationwide total of 2.4 per cent was furnished almost exclusively from the 11.1 per cent of the second votes which it won in the East. In the West it polled all of 0.3 per cent. Other parties, not represented in the Bundestag, totalled 4.1 per cent of the vote. With 2.1 per cent the Republikaner stands out as the largest among them, scoring markedly better in the Western electoral region with 2.3 per cent than in the Eastern with 1.3 per cent.

Unification brought about an increase in the number of electoral districts in Germany from 248 (excluding West Berlin) to 328. An equal number of seats are distributed according to the second (party list) vote. In addition, the complex workings of the German electoral system produced six extra seats (*Überhangmandate*) for the CDU, giving a total of 662 seats. The election gave the Union parties what is known as a structural majority. Against them the SPD, FDP and Alliance 90–Greens would not have had the 332 seats necessary for the election of a Chancellor (see Figure 2.4).

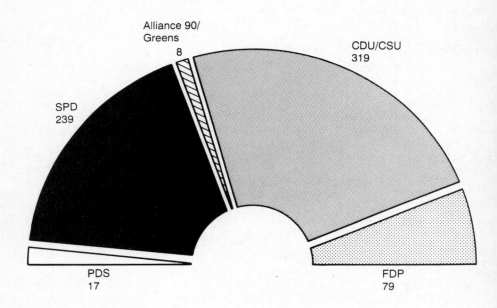

Figure 2.4   Distribution of Seats in the 1990 Bundestag (662 Seats)*

* Including six additional seats for the CDU in Mecklenburg–Vorpommern (2), Saxony–Anhalt (3) and Thuringia (1).

The overall election results do not reveal what were in some cases markedly different showings by the parties in East and West Germany and in the *Länder*. For the purposes of comparison it is necessary to assess voting behaviour in the West against the results of previous Bundestag

Table 2.3 1990 Bundestag Election Results and Changes in the *Länder* (percentage of second votes; change in percentage points)

	Turnout		CDU–CSU		SPD		FDP		GREENS		B90/Gr.		PDS		REP		Other	
	%	Diff.	%	Diff.	%	Diff.	%	Diff.	%	Diff.	%	Diff.	%	Diff.	%	Diff.	%	Diff.
Bavaria[1]	74.4	– 7.3	51.9	– 3.2	26.7	– 0.3	8.7	+ 0.6	4.6	– 3.1	–		0.2	*	5.0	*	3.0	+ 0.9
Saxony[2]	76.2	– 17.4	49.5	+ 6.1	18.2	+ 3.1	12.4	+ 6.7			5.9	+ 1.2	9.0	– 4.6	1.2	*	3.8	– 13.7
Baden-Württemberg[1]	77.4	– 5.7	46.5	– 0.2	29.1	– 0.2	12.3	+ 0.3	5.7	– 4.3	–		0.3	*	3.2	*	2.9	+ 0.8
Rhineland–Palatinate[1]	81.7	– 5.0	45.6	+ 0.5	36.1	– 1.0	10.4	+ 1.3	4.0	– 3.5	–		0.2	*	1.7	*	1.9	+ 0.6
Thuringia[2]	76.4	– 18.1	45.2	– 7.3	21.9	+ 4.4	14.6	+ 10.0	–		6.1	+ 2.0	8.3	– 3.1	1.2	*	2.6	– 7.2
Lower Saxony[1]	80.6	– 4.4	44.3	+ 2.8	38.4	– 3.0	10.3	+ 1.5	4.5	– 2.9	–		0.3	*	1.0	*	1.2	+ 0.4
Schleswig–Holstein[1]	78.6	– 5.8	43.5	+ 1.6	38.5	– 1.3	11.4	+ 2.0	4.0	– 4.0	–		0.3	*	1.2	*	1.1	+ 0.3
Hesse[1]	81.1	– 4.6	41.3	0	38.0	– 0.7	10.9	+ 1.8	5.6	– 3.8	–		0.4	*	2.1	*	1.8	+ 0.4
Mecklenburg Vorpommern[2]	70.9	– 22.0	41.2	+ 4.9	26.5	+ 3.1	9.1	+ 5.5	–		5.9	+ 1.5	14.2	– 8.6	1.4	*	1.5	– 8.0
North Rhine Westphalia[1]	78.7	– 6.7	40.5	+ 0.4	41.1	– 2.1	11.0	+ 2.6	4.3	– 3.2	–		0.3	*	1.3	*	1.5	+ 0.6
Berlin[3]	80.6	– 3.3	39.4	+ 9.8	30.6	– 5.7	9.1	+ 5.6	3.9	– 2.9	3.3	– 0.5	9.7	– 2.9	2.5	– 1.9	1.5	– 1.5
West[4]	83.4	+ 3.8	47.8	+ 10.1	30.2	– 7.1	9.9	+ 6.0	5.4	– 6.4	1.0	*	1.3	*	3.0	– 4.5	1.4	– 0.3
East[2]	76.0	– 14.8	24.3	– 6.0	31.3	– 3.5	7.7	+ 4.7	1.4	*	7.4	– 1.6	24.8	– 5.4	1.5	*	1.5	– 3.2
Saxony Anhalt[2]	72.2	– 21.2	38.6	– 5.9	24.7	+ 1.0	19.7	+ 12.0	–		5.3	+ 1.3	9.4	– 4.6	1.0	*	1.4	– 4.7
Saarland[1]	85.1	– 2.2	38.1	– 3.1	51.2	+ 7.7	6.0	– 0.9	2.3	– 4.8	–		0.2	*	0.9	*	1.4	+ 0.1
Hamburg[1]	78.2	– 4.8	36.6	– 0.8	41.0	– 0.2	12.0	+ 2.4	5.8	– 5.2	–		1.1	*	1.7	*	1.8	+ 1.1
Brandenburg[2]	73.8	– 19.7	36.3	+ 2.7	32.9	+ 3.0	9.7	+ 5.0	–		6.6	+ 1.2	11.0	– 7.3	1.7	*	1.8	+ 6.3
Bremen[1]	76.5	– 6.2	30.9	+ 2.0	42.5	– 4.0	12.8	+ 4.0	8.3	– 6.2	–		1.1	*	2.1	*	2.3	+ 1.0
Germany[5]	77.8	– 8.3	43.8	+ 0.5	33.5	– 0.1	11.0	+ 2.9	3.8	– 2.7	1.2	+ 0.1	2.4	– 1.3	2.1	+ 1.9	2.1	– 1.4

1 Change from 1987 Bundestag election (BE).
2 Change from 1990 People's Chamber election (PCE).
3 Change from 1989 Berlin elections + 1990 PCE.
4 Change from 1989 Berlin elections.
5 Change from 1987 BE + 1989 Berlin elections + 1990 PCE.
* Did not participate in previous election.

Source: Calculations of the Research Institute of the Konrad Adenauer Foundation.

elections and to compare the outcome in the East with the March 1990 election to the People's Chamber. The latter comparison is not without its problems, for in the case of the People's Chamber election (inclusive of East Berlin) there was only one ballot and no five-per-cent. However, the October 1990 Landtag elections in the East are even less suitable as a means of comparison, since not only was there no vote in populous East Berlin, but they were also decided to a remarkable degree on the basis of local issues and personalities – for instance, in Brandenburg in favour of the SPD's Stolpe and in Saxony in favour of the CDU's leading candidate, Biedenkopf (Veen *et al.*, 1990).

In comparing East and West by means of Table 2.3, one is struck initially by the fact that the voting was marked by a greater dynamism and sharper definition in the five new *Länder* than in the old Western *Länder*. Apart from the Greens' heavy losses in the West, the result was similar to the Bundestag election of 1987.

Trends in the West

Compared with 1987, the Union remained stable in the West. Over the past decade, in fact, it has been able more or less to maintain its level of support, albeit with some fluctuation from one election to another. In this election the substantial losses suffered by the Bavarian CSU (–3.2 per cent) were offset by CDU gains in Lower Saxony, Schleswig–Holstein, Bremen, Rhineland–Palatinate and North Rhine–Westphalia.

The SPD continued the long downturn that had begun in the 1970s, falling another 1.1 per cent from its 1987 showing. Its 35.9 per cent share of the vote represented its worst results since 1957. In the Western *Länder* the SPD gained only in the Saarland (+7.7 per cent), the home *Land* of its candidate for Chancellor. Otherwise it lost support in all the *Länder*, most heavily in Bremen (–4.0 per cent), Lower Saxony (–3.0 per cent) and North Rhine–Westphalia (–2.1 per cent). The FDP has been gaining steadily since 1983, up 1.5 per cent from just the previous election.

The considerable losses sustained by the West German Greens (–3.5 per cent) are attributable, first, to poor mobilization of their constituency. Right up to election day virtually none of the West German Greens supporters recognized any threat to their party, and simply assumed that it would be returned to the Bundestag. In addition, few of its supporters were particularly motivated by the overriding election theme of unification, and remaining Greens supporters were further demotivated by serious splits in the Greens' leadership. Right up to the end many supporters, especially the young, were unsure how they would vote (Veen *et al.*, 1990b).

Nevertheless, the potential of the West German Greens is greater than the results of this election would indicate. The fact that the Greens must still be regarded as an established party in the West German party system is confirmed by the Greens' showing in subsequent Landtag elections in the first six months of 1991 in Hesse, Rhineland–Palatinate and Hamburg. In future they may well rise above the five-per-cent mark nationally, especially since the East and West Greens united in December 1990.

Considerable gains were made by the splinter parties, who won a total of 4.7 per cent of the vote in the Western electoral region, with distinct advances mostly on the far Right. Running for the first time the Republikaner received 2.3 per cent of the vote. With their strongholds in Bavaria (5.0 per cent), Baden–Württemberg (3.2 per cent) and West Berlin (3.0 per cent) they have a stabilizing core of voters that could be enlarged by drifting protest voters in times of economic and social crisis.

Trends in the East

In the Eastern electoral region the CDU improved its position slightly (+1.0 per cent) over the People's Chamber election. It obviously profited little from the decline of the right-wing conservative DSU, which dropped 5.3 per cent and fell into the ranks of the splinter parties with 1.0 per cent of the total vote. Regionally the CDU's results were chequered. While it made large gains in Saxony (+6.1 per cent) and in Mecklenburg–Vorpommern (+4.9 per cent), it also sustained heavy losses in Thuringia and Saxony–Anhalt (−7.3 and −5.9 per cent respectively), which were clearly connected with the particular gains for the FDP in these two *Länder* (+10.0 and +12.0 per cent respectively). With 12.9 per cent the FDP was able to more than double its share of the vote in East Germany; it made strong gains in all the *Länder*.

The SPD, which had made an astonishingly weak showing in the People's Chamber election with 21.9 per cent, was able to gain a further 2.4 per cent to a total of just 24.3 per cent, over 10 per cent less than in West Germany. Above-average gains were made in Thuringia (+4.4 per cent), Mecklenburg–Vorpommerania (+3.1 per cent), Saxony (+3.1 per cent) and Brandenburg (+3.0 per cent). Bündnis 90–Greens improved by 1.3 per cent over the People's Chamber election and, with that, appeared to consolidate their position at a low level, analogous to the establishment of the Greens in West Germany.

The PDS, whose virtually only base of support is among East German voters, lost substantially from the People's Chamber election – roughly one-third of its previous vote. Its losses were especially heavy in Mecklenburg–Vorpommern and Brandenburg, where it nevertheless recorded its best results (14.2 and 11.0 per cent respectively) outside its East Berlin stronghold. In the next Bundestag, when the five-per-cent clause will be applied universally, the PDS will probably not be represented, although it will probably continue to play a role as a regional party in *Länder* parliaments and at the communal level in East Germany. Finally, with 1.3 per cent the Republikaner party garnered distinctly fewer votes in East Germany than in West. And, with 0.3 per cent, the NPD received no more than marginal support.

The Situation in Berlin

The party landscape in the new federal capital deserves greater attention since it does, after all, establish the political setting and atmosphere in which parliamentarians and the German government will conduct business and make decisions. If, in some cases, the parties made very different showings in West and East Germany, this was true to an even greater extent – and with peculiar twists – in East and West Berlin.

Table 2.4   Bundestag Election in Berlin, 1990 (percentage of second votes)

	All Berlin %	West Berlin %	East Berlin %
Voter turnout	80.6	83.4	76.0
CDU	39.4	47.8	24.3
SPD	30.6	30.2	31.3
FDP	9.1	9.9	7.7
Greens/AL	3.9	5.4	1.4
A90/Greens	3.3	1.0	7.4
PDS	9.7	1.3	24.8
DSU	0.2	0.2	0.2
Republikaner	2.5	3.0	1.5
Other	1.2	1.2	1.3

Source: Statistical Office of Berlin.

As can be seen in Table 2.4, with 39.4 per cent of the vote the CDU was the strongest party in Berlin as a whole, although it clearly fell short of its results nationwide. With 30.6 per cent the SPD also made a weaker showing than its overall result in the rest of the country. The third strongest party in all of Berlin, however, was the PDS with 9.7 per cent, just ahead of the FDP with 9.1 per cent. These results highlight the completely different electorates in the two parts of the city. Whereas party representation in West Berlin roughly corresponds with that in the old Federal Republic, quite a different picture emerges in East Berlin, not only compared with the west of the city, but also in relation to the East German *Länder*. The CDU's results in the East and West differ by over 20 per cent. In West Berlin the CDU took 47.8 per cent of the vote, in East Berlin just 24.3 per cent; thus, in the eastern part of the city it came in third, behind even the PDS. In East Berlin the CDU holds a considerably weaker position than in the new *Länder* as a whole. The same is true, to a lesser extent, of the FDP. The SPD had almost identical results in East and West Berlin. In East Berlin, with 31.3 per cent, it was in fact the strongest party, thus faring markedly better than in the other East German *Länder*, with the exception of Brandenburg where it won 32.9 per cent. With its atypical sociopolitical structure, East Berlin remains the principal stronghold of the PDS. Here the successor to the SED won nearly a quarter of the vote, more than twice as much as in East Germany.

Voter Turnout: Non-voters, Party Faithful, Swing Voters

The electoral turnout of 77.8 per cent was the lowest recorded for any Bundestag election. In the Eastern electoral region it was even lower at 74.5 per cent (including East Berlin) than in the old West German *Länder* (78.6 per cent including West Berlin). A particularly large number of those between the ages of 18 and 35 chose not to vote – even more so in East Germany than in West – and among young voters (18–24), the turnout nationwide fell below 65 per cent. The number of non-voters was especially high among young East Germans. Just a little more than half of them (56 per cent of young men and just 54.6 per cent of young women) made use of their right to vote, nearly 10 per cent less than in the same age group in the West. On the other hand, voter turnout traditionally runs well above average among voters between 50 and 70 years of age. After that it falls off again, partly due to health reasons and partly from growing distance from day-to-day political affairs. In contrast to young voters, the older voters (50–70) went to the polls in equally strong, above-average numbers (cf. Statistisches Bundesamt, 1991).

Within the old Federal Republic, decreasing voter turnout has been a growing trend for a number of years; this has been more marked, up until now, in Landtag rather than in Bundestag elections and is related to the increase in voters who swing from one party to another. These are both manifestations of profound changes in the voting behaviour of West Germans – changes that have gathered momentum in the latter half of the 1980s. A loosening of party ties is part and parcel of the continuing break-up of the traditional sociopolitical milieu in which social and economic interests and religious and philosophical orientations came together with intense party identifications in a way that was mutually stabilizing, and to a certain extent remains so today. In general, the younger generation (the under-40s) stay more aloof from the parties and make decisions on a more flexible, short-term and, above all, pragmatic basis geared to the prevailing problems and the parties' perceived capabilities for solving them. As Table 2.5 shows, the readiness to switch one's vote to another party is growing. Political protest is becoming increasingly sharp and quick to emerge, and may be articulated through populist protest parties such as the Republikaner. Or, as happens with increasing frequency, people simply do not vote (Veen, 1991).

Table 2.5   Party Loyalists and Swing Voters

	Sept. 1980	Jan. 1983	Jan. 1987	March 1989	Oct./ Nov. 1989	March 1990	Sept. 1990
	%	%	%	%	%	%	%
In the past ... Always voted the same party	60	59	48	48	47	45	44
Sometimes voted for another party	24	30	38	36	39	36	41
Voted for the first time	3	3	3	2	3	3	2
Never voted yet	11	6	7	7	4	7	6
No indication	2	2	3	7	7	9	7

Source: Research Institute of the Konrad Adenauer Foundation, file control no. 8012, 8302, 8701, 8901, 8902, 9003, 9007.

In line with these developments in voting habits and patterns, the proportion of non-voters has increased rapidly in the old West German *Länder* from about the mid-1980s onwards (see Table 2.6).

Table 2.6   Non-Voters in Bundestag Elections, 1972–90

	1972 %	1976 %	1980 %	1983 %	1987 %	FRG %	1990 West %	East %
Total	8.9	9.3	11.4	10.9	15.7	22.2	21.4	25.5
18–24 year-olds	15.5	16.6	20.4	17.4	25.7	37.1	35.2	44.7
25–34 year-olds	10.3	12.2	15.8	14.7	22.1	31.3	30.1	35.6
35–44 year-olds	7.3	8	10.4	9.7	15.2	22.5	22.0	24.1
45–59 year olds	6	6.3	8.1	7.5	11.2	16.2	15.9	17.4
60 years and older	9.8	8.9	11.2	11.7	15.5	19.3	19.3	19.5
Men	8.6	9.2	11.8	10.9	15.8	23.0	22.2	26.1
Women	9.8	10	12.9	12.2	17.9	24.3	23.9	25.9

Source: Amtliche Repräsentativstatistik/Research Institute of the Konrad Adenauer Foundation. Age and gender distinctions have been compiled without regard to absentee ballots.

It would be unhistorical to say that the new *Länder* had undergone an analogous development (in double time, as it were) for under SED totalitarianism the sociopolitical milieux remaining from the Weimar period were systematically destroyed. Nonetheless, the two parts of Germany display quite similar patterns of behaviour. The new kind of voting behaviour that is increasingly prevalent in West Germany is also evident in the East, and these conditions may produce even greater swings in future elections.

In the past there has been little well-founded and up-to-date information on the social background of non-voters and of their reasons for not voting. However interesting data on the origins and motives of non-voters has recently emerged from a broad-based survey of non-voters in the 1990 Bundestag election in the Greater Stuttgart area. Conducted by Michael Eilfort as part of a dissertation project, the survey involved interviews with more than 1,750 non-voters and is scheduled to for publication in 1992 in the *Studien zur Politik* series, Schöningh, Paderborn.

Whilst swing voters are found predominantly in the new middle class of white-collar workers with higher levels of education, non-voters more frequently come from lower social classes and have less formal education and training. As a general rule, voters of higher social status participate more actively in elections, although they are also more disposed to switch parties. In addition, the degree of social and cultural integration plays a role in voting behaviour. Thus, trade union members, practising Christians of either denomination and the gainfully employed vote more frequently than non-union members, non-churchgoers and the unemployed. Gender has little influence on inclination to vote.

There is obviously no one type of non-voter, but rather a plurality of reasons for not voting which play different roles under different electoral circumstances. However, on the evidence of the Stuttgart study of 1990, we can assume that voting is still regarded as a special responsibility, at least in West Germany. For many people, therefore, not voting has to be seen as an intentional act – as a way of expressing one's opinion on the political parties. Four basic reasons can be distinguished empirically: a feeling of political impotence, frustration or a tendency toward general apathy; a view that there are no important issues at stake or genuine alternatives available; a belief that the race has already been decided in favour of one party; and, finally, dissatisfaction with the policies or with the candidates and platforms of the party closest to one's own position and a consequent desire to demonstrate this by refusing to vote. Although, in theory, it is conceivable that the refusal to vote signals a discontent with democracy, in view of the continued high level of support for the German political system this currently does not appear to be a very cogent argument.

As neatly as we can analyse motives for non-voting, they appear much more entangled in real life. Among various sets of voters in East and West Germany, altogether different motives may have prompted abstentions and affected the outcome to varying degrees. First, the general conviction in West and East Germany that, from August onwards, the election had already been decided in favour of Kohl and the parties in power probably played an important role. As a result, the SPD and the CDU–CSU (to a lesser extent), both lost votes. Along with the awareness that the SPD no longer had a chance, another important factor was probably that many social democratic sympathizers were not happy with their candidate for Chancellor, nor with his approach to unification, and therefore denied the party their vote.

The fall-off in turnout among the Greens supporters in the old West German *Länder* had the most telling impact. The two reasons for this have already been mentioned: the belief that the party would pass the five-per-cent barrier anyway, combined with low motivation regarding the national question. On the other hand, the Republikaner party was apparently able to profit by the other parties' relative inability to mobilize. The greater the decline in turnout in specific electoral districts, the better the party fared. This might suggest a relatively stable core of Republikaner voters at about two per cent nationwide (Veen *et al.*, 1991). Another interpretation points to the mobilization of independent protest voters by the Republikaner party (Gibowski and Kaase, 1991: 9).

Another major contributory factor to voter abstention in the West was probably sheer election fatigue and a surfeit of politics; this was probably the case in the East after a politically riveting year that had already seen three elections. Finally the East Germans may have been showing the first signs of disappointment with the process of economic and social renewal.

Greater attention will have to be devoted to patterns of voting as a form of political participation. Up to a point, not voting may be a reflection of political poise and maturity, since the turnout in German elections remains high by international standards. However, in view of the importance accorded to voting as a citizen's obligation in German political culture, the growing trend of abstention, especially among younger voters, has to be interpreted as an early sign of crisis in the state of the parties and the legitimacy and credibility of the party system. Even if, overall, abstention did not play an extraordinary role in the 1990 elections, the parties will have to pay more attention than they have in the past to the critical signals of very low voter turnouts. Otherwise the latent alienation from parties and politics could imperceptibly turn into a dangerous alienation from democracy.

In addition to the mobilization of previous voters, the number of voters who swing from one party to another also determines how the parties fare. Although exact figures on these crossovers are almost too difficult to obtain, exit polls do, however, yield important data (Forschungsgruppe Wahlen, 1990: 25 ff: Infas, 1991: 100 ff). Here, too, it is imperative to analyse the Western and Eastern electoral regions separately, as the parties are founded on entirely different electorates in the two parts of Germany, with different predispositions to switch party allegiance. The CDU–CSU and the SPD still find their main base of support in the traditional party faithful from traditional social backgrounds, although this is less and less the case. In the new *Länder* these social–historical ties are almost completely absent, apart from the narrow segment of Catholic voters with their strong affinity to the CDU and the larger group of orthodox socialist voters of the old SED establishment who make up the PDS party faithful.

Thus, in West Germany more than three-quarters of previous CDU–CSU and SPD voters opted for their old party in the 1990 Bundestag election.

The constituencies of the FDP and Greens are far less solid. Two-thirds of the FDP voters in 1990 were new voters – in part an effect of its major gains. But the large proportion of swing voters for the FDP confirms, once again, that the party in the West has a relatively narrow electoral base of its own and that the majority of its voters vote instrumentally, with a view to a desired coalition and to strengthen checks and balances within the government. The FDP made its greatest gains from former CDU voters, but also took votes from the SPD and Greens.

The West German Greens could rely on the support of just half of its steady voters. One-third of former Green voters in 1990 favoured the SPD. To a lesser extent, votes also went to the Union, the FDP and the PDS–Left list. The CDU and CSU lost considerably to the SPD and FDP. The SPD in turn relinquished even more votes to the Union and the FDP. On balance the SPD lost substantially to the two coalition parties, in more or less equal measure. What is more, it lost to the Republikaner. On balance, in West Germany it won only from former Greens voters. The Union ended up with marked gains from the SPD and the Greens. In this way it was able more or less to offset the defections to the Republikaner and other splinter parties on the right. Between the Union and the FDP there was considerable crossing over, but on balance this produced no major Union losses. Republikaner voters in the 1990 Bundestag elections were primarily former Union supporters, although they also came in larger numbers from the SPD. In addition, the Republikaner party drew particularly well among young, previous non-voters and first-time voters.

The balance sheet on voter defections reveals the customary complexity of crossover concealed under the surface of the essentially unaltered final results in West Germany. In East Germany, given weaker party ties, the swing potential was substantially greater. The pattern of shifting allegiances among followers of all the parties, except the PDS, was even more varied, with extensive crossover between former CDU and SPD voters. Moreover, both parties lost votes to the FDP, which made gains from all parties. The strongest draw was from previous Union voters, followed by SPD, PDS and previous Bündnis 90–Greens voters. The FDP also gained from smaller parties that had made a stronger showing in the March 1990 election. The CDU was able more or less to compensate for the heavy defections to the FDP largely through gains from the DSU and votes from other small parties such as the Democratic Farmers' Party. The SPD's gains came mainly from previous PDS voters. Crossovers involving the PDS were least common, its previous voters again voting PDS with exceptional frequency. Compared with the March election it lost mainly to the SPD and Bündnis 90–Greens.

Social Structure and Voting Behaviour

The large national parties find the basis of their support in very different voter groups in East and West Germany. In this election the West German returns present a familiar picture. Since the Union parties have particularly strong backing in Catholic and rural areas, their strongholds thus lie in the north-east of Lower Saxony, in southern Baden–Württemberg, in northern Rhineland-Palatinate and, of course, in Bavaria. However, the breakdown of the milieu-dominated strongholds continues. The CDU made some slight gains in the Ruhr conurbation. Those belonging to agricultural professions, the self-employed, white-collar workers and civil servants, as well as professional groups with higher academic qualifications, voted in above-average numbers for the Union. On the other hand, the CDU–CSU was underrepresented among West German workers. Furthermore, although blue-collar workers and trade union members comprise part of the classical SPD milieu, the large lead among unionized workers which the SPD had over the CDU–CSU shrank perceptibly in this election (Gibowski and Kaase, 1991: 15 ff).

Whereas the middle class dominates the voter profile of the CDU and CSU in the West, blue-collar workers constitute the dominant group in the CDU's East German constituency. Half of all East German workers, especially those in rural areas and small towns, bucked the Western party tradition by voting CDU, and so made the most substantial contribution to the CDU victory in the new *Länder*. By contrast, the overrepresentation of those in agricultural professions and the self-employed in the CDU constituency in East Germany conforms to the West German pattern. The connection between religious denomination and the CDU vote is also similarly strong, although of a specifically Eastern character. Here the CDU is not just the party of the few Catholics but is backed in above-average numbers by Protestants, who make up about 35 per cent of the electorate and by far the largest religious community. (In West Germany the Protestants vote for the two large national parties in roughly equal numbers.) Finally, because the majority in the former GDR belong to no Church, the number of those in the Union nationwide who do not belong to any denomination has risen considerably. In fact, every third CDU voter in East Germany falls into this category.

In some ways, the SPD also shows markedly different voter profiles in East and West Germany. In West Germany it has its strongest backing in large urban areas with sizeable concentrations of workers. SPD strongholds have also progressively broken down over time, though not so much as those of the Union. Blue-collar workers still figure strongly among its voters, while white-collar workers are slightly underrepresented. Catholics rarely vote SPD, and the proportion of those who do not belong to any Church is distinctly above-average in the SPD electorate.

In East Germany, on the other hand, the SPD has not yet established a distinct voter profile. The social democrats are in dual competition with the PDS and Bündnis 90–Greens, and all three parties recruit their voters from similar social strata, espousing a related political ideology. Yet the voter profile of the PDS is clearly demarcated from the other left-of-centre parties, and is sharply defined. The PDS has its strongest hold among the so-called 'intelligentsia' of the old GDR – the better educated, managerial staff and academic professions – but it is also supported by above-average numbers of young voters, male and female, students and apprentices. Consequently, the PDS fares far better in the big cities than in rural areas. PDS voters, almost without exception, do not belong to any Church.

The SPD in East Germany is also largely a party of non-churchgoers. Its voters are more from metropolitan than rural, small-town areas. Here white-collar and blue-collar workers have an almost equally strong, or rather weak, representation, since the SPD has yet to firmly establish itself in East German society. Apart from the scant sympathy for Lafontaine's policy on Germany, this lack of support might also have been due to the rejection of anything that could be construed as 'socialist' as well as to the absence of trade unions as auxiliaries of the SPD. With the build-up of the DGB (German Trade Union Federation) unions already underway in the Eastern *Länder*, the SPD became increasingly attractive.

The FDP electorate is similarly structured in East and West Germany: the self-employed, civil servants, white-collar workers (particularly executive staff) are in some cases considerably overrepresented; blue-collar workers are distinctly underrepresented. The self-employed are even more strongly overrepresented in the East German FDP than in the West. Also, the proportion of voters in professions necessitating a university degree is similarly high in both the East and West. Traditionally Protestants vote FDP far more frequently than do Catholics.

The voter profile of Bündnis 90–Greens does not differ appreciably from that of the Greens in the West. These parties have a very clear-cut base of support mostly among young academics, white-collar workers in demanding professions and young voters who have not yet completed their education. In both parts of Germany, those who do not belong to any Church vote in above-average numbers for the Greens and Bündnis 90. Alliance 90/Green voters are more likely to be resident in big cities.

The Republikaner party is supported chiefly by younger workers with lower levels of education, with no differences between East and West Germany. In the West the party has regional strongholds mainly in rural areas, but also in specific districts in the big cities.

In some cases, the voter profiles of the parties also reveal marked differences in their age structures and male–female ratios (Statistisches Bundesamt, 1991). The 1990 election largely confirmed the trends so long evident in the old Federal Republic. Strikingly, the age structures of the CDU and SPD electorates in East Germany have developed along very similar lines to those in the West. In this last election the Union made its strongest showing among those over 45, with approximately 45 per cent of this age group voting CDU–CSU. The Union vote then rose in step with increasing age, with more than half of the over-60s supporting it, especially in West Germany. In particular, women of middle age and older (45–60) placed their confidence in the Union.

In contrast, the SPD has a more balanced ratio of men and women voters, their age profile is also more balanced, compared with the Union. One the whole the SPD electorate is younger, the party receiving above-average support from the 25–45 age group and from men and women equally. In West Germany the SPD is somewhat underrepresented among those over 60, while in East Germany it enjoys relatively stronger backing from that age group. The opposite is the case among young SPD voters: their proportion is higher in West than in East Germany.

The FDP receives most support from the 35–60-year-olds, both men and women. It also gets slightly above-average support from young voters (18–25).

The Greens and Bündnis 90–Greens have by far the youngest voter profile, with both parties scoring their best results among 18–35-year-olds. In West Germany, despite their sizeable losses, the Greens won about 10 per cent of the vote in this age group. In East Germany they came out even higher, as they were able to gather more than 12 per cent of the 18–25-year-old vote alone. In both East and West, young women contributed most to the strong showing of the Greens and Bündnis 90 in the younger age groups.

The Republikaner too are largely a party of young voters, although with a completely different social structure. The party's backing is exceptionally strong among young men between the ages of 18 and 25 – in the East even more than in West Germany. Almost every third East German Republikaner voter is younger than 25 years old. Women are rare among Republikaner supporters, as are voters over 60 years of age.

Although the PDS has a relatively balanced age structure, age and gender in combination show two distinctive areas of strength: among men over 60 and among 18–25-year-old women. These patterns were discernible in the October Landtag elections and were maintained in December 1990. The first group probably included many of those belonging to the old establishment, while the younger women were probably drawn to the PDS for more concrete motives of a social and professional nature. Indeed, the PDS geared much of its campaign directly to this group.

The Election Campaigns

Seldom has a Bundestag election been so dominated by one theme as was the first all-German election. With the opening of the Wall in early November 1989, and with Chancellor Kohl's early initiative in the 10-Point Plan the following month, it was clear that German unification was on the political agenda. At this stage, however, there was no telling what sort of dynamic the unification process would develop. The polls signalled a desire for unity, but public opinion was by no means unanimous on the question of timing or concerning the attendant financial burdens and economic and social risks. In the late spring of 1990 more Germans found the Kohl government's unification policy to be too hasty than appropriate (cf. Infas, 1991: 128).

At this stage the SPD's Chancellor candidate Oscar Lafontaine, who wanted to make unification a slower process and who stressed the economic problems it involved, was leading Chancellor Kohl in the polls. Almost up to the midway point in this election year, public opinion in West Germany, unlike in East Germany, was ambivalent, unstable and open, torn between the basic desire for unity and anxiety over possible dangers of a rapid process. By June–July, however, there was a prevailing sense that Kohl's rapid unification policy was the better course, and that the coalition was more capable of managing unification and economic reconstruction in the East. This was largely the result of government's ability to make use of its prerogative to take action and to put forward initiatives. Once the course had been set toward unity, there was virtually no alternative to the government's approach.

Lafontaine was evidently surprised by the dynamic of this process. From the outset, as was evident in public, he had failed to come to terms with unification and, after Economic, Social and Monetary Union, he was no longer in a position to readapt. Although he maintained his policy of misgivings and warnings, this never represented a real alternative to government policy after 1 July.

The SPD's main campaign slogan, 'The New Road', completely missed the political agenda. Building on the party's original campaign planning, with the theme of 'Progress 90', the focus was entirely on Oscar Lafontaine and the theme of modernization. Under other circumstances this might have made for a promising offensive. The new 'socially and ecologically responsible road' would, for example, be financed by introducing a 'green

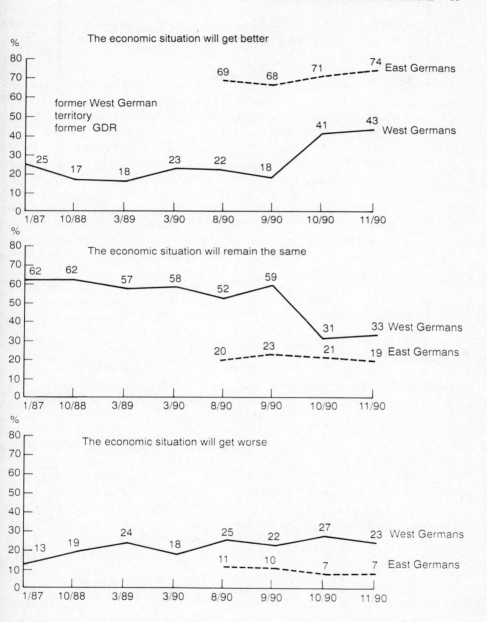

Figure 2.5 Expectations of the Economic Future, 1987–90

Source: Research Institute of the Konrad Adenauer Foundation.

tax' and by raising the severance tax. At this historic moment, however, the modernization discussion passed by the burning questions of unification which preoccupied the electorate, especially in the East.

In contrast, the Union focused the campaign entirely on Chancellor Kohl as the undisputed architect of unity, and drew the analogy with the early years of the Federal Republic and the historic decisions of the Union-led government for economic reconstruction. Thus, one key slogan under the large poster portrait of Helmut Kohl read: 'Chancellor for Germany'. The other, with the slogan 'Together we'll do it – Freedom, Prosperity, Security' appealed on the one hand to the new sense of national identity, and on the other to the prevailing optimism about Germany's self-ability to manage the problems of unification. As demonstrated in Figure 2.5, in November 1990 roughly 50 per cent of the electorate were convinced that things would continue to move ahead in Germany, 30 per cent expected the situation to remain the same, and only 20 per cent anticipated things getting worse. Here, of course, the West and East Germans were setting out from very different starting-points.

The Union's election campaign was in harmony with the climate of opinion and expectation and simultaneously reinforced it. In this respect the Union campaign was a model of focused political communication, on

Table 2.7   Perceptions of Economic Reform in the East

	The Federal Republic is capable of rebuilding the East German economy		This is beyond our means	
	March–April 1990 %	August 1990 %	March–April 1990 %	August 1990 %
FRG total	72	80	25	20
CDU–CSU supporters	81	86	18	14
SPD supporters	70	75	28	24
FDP supporters	79	92	20	8
Greens supporters	72	83	28	17

Source: Research Institute of the Konrad Adenauer Foundation, file control no. 9002, 9005.

which theorists and practicioners of election campaigns frequently reason, but which are seldom realized (Radunski, 1980). In the heat of the campaign the Union was cited four times as often as the SPD as conducting the best election campaign. This opinion was shared by supporters of all parties. Table 2.8 gives a detailed breakdown of the electorate's perceptions of all the party campaigns.

Table 2.8   Perceptions of Party Campaigns

| | The best election campaign is being waged by ... | | | | | | | | | |
| | CDU–CSU | | SPD | | FDP | | Greens–Bündnis 90 | | No answer | |
	Oct. 1990 %	Nov. 1990 %	Oct. 1990 %	Nov. 1990 %	Oct. 1990 %	Nov. 1990 %	Oct. 1990 %	Nov. 1990 %	Oct. 1990 %	Nov. 1990 %
United Germany	44	42	13	10	3	2	2	3	35	40
CDU supporters	38	59	6	5	5	2	0	2	30	33
SPD supporters	37	32	25	22	1	2	2	3	35	40
FDP supporters	46	45	5	5	13	11	1	1	35	37
Supporters of the Greens – Bündnis 90	36	31	16	11	0	3	16	14	22	40
Supporters of the Left List/PDS	48	30	4	13	4	4	4	0	9	26
West Germany	40	37	11	9	3	1	2	3	43	48
East Germany	60	62	19	14	5	6	3	3	9	12

Source: Research Institute of the Konrad Adenauer Foundation, file control no. 9010, 9011, 9012, 9013.

As coalition partner, the FDP did not conduct a self-aggrandizing campaign, preferring to rely entirely on the prestige of Foreign Minister Genscher and his role in the negotiations to secure foreign backing for German unity. FDP posters, featuring Genscher's portrait, proclaimed 'The Germany the world trusts'. On a second level, however, the FDP disassociated itself from its government partner in two ways: by its demand for a low-tax regime in the new *Länder* and, more aggravating still, by its rather subliminal campaign to prevent an absolute majority for the Union. To judge from the polls this was never a real possibility, yet the German aversion to absolute party majorities had already helped the FDP to mobilize coalition voters in the Bundestag election of 1983.

The only other party to wage a campaign accentuating policy on Germany was the PDS, which presented itself as a 'left, radical democratic, ecological and feminist force' for a united Germany. Especially for East German voters, it portrayed itself as a guardian of the emancipatory and 'social achievements' of the ex-GDR.

The election campaigns of the Greens, Bündnis 90 and the Republikaner followed well-worn paths. Ultimately, the Greens in the West failed to come to grips with unity, their leaders (far more so than their followers) being polarized on the question of dual statehood. Upholding 'anti-imperialist' standards and promising rigorous rejection of any calculated power politics, they wanted no part of combined electoral lists with the East German Greens. Nevertheless, in their campaign themes, the Greens and Bündnis 90–Greens were already on the same track: ecology, peace, feminism, grass-roots democracy, but with no discernible thematic focus. The Republikaner campaign was tailored to Schönhuber, who reiterated the party's populist themes: law and order and the menace of foreigners, and furthermore, claims over the formerly German Eastern territories beyond the Oder and Neisse rivers.

As always in Bundestag elections, the campaigns were conceived in the national party headquarters, and (with the exception of the Greens and Bündnis 90) directed from the centre at all stages. In the case of the national parties and the FDP the campaigns were implemented through direct collaboration between national party headquarters and district organizations, which are responsible for the nomination of candidates in the electoral districts. However, this process – well established in the Western districts – was scarcely realizable in the new *Länder*. One exception was the PDS, which could rely on the far-reaching organizational structures of the SED and commanded by far the most developed party organization in East Germany. In the other parties, active district and local party organizations are only now beginning to take shape. Where the administrative machinery was taken over from the old bloc parties, there was such a dearth of experience in the organization of election campaigns that, on the whole, the West German national committees of the CDU, SDP and FDP had to take a direct hand in the Eastern campaign.

The organizational weakness of nearly all the parties in the new *Länder* is of course scarcely surprising. However, it does refute some assumptions about the allegedly big organizational advantage of the former bloc parties, namely the CDU and the LDPD (Liberal Democratic Party of Germany). In the spring of 1990 the latter became the LDP and later merged with the FDP. Even if the former bloc parties initially wielded a grossly oversized party apparatus, this proved increasingly unsuited for party work and campaigning under the new conditions of democratic communications and competition. The erosion of the old party organizations had already begun by late autumn 1989 and, since then, membership has fallen drastically. In retrospect one must question whether the official membership figures for the former bloc parties were ever anywhere near correct, since summer 1990, it was clear that their organization and membership existed only on paper (see below).

Themes and Chancellor Candidates

During the months immediately before the election, unification forced all other political problems into the background. Some of these had still been very prominent in the spring: environmental protection; political asylum and foreigners; and housing construction and rents. From their extremely different point of departure, of course, the issue of unification was accentuated very differently in the East, as Figure 2.6 shows. Whereas West Germans were primarily concerned about the financial consequences of unification, East Germans very distinctly focused on the question of jobs, social security, rebuilding the economy, wages, pensions and matters of law and order. Environmental protection was ascribed far less importance than in West Germany, where it took second place to unification in terms of political priority. In unification year, issues of foreign and security policy were left out of the political picture in East Germany. The Gulf War and peace issues were important for West Germans only.

There is no doubt that the result of the December election was a vote for Chancellor Kohl, who was regarded as far more capable than Lafontaine of solving the problems of unification. Shortly before the election nearly 60 per cent of all voters, and almost a quarter of SPD supporters, believed that Chancellor Kohl would best be able to solve the problems of the nation as a whole. Less than one-third of all those polled expected this of Lafontaine. In East Germany the Chancellor's rating was even higher, at 65 per cent, than in West Germany (58 per cent).

The choice for Chancellor had developed accordingly. In August, 50 per cent in both East and West Germany preferred Kohl, while 42 per cent (41 per cent in the East) wanted Lafontaine as Chancellor. Immediately prior to the election, Kohl's lead in the West reached 56 per cent against Lafontaine's 38 per cent. Ultimately the Chancellor's rating exceeded that of his party. Yet the CDU–CSU also contributed to the victory through its long-standing

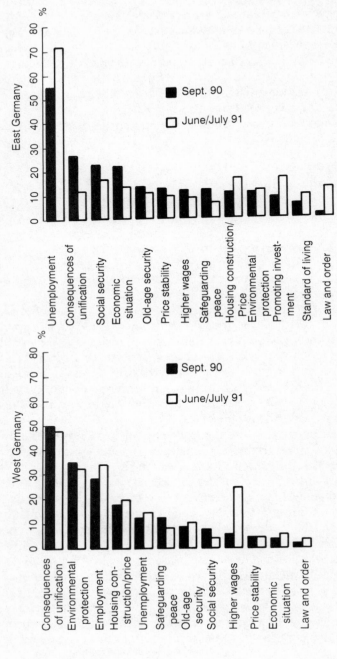

Figure 2.6   Important Political Issues, 1990–91 (spontaneous answers with multiple answers)

Source: Research Institute of the Konrad Adenauer Foundation, file control no. 9007, 9008, 9101, 9102.

74

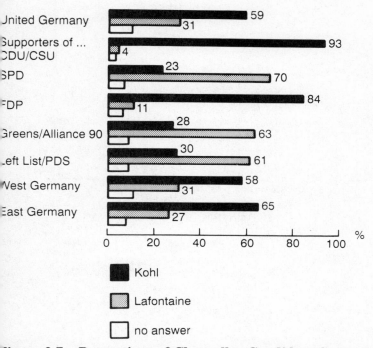

Figure 2.7   Perceptions of Chancellor Candidate Competence

Source: Research Institute of the Konrad Adenauer Foundation (Nov. 90).

image of competence. In both parts of Germany the Union was seen, markedly ahead of the SPD, as the party that could best solve the problems arising in West Germany as a result of unity and that could bring about economic reconstruction in the East.

The preponderance of economic and financial issues in the public discussion during this year of unification certainly was a major factor contributing to the vote of confidence in the Union. Ironically, this emphasis had actually been initiated by Lafontaine but, given the economic optimism prevailing before the election, it clearly benefited the Union. The CDU is traditionally considered the most competent party in economic and financial matters. In 1990 it was also deemed the most competent party on the security of jobs and pensions and – again in keeping with its traditional image – on law and order (see Figure 2.8).

Prior to the election the SPD – consistent with its traditional sociopolitical image – showed a lead in perceived competence for preserving social

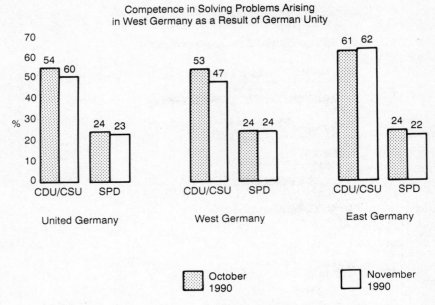

Source: Research Institute of the Konrad Adenauer Foundation, 1990.

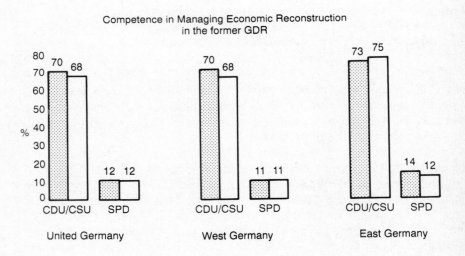

Figure 2.8   **Perceptions of Party Competence**

Source: Research Institute of the Konrad Adenauer Foundation, 1990.

programmes and in promoting housing construction. However, these reflected advantages solely in West Germany. In East Germany at this time, the SPD was behind the CDU even in its classical domains of social policy. Table 2.9 illustrates the CDU–CSU lead over the SPD on major election issues.

Table 2.9   Perceptions of Party Competence by Issue (CDU–CSU lead over the SPD)

	United Germany %	West Germany %	East Germany %
Job security	+15	+15	+15
Impetus to economy	+48	+46	+53
Security of pensions	+10	+8	+15
Combating crime	+27	+29	+19

Generally what is striking is the singularity of factors determining the outcome of this election. It was an election with two candidates and a single theme of truly historical dimensions. A decisive government and its parties turned this theme to their advantage: four months before election day they had put an end to the 'race'.

As a result of the exceptional single-issue character of this election, some of the historical identities and old party loyalties had less of a bearing than usual on the outcomes. The poor showing of the SPD among West German workers would be one indication of this. In future, the areas of political conflict will again be more complex and problems will once more present themselves as issues sharply contending for attention. Two years after the historic election, a critical public is once again fully aware of the entire spectrum of political problems. The high tide of sentiment for the Union parties has passed, and public opinion fluctuates as usual (Noelle-Neumann, 1991a: 5).

Unity and National Consciousness

One theme, however, had no currency either in the year of unification or afterwards: new German nationalism. The moments of national feeling

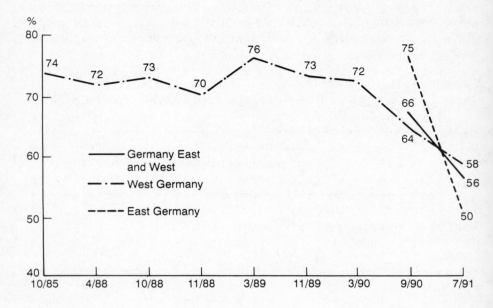

Figure 2.9   National Self-confidence*

Source: Research Institute of the Konrad Adenauer Foundation.
* 'How proud are you to be a German?' (The curve is a combination of two responses:
  'Very proud' and 'Quite proud'.)

welling up after the Wall had come down failed to inflame any heightened
national pride during the year of unification. Increasing restraint, rather
than triumphant self-confidence, has characterized the sense of national
self-awareness in the West since the election, and there has been a steep
decline in national pride among East Germans (see Figure 2.9). The very
different trends in East and West require a more thoroughgoing consideration of their causes. The two parts of Germany must be seen in terms of
very different political psyches and experiences, bound up, on both sides,
with the problems of unification. Most disconcerting of all is the critical
decline of national identity in the new *Länder*, reflecting as it does the full
magnitude of the recent upheavals. For many, the early elation has evidently
given way to depression and 'unity shock' (Schröder, 1991: 18).

From the outset, the citizens of the old FDR regarded the unification process with a large measure of emotional reserve and pragmatic deliberation, quite unlike those of the former GDR, the vast majority of whom wanted rapid unification. In West Germany an awareness of the accompanying burdens and responsibility, nationally as well as internationally, has meanwhile led to even greater pragmatism on matters of national interest. The nationalist temptation to chart a uniquely German course, which Germany's allies have occasionally feared, did not materialize either before or after unity. It was repeatedly suggested that the Germans were wavering between ties with the West and nationalist neutralism. In fact, they wavered and hesitated most between the fear of the costs of unity and the expectation of future benefits. Uniting the nation at the price of neutralism – by leaving NATO or the European Community – had already been rejected by the majority of the West German people in the polls of December 1989. On the contrary, as shown by Table 2.10, there was a growing awareness that the Western Alliance and the European Community would be needed even more after unification than before.

Table 2.10   The Importance of European Unification

	After the unification of Germany, the importance of European unification is …					
	rather greater		the same		rather less	
	Sept. 1990 %	June/ July 1991 %	Sept. 1990 %	June/ July 1991 %	Sept. 1990 %	June/ July 1991 %
United Germany	49	50	38	38	12	11
West Germany	47	48	40	41	13	11
East Germany	56	56	31	30	11	12

Source: Research Institute of the Konrad Adenauer Foundation, 1991.

Implications for the Party System: Diversification or Stabilization?

Given the exceptional nature of this election, it is extremely difficult to draw conclusions, from its results, as to the future development of the party landscape in Germany. It therefore remains an open question whether unification will result in a new social synthesis, and what form this might take. The future development of the parties and party system as a whole is equally uncertain. In a number of ways the first all-German election has already given the party system and the parliament something of a new cast, although at present it is hard to gauge whether this will mark a long-term, or merely a short-term, change. As yet the tendencies point in different directions.

The extraordinary stability of the West German systems of politics and government has been based on the decades-long dominance of two large peoples' parties (*Volksparteien*), which since the Bundestag election of 1957 have always been able to attract between them over 80 per cent of the voters, and at the highwater mark in the 1970s even reached a combined total of 90 per cent. As was shown in Chapter 1, the *Volksparteien* have now lost some of their appeal, and their share of the electorate has consequently steadily declined.

Corresponding to the relative decline in the *Volksparteien* vote is the increased number of small splinter parties below the threshold for Bundestag representation. In the 1990 Bundestag election the latter polled a total of 4.2 per cent of the votes cast. In the past this splintering stemmed largely from fringe parties on the extreme right in the old Federal Republic. On the other hand, as a specifically East German contribution, the PDS with its 2.4 per cent nationwide must also be included, so that the sum of all the splinter parties actually comes to 6.6 per cent of the votes cast.

Unlike the centre-right parties, all the so-called centre-left parties – the SPD, Greens and Bündnis 90, plus the PDS – sustained losses. As a result, not only is the party spectrum from the left-centre to the radical left smaller today than the SPD and Greens segments from the previous Bundestag election, but it is also more diversified than the centre-right camp. Here a new structural asymmetry could develop in the party system, although this is by no means certain.

Finally, it is obvious that with the greater fragmentation of parties, though clearly below the five-per-cent hurdle, the ideological spectrum has broadened, marked on the Right by the Republikaner party, on the Left by the PDS, in each case with regional strengths and of roughly the same magnitude. Regional concentrations of this kind generally afford favourable conditions for parties to develop their organizational structures and to broaden their electoral base.

Although the Republikaner party can currently attract only about 2 per cent of the voters nationwide, its successes should not be disregarded. In the past few years it has been able to develop into by far the largest and most successful party on the right of the West German party spectrum. Until now it has lacked an organizational basis and significant numbers of party members in East Germany, although it obviously draws well there among young poorly educated men. Moreover, there has recently been increasing evidence of roving right-wing radicalism in the new *Länder*. Certainly, a receptivity to right-wing populist and radical appeals could quickly spread during the difficult phase of economic and social restructuring. Pressing social problems for the individual coincide with profound disorientation on questions of values and of political culture in a democratic political system with a free-market economy. The West German experience of grappling with these essential multicultural learning processes over many years has largely been lacking in the East. Political resentments and radical slogans can, of course, flare up just as quickly in the old West German *Länder* and raise protest potential to the five-per-cent level. In the new *Länder* especially, much will depend on how the parliamentary parties respond to urgent problems and how the government and opposition parties interact and work together.

At present it is hard to say whether the process of diversification and splintering will increase or whether these trends will subside and return to past levels. Sometimes comparison is ventured with the early years of the Federal Republic, when the party system underwent an extremely rapid process of concentration, and parties progressively abandoned ideology. Yet this analogy underestimates the historical difference in economic and social circumstances, and the political experience specific to the prevailing international conditions of the 1950s. Moreover, the analogy obscures the new factors at work today in shaping the all-German electorate.

The Retarded Development of the Parties in the New *Länder*

In the above analysis of the 1990 election, it has been necessary to distinguish between the electoral regions, and to take account of differences in political cultures and social structures in West and East Germany. The national parties have to reconcile very different sets of voters with very different expectations and political objectives. With unification, the electorate has become even more heterogeneous and the major parties are increasingly faced with the problem of overextending themselves in attempting to reach both their traditional voters and new strata in the electorate.

Yet it remains to be seen how East German society is politically re-formed, and, for the moment, the voter profiles of the national parties remain somewhat blurred. In a largely destructured society, electoral structures and political culture can develop only gradually. In the meantime the democratic parties in East Germany are participants in the process of re-structuring society, thereby reversing the historical pattern of party-building. In the nineteenth century, the parties originally formed as social groupings that reflected the basic attitudes and ideologies of social and economic communities formed along the fault lines of industrial development. Now the parties themselves, by virtue of their social restructuring role, have a part in shaping their own electoral base.

The fact that the CDU and, to some extent, the SPD, have different images and are preferred by different groups of voters in East and West Germany must not, however, at the present stage of party development in the new *Länder*, be taken as indicative of independently defined political programs. The causes lie, as indicated above, in the specific circumstances of this election. Moreover, in the East, the large national parties are as yet barely understood as historical entities with philosophical traditions and long-standing social cleavages. They have yet to fully establish their own political profile in the East. In none of the major national parties has there been any scope for a distinctly Eastern influence on the party as a whole, although in the case of the CDU, this may change following the discussion begun in 1991 on reforming the basic party programme. The establishment of a distinct party identity incorporating specifically East German ideas and interests requires the construction of broad-based party organizations with active membership bodies. As will become clear from Part Two of this volume the construction work has just begun.

For all the parties rebuilding and reorganization is fully underway. For the foreseeable future integration will tax their resources, although the problems differ from one party to another. It can also be concluded that a specifically East German voice is likely to be heard within the national parties. It is unlikely, then, that the polished images of the traditional West German parties will be thoroughly revised, although new emphases may appear within party programmes and thus new lines of conflict may emerge both within the parties themselves and in the public debate.

Conclusion: Two Political Cultures

The cultural factors that shape attitudes towards politics, the state and democracy, political parties and elections could well have a long-lasting impact. The SED regime destroyed not only social and economic structures, but intellectual and moral traditions as well. The contextual knowledge that sustains the Western democracies is largely lacking in the East after two generations of totalitarianism and ideological deformation. Moreover, the independent social institutions which comprise 'civil society' were suppressed under totalitarianism.

Today, East German society is made up of a large, approximately two-thirds majority of people who do not belong to any Church, and, as yet, there is no countermovement in sight. Thus the growing secularization in West Germany will probably be solidly reinforced nationwide (Gauly, 1991: 51 ff). The turn away from denominationalism that has begun among CDU voters will continue. The great majority of East German voters vote radically 'modern', disregarding the traditional moorings of social background and party ties. Voting is more uninhibitedly pragmatic and distinctly issue-oriented than in the West. As a result the potential for flexible voter behaviour is considerably greater in the German electorate (Roth, 1990: 369 ff).

Finally, the distinctly East German conception of democracy and confidence in institutions gives rise to imponderables in party development. The East German understanding of democracy, as Ursula Feist has pinpointed it, is more emphatically bipolar than in the West (Feist, 1991: 21 ff). Demands for grass-roots, direct democracy run directly counter to representative and authoritarian conceptions of democracy. Trust in institutions is considerably weaker among East Germans than in the West, where widespread trust in the system is reflected in the high level of confidence expressed in virtually all essential institutions (see Figure 2.10). In some cases, the differences are glaring. In East Germany, television enjoys by far the greatest confidence, which is not surprising for a people that has suffered for many years under press censorship and domestic spying. Above-average confidence is otherwise reserved solely for political institutions, the Federal government and the Bundestag. Everything else apparently recalls the old GDR reality, seen in

> ... the cooperation between the police and the judicial system – perhaps a reminder of the old police state – and in the combination of trade unions with municipal administrations, where many GDR citizens experienced up close and first hand how the power of the SED state penetrated businesses and municipalities. (Feist, 1991: 28)

The widespread distrust among East Germans toward public institutions demands the utmost attention. It signals that integration into the basic political and social order of the Federal Republic has not yet been consummated and that the affirmation of its principles and procedures has yet to be firmly established in political thought (Noelle-Neumann, 1991b: 13). When

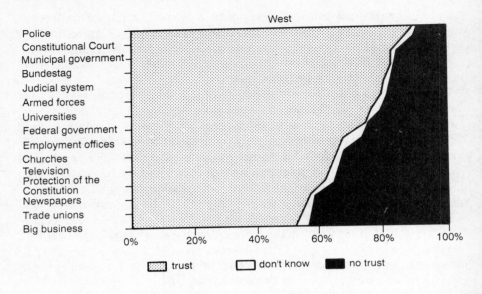

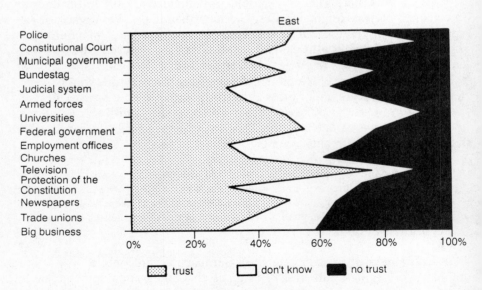

Figure 2.10   Trust in Institutions: West and East

Source: Infas Deutschland-Politogramm 89-40/1990.

confidence in the system is lacking, political frustration can not only turn more quickly, and with fewer checks, into protest and anti-positions and into apathy and non-voting, but also into radical forms of political articulation that could develop a political dynamic of their own, crossing old borders. As a result, greater importance will probably have to be attached to the impetus for social, cultural and political change deriving from unification than has as yet been recognized in West Germany.

The dynamics of social integration may create stronger forces for change in the larger but also more heterogeneous society in the West than in the East. A number of social-emancipatory and secular impulses from East Germany give impetus to and broaden already existing currents in the pluralistic West. If German society is further pluralized and drifts away from its traditional social contexts and philosophical bearings, this would have consequences for the parties, the party system and the stability of the new German polity. The push for change sketched here need not inevitably lead to a further splintering of the party system, but it seems, however, that the likelihood of further diversification involving a diminution in the large national parties and the growth of small parties above and below the five-per-cent mark is greater than the likelihood that the traditional four- or five-party parliamentary system can be maintained.

For the national parties to meet this development, they will have to devote a great deal more energy to discussing their self-conception, competitive edge and readiness to remain on top of developments. Building upon this, they need to re-establish their integrative capability in terms of programmes, personnel and organization.

The first all-German Bundestag election marks the end of the old Federal Republic and, at the same time, a new beginning and transition for all Germans. The social and political system has begun to move in a fundamental way, but the direction is not yet clear. Analysis of the results of this election suggests the acceleration of change, new lines of tension and conflict and even fewer long-standing certainties. The difficult process of internal unification has just begun.

References

Feist, U. (1991), 'Zur politischen Akkulturation der vereinten Deutschen' in *Aus Politik und Zeitgeschichte*, B11–12, p. 21ff.

Forschungsgruppe Wahlen e.V. (1990), *Bundestagswahl 1990. Eine Analyse der ersten gesamtdeutschen Bundestagswahl am 2. Dezember 1990*, Forschungsgruppe Wahlen e.V. Report, no. 61, Mannheim, October.

Gauly, T. M. (1991), 'Konfessionalismus und politischen Kultur in Deutschland', in *Aus Politik und Zeitgeschichte*, B20, 10 May.

Gibowski, W. and Kaase, M. (1991), 'Auf dem Weg zum politischen Alltag. Eine Analyse der ersten gesamtdeutschen Bundestagswahl vom 2. Dezember 1990' in *Aus Politik und Zeitgeschichte*, B11–12, p. 3 ff.

Infas-Report Wahlen (1991), *Bundestagswahl 1990*, Bonn-Bad Godesberg, April.

Noelle-Neumann, E. (1991a), 'Der Einigungsprozess wirft einen langen Schatten', *Frankfurter Allgemeine Zeitung*, 11 September, p. 57.

Noelle-Neumann, E. (1991b), 'Die Vorzüge der Freiheit stehen noch nicht im Mittelpunkt. Die neuen Bundesbürger und die Demokratie', *Frankfurter Allgemeine Zeitung*, 30 September, p. 76.

Radunski, P. (1980), *Wahlkämpfe, Moderne Wahlkampfführung als politische Kommunikation*, München-Wien, p. 45.

Roth, D. (1990), 'Die Wahlen zur Volkskammer der GDR. Der Versuch einer Erklärung' in *Politische Vierteljahresschrift*, p. 369 ff.

Schröder, R. (1991), *Die Ziet*, 12 September, p. 59.

Statistisches Bundesamt (1991), *Wahl zum 12. Deutschen Bundestag am 2. Dezember 1990, Heft 4: Wahlbeteiligung und Stimmabgabe der Männer und Frauen nach dem Alter*, Wiesbaden, May.

Veen, H-J. (1990), 'Die schwankenden Westdeutschen. Ein Vorlaufiges Meinungsbild zur Einigung' in *Die politische Meinung*, no. 250, May–June.

Veen, H-J. (1991), 'Wählergesellschaft im Umbruch' in E. Noelle-Neumann (ed.), *Wählerverhalten im Wandel. Bestimmungsgründe und politisch-kulturelle Trends am Beispiel der Bundestagswahl 1987*, Paderborn, Munich, Vienna Zurich.

Veen, H-J. *et al.* (1990a), *DDR-Parteien im Vereinigungsprozess. Profil und Organisationstruktur der SPD der Liberalen, der Grünen/Bündnis 90 und der PDS*, St Augustin: Forschungsinstitut der Konrad-Adenauer-Stiftung, Interne Studien, 20.

Veen, H-J. *et al.* (1990b), *Die erste gesamtdeutsche Bundestagswahl am 2. Dezember – eine erste Wahlnachtsanalyse*, St Augustin, 3 December.

Veen, H-J. *et al.* (1991), *Die Republikaner-Partei zu Beginn der 90er Jahre. Programm, Propaganda, Organisation, Wähler- und Sympathisantenstrukturen*, St Augustin: Forschungsinstitut der Konrad-Adenauer-Stiftung, Interne Studien, 14.

3 Dimensions of Change in the German Party System

Gordon Smith

The *Volkspartei* and a 'Frozen' Party System

In Germany, as elsewhere in Western Europe, certain parties have been able to maintain a prominent position for themselves apparently regardless of changing social conditions and political circumstances. These parties – perhaps only two or three – constitute the 'core' elements of a party system (Smith, 1989: 15–16): they, in combination, determine how the system functions and decide the composition of government. The core parties give a party system its long-lasting characteristics, and for the earlier decades of the present century this stable patterning was widely interpreted in terms of the 'freezing hypothesis' formulated by Lipset and Rokkan. This proposition held that European party systems of the late 1960s 'reflected, with few but significant exceptions, the cleavage structure of the 1920s' (Lipset and Rokkan, 1967).

Germany obviously proved to be one of these 'significant exceptions'. The Nazi dictatorship and other sharp breaks in the form of regime severed the continuity of party and institutional structures, and these upheavals also brought about fundamental changes in German society. The full extent of the transformation became evident only after 1945, and the party system that took root in the Federal Republic had virtually nothing in common with its forerunner of the Weimar Republic: the bitter political polarization vanished, the number of parties rapidly diminished, and governing coalitions became highly stable. These features resulted from the pre-eminence achieved by the core parties, and in particular by the two *Volksparteien*, the CDU and SPD. Spanning more than four decades the core parties have controlled – and at times have even been equated with – the party system.

Yet this apparent 'freezing' of the German party system bears no resemblance to the more general proposition: the rise to dominance of the

87

Volkspartei occurred in the era of declining social cleavages, and its success was based precisely on its capacity for making a wide appeal – in principle to all sections of the population. Since the cleavage model is clearly inappropriate to an explanation of the West German case, it is necessary to look at specific factors that help to account for the *Volkspartei* being so successful as to become, in Kirchheimer's description, a formidable 'competitive phenomenon' (Kirchheimer, 1966: 188). These factors – political and organizational resources – can be summarized as follows.

1   Despite the lack of political continuity, the core parties – the CDU, SPD and FDP – all belong in the major European party families of christian democracy, social democracy and liberalism. These political traditions provide a secure point of reference for the three established parties.
2   Even though the *Volksparteien* are not based on strong cleavages in society, both the CDU and SPD have been able to rely on particular kinds of social support, for which church attendance and trade union membership respectively are the most reliable indicators.
3   In organizational terms, the CDU and SPD have been successful in maintaining themselves as mass membership parties, despite the necessarily looser commitment and party identification that non-ideological parties can achieve.
4   A vital contribution to the organizational resources of the core parties is made by the system of state financing of political parties. The amounts allocated to the parties depends on the share of the vote each receives, and this strict proportionality is nominally equitable, but in reality the system has helped to sustain a permanent imbalance. The parties that were largest initially can use the state funding to strengthen their position further, so that the gap between them and small new parties remains.
5   Because it is not constrained by a firm ideology, the *Volkspartei* can act flexibly to changing circumstances, react to electoral pressures, and take up issues put on the agenda by other parties. Parties are 'strategic and adaptive actors', and the *Volkspartei* has the attributes to manoeuvre successfully.

The Electoral Dimension

A measure of the strength of the CDU and SPD is the size of the electoral following they have been able to attract, and that is most evident when the votes of the two parties are combined. Their aggregate share followed a rising course from 1949 onwards to reach a peak of 90 per cent in the mid-1970s. Since then there has been a steady decline. Does this downward movement indicate that the German party system is at last becoming 'unfrozen'? This question can be applied to several European party systems at the present time: new parties have made inroads into the support for established ones, and voters are less inclined to identify strongly with parties. These changes are interpreted in different ways, either as a process of electoral dealignment which would imply a permanent fluidity in electoral behaviour, or else as the beginnings of an electoral realignment and the rise of new political cleavages (Dalton, 1992: 52–76). Yet the extent of change that has occurred in party systems up to now can easily be exaggerated. As Peter Mair has argued:

> The old parties which were around well before Rokkan elaborated his freezing proposition are still around today and, despite the challenges from new social movements, most still remain in powerful, dominant positions. They have not suffered substantial electoral erosion. The electoral balance is not substantially different from that thirty years ago, and, in general, electorates are not more volatile than once they were. (Mair, 1992)

This comparative assessment applies with equal force to the Federal Republic. Moreover there are further grounds for holding that the 'old' parties in West Germany have been able to absorb pressures without substantially losing their grip on the electorate. One important piece of evidence is detailed by Mair in considering the increase in the size of West European electorates over the past 30 years. The really remarkable achievement of the 'old' – core parties has been their ability to attract a high proportion of new generations of voters at successive elections in an era of fairly rapid social change (see Table 3.1). For the Federal Republic the operative election years are 1961 and 1990 (the latter excluding East Germany).

Tables 3.1 'Old' Parties and New Electorates

	1961 % Vote for 'Old' Parties	1990 % Vote for 'Old' Parties	Change % Vote Share 1961–90	Change % Electorate 1961–90	Change in Total 'Old' Party Vote 1960–90
Germany	94.4	90.6	–3.8	+28.5	+13.9
All countries	94.0	85.0	–9.0	+31.7	+12.1

Note: 'Old' parties are those contesting the most recent election and which *also* contested the first election. For Germany these parties are the CDU–CSU, SPD and FDP.
Source: Adapted from Mair, 1992.

It is clear that the 'old'–core parties in Germany have lost ground (–3.8 per cent) over the 30-year span, but much less ground than their counterparts elsewhere in Western Europe (–9.0 per cent). Furthermore, the German parties managed to increase their total vote (+13.9 per cent) significantly – better than the European average and with a smaller increase in the size of the electorate (28.5 per cent compared with 31.7 per cent for Western Europe as a whole). Seen in a comparative perspective, the German core parties have performed well, and they can by no means be described as having lost their hold on the electorate.

In considering the core parties, the contribution of the FDP in maintaining its position should not be neglected. Its role was less significant when the aggregate of the two major parties was still on the increase, and at all the elections until 1987 even when either the CDU–CSU or the SPD lost support, the other one gained. However, at both the 1987 and 1990 elections, the pattern changed with both parties losing ground, whereas the FDP made appreciable gains. To an extent, what has occurred is an exchange of voters among the core parties, and it is the resilience of the core rather than fluctuations in support for the individual members that is important in examining the development of the party system.

Mair's contention, that the performance of old parties should be considered in relation to their ability to win a sizeable share of a growing electorate, applies with particular force to the German situation consequent upon unification. The electorate in the 1987 West German election totalled 45 million; in the 1990 all-German election it increased to 60 million – an increase without parallel in Western Europe. Against this background, the share of the total vote (88.3 per cent) taken by the core parties (79 per cent in East Germany) should be rated as a considerable achievement.

It can, of course, be said that the 'unification election' was held in somewhat artificial circumstances and that a normalization of political life will produce a different pattern. But the abnormality was one that may have disproportionately benefited the CDU and disadvantaged the SPD, so that in the future the losses of one party in East Germany could partly accrue to the other party: in other words, the total support for the core parties need not be too greatly affected especially if, as widely anticipated, the PDS disappears from the federal scene.

Marginal Changes and System Deconcentration

To summarize the case for the durability of the core of the German party system, it can be seen that, although the individual parties have experienced changing fortunes, the core as a whole has so far been relatively unaffected. It is true, however, that some decline has been evident since the mid-1980s, and, as Stephen Padgett has already shown, electoral dealignment is having an erosive effect. But the ability of the core parties to absorb a very high proportion of an electorate that has doubled in size since 1949, and grew by a quarter in 1990, puts the relative decline into a better perspective.

On these grounds – that is, the electoral performance of the *Volksparteien* or, more broadly, the core – the evidence may point to a condition of stasis rather than change. Yet this concentration on the electoral level, and in particular on large aggregates, is likely to be misleading if it is concluded that the party system is immune to change. It may appear contradictory to say that the stability of the core could well be a continuing feature concurrent with a basic restructuring process, but the two are compatible: the maintenance of a high aggregate can be accompanied by *critical shifts at the margin*. The marginal changes may not, in themselves, be particularly momentous, but the nature and the functioning of the party system can be fundamentally altered.

The Federal Republic has experienced several decades of a highly concentrated party system, with few parties, scarcely separable in ideological terms, and with a strong coalition compatibility. A move towards a deconcentrated system would require one or more of these elements to change. Because there is little sign that the core parties themselves would contribute to a deconcentration through polarization and coalition incompatibility, the most probable development is for the number of parties to increase. However, given the persistence of the core, it is unlikely that there could be a substantial increase in the number of non-core parties; the five-per-cent electoral threshold to Bundestag representation sets an effective barrier to entry for most new parties anyway. The most probable scenario, therefore, is that one or two parties will be in a position to upset the balance at the federal level.

A good illustration of how such a shift could occur was during the 1980s after the entry of the Greens into the Bundestag. The emergence of a party broadly to the left of the SPD raised the possibility of a new left-wing alignment of SPD and Greens coming about, thereby counterbalancing a centre-right CDU–CSU and FDP alignment. Such a two-bloc system would not necessarily be strongly polarized but would nontheless break the existing core domination of coalition formation which has operated by means of the 'alternation' between the CDU and SPD practised by the FDP. In the event, the new line-up did not materialize at the federal level: the SPD and the Greens did not share sufficient common ground, and the two parties were never able to command a parliamentary majority. The example, however, is instructive in showing how a party with, say, between 5 and 10 per cent of the total vote could have a decisive influence on the functioning of the party system. The possibilities can be illustrated by looking, first, at the recent rise of the radical Right, and then more generally at the changes in *Länder* party systems.

The Party System and the Radical Right

In assessing the possibilities for deconcentration at the federal level, it is best to focus on areas where non-established parties have most competitive space, namely, on the left and right flanks of the core parties. The Greens, now mostly representing the 'New Left', have been prominent on the federal stage since the early 1980s and, because in this period they have failed to make a decisive breakthrough (emphasized by the poor performance of the West German Greens at the 1990 federal election), it is doubtful whether they have the potential to attract much more than 10 per cent of the vote. The position of the radical Right, however, is still far from clear. Throughout the life of the Federal Republic, right-wing parties have come and gone without making a permanent impact. The most successful was the National Democratic Party (NPD) in the late 1960s, with a best *Land* vote of 9.8 per cent in Baden–Württemberg, and 4.3 per cent in the 1969 federal election. After this initial showing, however, the NPD quickly became just one more fringe party (Stöss, 1988: J4–46).

A new upsurge occurred in the late 1980s when the Republikaner took only 3 per cent in their home state of Bavaria in 1986, but 7.5 per cent in West Berlin in January 1989, and 7.1 per cent in the June 1989 elections to the European Parliament (in Bavaria alone the Republikaner scored no less than 14.6 per cent). It is worth noting that throughout the first half of 1989, dissatisfaction with the Christian Democrats, and in particular with Kohl's leadership, ran high. Shortly afterwards the issue of national unification rescued the CDU, and the radical Right went into a temporary eclipse. Its renewed appeal subsequently poses problems of interpretation: is it about to gain a secure foothold in the party system or likely to revert to its normal fringe status?

Although not clearly separable, four elements in the appeal of contemporary right-wing radicalism can be distinguished (Falter and Schumann, 1988: 91–110):

1   a mainly latent, but sometimes overt, expression of neo-Nazism, and the exculpation/rehabilitation of National Socialism;
2   the invocation of traditional German values – diligence, law and order, nationalism, and anti-EC;

3   the harnessing of specific discontents – the size of the immigrant population (anti-foreigner), housing and related social problems, economic difficulties, all issues typical for right-wing protest parties;
4   the expression of a general disillusionment with established parties and their performance – a diffused protest symptomatic of the process of electoral dealignment.

Although the CDU–CSU is particularly vulnerable to a loss of support due to the appeal of the radical Right, none of the core parties is immune because the two elements of 'protest' affect the electorate across a wide band of socioeconomic groupings including blue-collar workers as well as middle-class CDU adherents. Moreover both the DVU (German People's Union) and the Republikaner have proved attractive to younger voters. As yet, the potential of these parties in the new *Länder* has not been properly tested, but it appears that, with the high level of unemployment, social dislocation, and outbreak of anti-immigrant behaviour, the widespread anomie provides an ideal recruiting base for the radical Right.

The post-1990 performance of the DVU and the Republikaner shows that these parties have been able to recover the position they held in the first part of 1989. Indeed they have gained added impetus, given the tensions resulting from unification and the increased salience of immigration issues, as shown by the 1991–92 *Land* elections in Bremen; Baden–Württemberg, and Schleswig–Holstein. In themselves, however, these are marginal changes: it is only when they are allied with other changes that the effects on the party system are likely to be profound.

The Party System in the *Länder*

Apart from the possibility of a red–green formation at the federal level – now precluded by the failure of the West German Greens to win Bundestag representation at the 1990 election – the evidence of deconcentration in *Länder* party systems provides other indications of how the federal system could be affected. The dangers of extrapolating from *Land* to federal level are evident: in *Land* elections local issues and personalities are important factors, protest voters are easier to mobilize, and the extent of opposition to the major federal governing party – at what are effectively 'mid-term' contests in relation to federal elections – may distort the real picture.

Nonetheless, there have been two important changes at the *Land* level in the recent past. First there has been an increase in the incidence of so-called cross-cutting coalitions. Second there is a growing tendency towards new-style coalitions in the *Länder*. In one way or another both developments can be related to the weaker performance of the core parties, either the CDU or SPD, or occasionally both. The extent of the erosion in some *Länder* should not lead to the expectation that these developments will necessarily spread to federal level, but the direction of change is significant.

Cross-cutting coalitions – where the government at *Land* level contains parties that are opposed at federal level (that is, from both government and opposition) – have in the past tended to be sporadic occurrences. Recently, however, they have assumed increasing importance and in 1992 affected no fewer than five *Länder* (see Table 3.2). One direct consequence has been to complicate considerably the relationships between the federal government, with its majority in the Bundestag, and the Bundesrat with its increasingly variegated composition.

Table 3.2   The Composition of Governments in the *Länder*

Land	Governing Parties
Baden–Wurttemberg	CDU–SPD
Bavaria	CSU
Berlin	CDU–SPD
Brandenburg	SPD–FDP–Bündnis '90
Bremen	SPD–FDP–Greens
Hamburg	SPD
Hesse	SPD–Greens
Lower Saxony	SPD–Greens
Mecklenburg	CDU–FDP
North-Rhine Westphalia	SPD
Rhineland–Palatinate	SPD–FDP
Saarland	SPD
Saxony	CDU
Saxony–Anhalt	CDU–FDP
Schleswig–Holstein	SPD
Thuringia	CDU–FDP

Examples of 'new-style' coalitions are the three-party coalitions formed in Brandenburg (1990) and in Bremen (1991). In the former *Land* the governing parties are the SPD, FDP and Bündis '90 and in the latter the SPD with the FDP and the Greens. Both coalitions are of a cross-cutting character, and they were necessary in order to secure a parliamentary majority. Although, properly speaking, the alliance of the CDU and SPD in government is not 'new style', since the 'grand coalition' has been adopted occasionally in the past, its reappearance in the 1990s is significant – Berlin (1990) and Baden–Württemberg (1992).

A common element in these four *Länder* are the signs of electoral dealignment and the relatively weak showing of the core parties in the four elections: Berlin, with a three-party total of 77.9 per cent was the strongest, followed by Brandenburg (74.2 per cent), Bremen with 69.5 per cent, and Baden–Württemberg (69 per cent). In other words, once the core parties' vote falls below a critical point, it is necessary for them to look more widely in order to construct a minimum-winning coalition. In this context it is worth noting that although there is no constitutional rule to prevent the formation of a minority government, in the German context the expedient is not regarded as a legitimate option. Government should be representative of majority opinion otherwise it lacks legitimacy, and a government without an assured majority would also be weak and ineffective. The difficulties of forming a majority government are compounded if certain parties are treated as non-coalitionable: the PDS with 9.2 per cent in Berlin and 13.4 per cent in Brandenburg, the Republikaner with 10.9 in Baden–Württemberg, and the DVU with 6.2 per cent in Bremen and 6.3 per cent in Schleswig–Holstein.

These two factors – growing support for non-coalitionable parties and the decline of the core vote below a critical level – are the principal indications that the normal pattern of coalition formation is becoming less tenable, in so far as an increasing number of coalitions now have to include one or more non-core parties. The effects of deconcentration were thrown into sharp relief as a result of the 1992 Baden–Württemberg election. Both the CDU and SPD lost support (the CDU from 49 to 39.6 per cent, the SPD from 32 to 29.4 per cent), and the FDP share stayed the same at 5.9 per cent. Between them the Republikaner (10.9) and the Greens (9.5) took a fifth of the vote. The problems of coalition-building in this situation are apparent, since neither of the two 'normal' core combinations yielded a majority: CDU + FDP = 45.5 per cent; SPD + FDP = 35.3 per cent. A traffic-light alliance also failed to yield one: SDP + FDP + Greens = 44.4 per cent. There were thus two minimum-winning coalition possibilities: CDU + Republikaner = 50.5 per cent, and CDU + Greens = 49.1 per cent (but with majority of seats). However, the CDU would not deal with the Republikaner, and although there were preliminary negotiations between the CDU and the Greens, there was no real basis for agreement between them. One possibility remained, a grossly oversized coalition of the CDU and SPD with 69 per cent support. Ironically, the core formula was successful, but *faute de mieux*, and with the danger of encouraging radical opposition from both Left and Right.

How far can such a pattern of deconcentration at *Land* level be transposed to the federal stage? Granted that there are similarities in the trend, nevertheless the differences between the two levels are of importance, both with regard to the size of the core vote and the proportion of the electorates voting. Whether or not the differences are treated as of decisive significance depends on the kind of interpretation placed on the 1990 federal election.

The three-party core vote in *Land* elections has declined appreciably in recent years, and the same is true of federal elections. How safe is it, however, to take the 1990 federal election as part of a continuing trend? The downward movement looks convincing: 94 per cent (1983), 90.4 per cent (1987), 88.3 per cent (1990). But, for 1990, account has to be taken of the small East German parties; for instance, the PDS with 2.4 per cent. Moreover, the core-parties' vote in 1990 was between 10 and 20 per cent higher than their share in the four *Länder* where new-style coalitions had formed.

Electoral turnout in Germany is undoubtedly declining, and this growth in electoral dealignment is apparent for both federal and *Land* elections. A comparison of three *Land* elections held since unification with the ones held previously shows a steady fall, and a very sharp one for the federal elections (see Table 3.3).

Table 3.3   Declining Electoral Turnout, 1990–92

	1987–88	1990–92
Baden–Württemberg	71.8	70.2
Bremen	75.6	72.2
Schleswig–Holstein	77.4	71.4
Federal Election	84.3	77.8

Again, much depends on the weighting given to special factors in the 1990 federal election: *Wahlmüdigkeit* (election fatigue) may explain the low turnout in East Germany (74.7 per cent) following two other sets of elections in 1990 (the GDR election in March and the *Land* elections in October); the West German turnout (78.6 per cent) was low but could be accounted for by the terms of the campaign – the easy victory expected for the CDU and the negative image of the SPD caused abstentions by supporters of both parties. Although these considerations indicate that close parallels should not be drawn, the fact remains that any sizeable 'reservoir' of non-voters is evidence of a dealignment, and that those non-voters are more readily available for mobilization by non-core parties.

At this juncture it is impossible to say whether the federal party system is poised to follow the emerging pattern in the *Länder*. It is also difficult to specify the level to which the federal 'core vote' would have to fall to reach a 'critical level'. The fact that the core party vote at federal level is still far higher than in recent *Land* elections, however, shows that a rapid deconcentration is unlikely.

Trends in Party Membership

Rather indirect evidence of the increasing vulnerability of the *Volksparteien* concerns their falling membership. As can be seen from Table 3.4, both the SPD and the CDU have experienced a decline since their peak years – the SPD in 1977 and the CDU in the early 1980s. The decrease has been steady, but not dramatic and, in comparison with many other countries in Western Europe, they remain powerful mass parties. It may also be argued that the *Volkspartei* does not need a large membership and that the German system of state-financing enables them to speak directly to the voters via advertising and the media without having to rely on membership dues. Nonetheless, the continuing decline since unification does support the impression of a gradual move away from the large parties. Significantly, and in contrast, the membership of the smaller parties (taking only West Germany) has held up better.

Table 3.4   Party Membership in Western Germany ('000s)

	1972	1977	1982	1987	1991–92
SPD	954	1,006	926	910	892
CDU	423	664	719	705	658
CSU	107	159	179	184	185
FDP	58	80	74	65	68
Greens	–	–	25	42	38

Source: Der Spiegel 16/1992.

Table 3.5   Party Membership in the New *Länder* ('000s)

	1990	1991–92
SPD	24	31
CDU	134	111
FDP	114	65
Greens	1	2
Bündnis '90	–	2
PDS	285	185

Source: Der Spiegel 16/1992.

More informative, and more complex, is the developing situation in the new *Länder*. There the decline for most parties has been sharp in just two years (see Table 3.5), but the bare figures are misleading. Not unexpectedly, the drop for the PDS has been sharpest, and it is only a shadow of the former SED. But its present membership is still far larger than for any of the other parties, and it is unsafe to assume that the PDS will continue its spiral of decline. Thus, the Berlin city elections in May 1992 showed that the PDS in the eastern districts was able to rally considerable support with 29.7 per cent of the total vote as compared with only 0.9 per cent in the western districts. On this basis, the relatively large membership of the PDS fairly reflects the party's electoral support. Its appeal is twofold: on one level the PDS is a vehicle for protest against the policies that are held to be responsible for the economic malaise in the former GDR, and on another it can be interpreted as a form of 'cultural defence' expressing the resentment felt towards the perceived haughty disregard on the part of the West Germans for any positive aspects of all of East German society.

For both the CDU and the FDP the rapid falling away of party membership is a natural consequence of their origins in East Germany: that is, as products of amalgamation with the corresponding 'bloc' parties of the former regime. In effect, the high initial figures were spurious. Taking the membership levels as a yardstick, the erroneous impression might be gained that the FDP and its liberal values were more deeply entrenched in the new *Länder* than in the rest of Germany. For both parties the sharp downward trend is likely to continue. The problem of building up a viable party membership is best exemplified by the case of the SPD which, unlike the other Western parties, had to start from scratch: the minimal increase of just 6,000 from 1990 until 1991–92 shows the real weakness not only of party organizations, but also of the links between parties and voters.

The extent of the 'party deficit' in the new *Länder* was hidden in the course of the three elections held in 1990 because they were all overwhelmingly issue-based contests, focusing on national unification. Without any firm social base, the East German electorate was essentially unstructured (see Chapter 1). This lack of connection was disguised by the dominance of the national issue and by the outcome of the 1990 federal election, since the results for the core group of parties were broadly comparable in both parts of Germany (90.6 per cent in West Germany and 79 per cent in East Germany). It is doubtful whether the 'Western' parties can secure levels of organizational density in the East comparable to those they reached in the old Federal Republic.

Party Democracy and System Change

Declining party membership is one of a number of indications that the core parties are under pressure: the success of 'outsider' parties in the *Länder*; the increasingly mixed character of *Land* coalitions; falling turnout at elections; the decreasing share of the vote going to the core parties. The initial dominance of the core parties in the new *Länder* may prove to be a temporary respite – a pseudo-integration of the new electorate – and if the transplantation of the social market economy runs into severe difficulties, the political consequences for the established parties could intensify in both parts of Germany.

In all these circumstances, questions are naturally raised about the future of the *Volksparteien*. The critique is of two kinds. On one level, their predominance in the political system has come under fire ever since the earlier years of the Federal Republic. For instance, Karl Jaspers (1966) inveighed against their oligopolistic power and their virtual assumption of state authority as *Staatsparteien*, so that the concept of 'party democracy' came to have a pejorative ring. Yet so long as the *Volkspartei*-dominated system continued to show a high problem-solving capability, signs of alienation were restricted to minority movements. On the second level, however, if the core parties – collectively – are widely perceived as failing to provide the 'answers' to pressing social and economic problems, then the *Volksparteien* could forfeit their integrative power. Weakness on this level reinforces the kind of criticism made by Jaspers.

The vulnerability of the core parties is by no means entirely of their own making. Quite apart from the current difficulties they face – in particular those relating to German unification, European integration, and migration into the Federal Republic – the core parties are, in a sense, 'trapped' by the institutional structure of decision-making. Douglas Webber, in analysing the institutional context of German politics, concludes that they all

> ... tend to have the same impact, namely to grind down radical policy initiatives so that the end product, if one emerges at all in the form of an authoritative decision or policy output, represents the lowest common denominator between those corporate actors which command the potential to crush the initiative completely. Radical policy changes are only possible where they rest upon a consensus among all the relevant forces – which is very rare – or where there has been a massive mobilisation of public opinion in favour of a radical change of course. (Webber, 1992)

It can be argued that the 'consensus-inducing mechanisms' that served the old Federal Republic so well in the past may be less suited to the post-unification era, and further that, with the persisting social and economic divide between Eastern and Western Germany, a 'massive mobilisation of public opinion' could not come about because of the conflicting interests, and they are reflected within the parties themselves. If these wider perspectives are taken into account, it becomes apparent that a narrow focus on party system change is inappropriate: party fortunes, voting behaviour and attitudes towards 'party democracy' all have to be related to the structure and functioning of the wider political system.

References

Dalton, R. J. (1992), 'Two German Electorates?' in G. Smith, W. Paterson, P. Merkl and S. Padgett, *Developments in German Politics*, Basingstoke: Macmillan, pp. 52–76.

Falter, J. W. and Schumann, S. (1988), 'Affinity Towards Right-wing Extremism in Western Europe', *West European Politics*, **11** (2), April, pp. 91–110.

Jaspers, K. (1966), *Wohin treibt die Bundesrepublik?*, Munich: Piper Verlag.

Kirchheimer, O. (1966), 'The Transformation of the Western European Party Systems' in J. La Polombara and M. Weiner, *Political Parties and Political Development*, Princeton, NJ: Princeton University Press, pp. 177–200.

Lipset, S. M. and Rokkan, S. (1967), 'Cleavage Structures, Party Systems and Voter Alignments' in S. M. Lipset and S. Rokkan (eds), *Party Systems and Voter Alignments: Cross National Perspectives*, New York: Free Press, pp. 1–64.

Mair, P. (1992), 'The Myth of Electoral Change; The Survival of Traditional Parties in Western Europe', *Stein Rokkan Lecture*, ECPR Joint Sessions, Limerick, April.

Smith, G. (1989), 'Core Persistence, System Change, and the People's Party', *West European Politics*, **12**, (1), pp. 15–16.

Stöss, G. (1988), 'The Problem of Right-wing Extremism in West Germany', *West European Politics*, **11**, (2), April, pp. 34–46.

Webber, D. (1992), 'Kohl's *Wendepolitik* after a Decade', *German Politics* **1**, (2).

4 The Territorial Dimension of the New Party System

Roland Sturm

Germany's sub-national party systems are a neglected topic of political science research. It is a myth to believe that being well-informed about party competition on the federal level suffices to understand the *Länder* party systems, and this is especially true after unification. National party competition functions as an efficient party system filter, as can be demonstrated by the (at least temporary) demise of specifically East German political parties after unification. There are, however, three important factors leading to diversity in the *Länder*: differences of social structures, traditions and political cultures between the *Länder*: the influence of *Land* politics; and a turnout at *Land* elections, which is generally lower than that at federal elections. The latter gives strongly supported minority interests a greater chance for gaining party political representation in a *Land* government.

The Federal System and Party Politics

Sub-national and national levels of party systems are closely interconnected, although in a federal system the relative autonomy of the sub-national level is greater than in centralized political systems. The only German party with a central organizational structure older than the Federal Republic, is the Social Democratic Party. But even in the SPD, programmatic pluralism between the *Land* party organizations is easily discernible. Josef Schmid's in-depth study of the CDU (1990) has demonstrated pluralism in the Christian Democratic Union, both on the organizational and on the programmatic level.

For the period 1970–90 he distinguishes four types of *Land* parties in the CDU. This distinction is, as he shows, not at all static, since *Länder* parties have been able to transform themselves and acquire new roles. Schmid's first type of a *Land* party is the dynamic government party: Rhineland–Palatinate 1970–76, Baden–Württemberg (1978–91), Lower Saxony (1974–78) and Berlin (1981–89). The second type is the bare-knuckle fighting organization, which he found in Hesse (1970–80) and in Hamburg (1983–present). The third type consists of *Land* party organizations trying to follow a middle-of-the-road political strategy; the Lower Saxony party (1980–87), the Hesse party (1987–91) and the Rhineland–Palatinate organization (1976–91). A final category groups the 'sleeping giants' and 'unimportant gnomes': namely, Hamburg (pre-1983), Schleswig–Holstein (post–1970), the Saarland (post–1970), North Rhine–Westphalia (post–1970), Berlin (1970–80), and Bremen (post–1970).

The variety of *Land* parties, especially in the two big party organizations, can also be shown with regard to certain policies, and is, for example, reflected in their attitudes towards nuclear power plants, private TV broadcasting stations, or environmental questions. Another framework in which the strategies of *Land* organizations of the same party differ is in the European integration process, especially with regard to the respective *Land*'s preparation for the European single market (Sturm, 1991a; 1992b). Initiatives have been taken most effectively by the CDU-governed Baden–Württemberg, the SPD-governed North Rhine–Westphalia and the CSU-governed Bavaria. Typical latecomers, who profited from a process of policy diffusion, are among the CDU-governed *Länder*, Rhineland–Palatinate until 1991, and among the SPD-governed ones the Saarland and Bremen.

In addition to organizations and programmes, personalities compete on the federal level as heads of *Länder* party organizations. In particular, *Land* Prime Ministers are eager to carve out their own profiles, not only because they hope to get re-elected, but also because they often try to influence politics on the national level. They may seek an enhancement of their relative power position in their national party's organization, or they may try to position themselves for an office at the federal level. It is one of the characteristics of the German political system that it regularly recruits an important part of the national political élite (including some of the Chancellors) from the *Länder*.

The relationship between federal and *Land* elections is less direct and – amongst political scientists – more controversial (Schultze, 1991). *Land* elections provide an opportunity for the voter to 'correct' choices made at federal elections, and, since the 1950s, *Land* elections have been characterized by a pronounced anti-government effect. As a rule of thumb it was usually the bigger partner in the Bonn coalition which lost votes compared with performance at federal elections. This anti-government effect is produced by three factors specific to *Land* elections, but has also been an expression of long-term changes in the party systems of the *Länder*. The specific factors are: the above-mentioned consequences of a lower turnout at *Land* elections; the voters' calculation that at *Land* elections they can punish their preferred party for its mistakes without damaging its political position on the federal level; and a greater motivation for supporters of the opposition parties to turn out at *Land* elections to express their dislike of the Bonn coalition.

The long-term change in electoral behaviour, which election results on the *Land* level signalled in the 1960s and 1970s was an upswing for the Bonn opposition parties. Since the late 1970s however, anti-government protest found its expression increasingly outside the traditional party system. The number of non-voters has risen steadily, as has been the number of votes going to smaller political parties, including the Greens and right-wing extremists. In the 1990s, *Land* elections have been interpreted as massive votes of no-confidence in the traditionally dominating catch-all-parties, the CDU and the SPD.

With regard to the relationship between federal and *Land* elections there are also influential cyclical effects. The closer the date for a *Land* election is to the date of a federal election, be it shortly before or shortly afterwards, the greater is the similarity of results. Empirical research has shown that the mid-point, and the beginning of the second half of a federal government's period in office show the widest variation between federal and *Land* election results. This tendency is linked to the federal government's agenda-setting. Unpopular legislation tends to be brought into parliament at the beginning of a government's term, whereas, if possible, benefits are distributed shortly before the next election is due.

Voters have a clear idea about the relative importance of federal and *Land* elections. Although they perceive the latter as less important than the former, this has the paradoxical consequence of an increase in the political relevance of *Land* elections. Voters and parties are prepared to experiment, not at the 'more important' federal elections, but at *Land* elections. Consequently, hidden tendencies towards party realignment find their expression here. It is typical of the German political system that such realignments invariably begin at *Land* level. The permanence of these realignments has then to be finally tested at federal elections.

Land Party Systems in Western Germany

At first sight there are no far-reaching differences between the regional party systems in the *Länder* and the federal party system. Formal parallels, however, the same parties in parliament on both levels, the number of parties, or the relative stability of *Land* party systems, may be misleading. A closer look makes one realize that there is a degree of variety among the *Land* party systems, and that the differences matter. *Land* party systems continuously change, both as a result of the political dynamics of the *Länder*, and because of political influences from the federal level.

Party System Dynamics

As mentioned above, at *Land* elections the voter tends to be more innovative than at the 'more decisive' national elections. This can be demonstrated, for example, by the Green party, which, prior to entry into the Bundestag in 1983, found success easier at the *Land* level. After the Greens in the West had lost their seats in the Bundestag in 1990 the party was nevertheless elected into every *Land* parliament at the following *Land* elections (except for Schleswig–Holstein where the result for the party fell short of the five-per-cent hurdle by less than 400 votes). This was generally understood as a signal that, although the party was no longer represented in the Bundestag, it would continue to remain an important factor in German politics.

The 'experimental character' of *Land* elections can also be demonstrated by the fact that they have allowed right-wing parties to enter *Land* parliaments. The 1980s were in this respect, at least at first sight, a weak echo of the late 1960s when the NDPD (National Democrats) was represented in almost every *Land*. In Bremen in 1987 one member of the 'Liste D' (Germany ticket) was elected, and after the 1989 election in West-Berlin 11 so-called Republicans sat in the local parliament for one year until the all-Berlin election of December 1990. In 1990 it seemed that German unification had robbed the right-wing radicals of one of their central manifesto issues. But, as it turned out, unification euphoria (if it existed at all) was only temporarily successful in dominating the political agenda. By 1991 when the seriousness of post-unification problems had become clear, right-wing radicalism was back – and more successful than before – at *Land* elections. Although a number of right-wing parties contested the *Land* elections, often in competition with each other, a single party emerged as the dominant force with more than 5 per cent of the vote. In Bremen in 1991 the Deutsche Volksunion (German People's Union, DVU) secured 6.2 per cent; in Schleswig–Holstein the same party received 6.3 per cent of the vote in 1992, and, at the same time, in Baden–Württemberg, the Republikaner recorded 10.9 per cent. In the latter two parliaments right-wing parties became the third force after the two big parties. In Baden–Württemberg, governed since 1992, by a Grand Coalition of the CDU and SPD, the Republikaner have become the leading party of the parliamentary opposition. *Land* elections have thus served as early warning systems, indicating that the success of right-wing parties here may signal a transformation of the national party system.

The enlargement of the party spectrum in the *Länder* is not only a quantitative change, it also has important consequences for coalition formation and consensus-building. There is still an influential school of German electoral research (see, for example, Forschungsgruppe Wahlen, 1992) which regards right-wing voting as no more than the expression of political protest although, paradoxically, it argues that the rise of right-wing parties shows that Germany is on the road to normalcy compared to other European countries. If, as politicians like to believe, right-wing voting is only a form of protest against policy failures – currently against the way politicians have handled the political asylum issue – then the right-wing parties will disappear when the central problem in question is solved.

This interpretation underestimates, however, the structural problems of German society which seem to provide right-wing parties a more permanent base. A growing number of voters, victims of industrial modernization in both the West and East and who frequently also see themselves as victims of the unification process, no longer feel that the Bonn 'political class' represents their interests. (Significantly, this term which has its origins in Southern European democracies is now also used in Germany.) As they see it, Bonn politicians are inattentive to their problems – severe housing shortages, unemployment, a general threat to their already low social status by asylum-seekers and ethnic German immigrants, and the perceived economic burdens of both German and European unity. The ruling middle classes seem to have become estranged from the industrial workers, the urban lower classes and the rural farming communities. Consequently, these groups have largely stopped voting automatically for the SPD or the CDU and – if they do not abstain – support those right-wing populists who promise them a better future (Sturm, 1992c).

Other particular characteristics of *Land* party systems owe their existence to local circumstances. In city states, such as Hamburg and Berlin, the Greens have a strong anti-system faction, whose supporters tend to define themselves as 'alternative' – an expression which implies that they are not fully convinced of reform strategies and still have some sympathies with socialism. So instead of a Green party a Green Alternative List (GAL) competes for votes in Hamburg and an Alternative List (AL) competes in Berlin; in 1991 it joined forces with the Greens under the label Greens/AL. Particular to Schleswig–Holstein is the SSW, the South Schleswig Union of Voters, the party of the Danish minority. This party is the only one for which the five-per-cent hurdle for parliamentary representation was lowered to 1 per cent.

Coalition Formation in the Länder

In the 1980s there was a general tendency for the development of four-party systems at the *Land* level. The FDP has overcome the problems it experienced after changing its coalition partner at the national level in 1982, which led to the temporary elimination of the party from all but two *Land* parliaments. The Green party is now also a well-established political force, which in the 1980s was represented in every parliament except for the Saarland and Schleswig–Holstein where charismatic SPD leaders successfully mobilized the potential Green support by stealing their arguments. The advent of right-wing parties, however, may mark a transition from a *four*-to a *five*-party-system at the *Land* level, with potentially destabilizing consequences for coalition-building.

In the 1980s this tendency was foreshadowed in some of the *Länder* by an increasing instability in party majorities, creating uncertainty over coalition formation. Thus, for the first time in the history of the Federal Republic, *Länder* governments have tried to stay in power with minority support in parliament. In Berlin the 1981–83 SPD minority government was the result of the promise the FDP had given to form a coalition with the SPD, for which there was no majority after the election. The alternative, a CDU–Green coalition was out of the question for both parties. After the FDP had changed its coalition partner in Bonn, the Berlin FDP followed suit and agreed to a Conservative–Liberal government. In Schleswig–Holstein the unwillingness of the FDP to agree to a coalition with the SPD in 1987 (after an election campaign marked by 'dirty tricks' against the SPD's candidate, Björn Engholm) resulted in a parliamentary blockade. When the full scale of the scandal became public, an early election was agreed upon, the result of which broke the parliamentary blockade. In Hesse in 1982 no majority coalition was possible, because both big parties rejected the Greens as coalition partners. An election in the following year failed to break the deadlock. The FDP had pledged itself to a coalition with the CDU for which there was no majority, and the SPD still refused to join forces with the Greens. Only when SPD changed its mind in 1985 (and for the first time in German history a Green minister was appointed) were these parties able to form a majority government.

In 1986 Hamburg was confronted with a situation similar to the one in Hesse the previous year. Again, the Greens would have been needed for a parliamentary majority (but unlike in Hesse they themselves were undecided whether they wanted to become a government party) and again parliament was dissolved to find a 'better' majority. This time the FDP, now back in parliament, decided in favour of a coalition with the SPD.

When the Hesse situation repeated itself for a third time, in Berlin in 1989, the general mood had swung against making the voters vote twice merely because the politicians did not like or could not cope with the election result. In addition, the big parties were shocked by the electoral success of the right-wing Republikaner. Torn between the alternative of a 'Grand Coalition', with only the Greens and the Republikanes in opposition, and the 'Red–Green' model already tried out in Hesse, the Berlin SPD chose the latter to break the deadlock. It is interesting that in Bremen after the 1991 election and in Baden–Württemberg after the 1992 election, although government formation turned out to be extremely difficult (in Bremen the result was a traffic-light-coalition of SPD, FDP and Greens, in Baden–Württemberg a 'Grand Coalition'), still no serious politician advocated what had seemed possible in the 1980s: a new election.

As a general observation on parliamentary majorities at the *Land* level, the *Länder* can be grouped by the relative strength of governments and oppositions. As Tables 4.1 and 4.2 illustrates, in the 1980s there were *Länder* with very stable and relatively big majorities for the government, above all Bavaria (CSU) and, to some extent in the first half of the 1980s, North Rhine–Westphalia (SPD) and Berlin (CDU–FDP coalition). Majorities of 5–10 seats were characteristic for Hamburg (SPD and SPD–FDP), Rhineland–Palatinate (CDU–FDP and SPD–FDP) and Baden–Württemberg (CDU). Typically close was the race between political camps in Lower Saxony (CDU–FDP and SPD–Greens). Hesse (CDU–FDP and SPD–Greens), and the Saarland (CDU–FDP and SPD). Today, in the 1990s, the situation is in flux; the relative strength of political camps in the *Länder* seems to be gradually eroding.

With the exception of one-party dominated party systems (for example, Bavaria, dominated by the CSU; Baden–Württemberg dominated by the CDU until 1992, or Bremen, until 1991, and North Rhine–Westphalia dominated by the SPD) coalitions were needed in the *Länder* to form governments. The rational-choice solution of a search for a 'minimum winning coalition' (Riker, 1962) is not a good guide for predicting the outcomes of coalition formation in the 1980s. Minimum-winning coalitions rule out 'Grand Coalitions', but more effective than rational-choice arguments for ruling out such coalitions was the influence of party competition at the federal level on party competition at the *Land* level. The central role of the FDP in Bonn prevented a *rapprochement* of the two big parties, both because the FDP presented itself as the natural coalition partner, (usually for the Conservatives), and because the ideological gap between Conservative neoliberalism and Social Democratic welfare statism had temporarily widened. The latter can best be demonstrated with regard to the 1989 Berlin election, when the SPD's candidate, Walter Momper, was forced by

Table 4.1   Party Systems in the *Länder*, 1980–92

Schleswig–Holstein	1983	1987	1988	1992
SPD	34	36	46(G)	45(G)
CDU	39(G)	33(G)	27	32
FDP	–	4(G)	–	5
Greens	–	– ·	–	–
DVU	–	–	–	6
SSW	1	1	1	1
Total	74	74	74	89

Hamburg	1982	1986	1987	1991
SPD	64(G)	53(G)	55(G)	61(G)
CDU	48	54	49	44
FDP	–	–	8(G)	7
GAL	8	13	8	9
Total	120	120	120	121

Lower Saxony	1982	1986	1990	
SPD	63	66	71(G)	
CDU	87(G)	69(G)	67	
FDP	10	9(G)	9	
Greens	11	11	8(G)	
Total	171	155	155	

Bremen	1983	1987	1991	
SPD	58(G)	54(G)	41(G)	
CDU	37	25	32	
FDP	–	10	10(G)	
Greens	5	10	11(G)	
Liste D	–	1	–	
DVU	–	–	6	
Total	100	100	100	

North Rhine–Westphalia	1980	1985	1990	
SPD	106(G)	125(G)	122(G)	
CDU	95	88	89	
FDP	–	14	14	
Greens	–	–	12	
Total	201	227	237	

Hesse	1982	1983	1987	1991
SPD	49(G)	51(G)	44	46(G)
CDU	52	44	47(G)	46
FDP	–	8	9(G)	8
Greens	9	7(G)	10	10(G)
Total	110	110	110	110

Rhineland–Palatinate	1983	1987	1991
SPD	43	40	47(G)
CDU	57(G)	48(G)	40
FDP	–	7(G)	7(G)
Greens	–	5	7
Total	100	100	100

Baden–Württemberg	1980	1984	1988	1992
SPD	40	41	42	46(G)
CDU	68(G)	68(G)	66(G)	64(G)
FDP	10	8	7	8
Greens	6	9	10	13
Republicans	–	–	–	15
Total	124	126	125	146

Bavaria	1982	1986	1990
SPD	71	61	58
CSU	133(G)	128(G)	127(G)
FDP	–	15	7
Greens	–	–	12
Total	204	204	204

Saarland	1980	1985	1990
SPD	24	26(G)	30(G)
CDU	23(G)	20	18
FDP	4(G)	5	3
Greens	–	–	–
Total	51	51	51

Berlin (West)	1981	1985	1989
SPD	51	48	55(G)
CDU	65(G)	69(G)	55
FDP	7(G)	12(G)	–
AL	9	15	17(G)
Republicans	–	–	11
Total	132	144	138

Note: (G) = Parties in government.
Source: Wahlstatistik des Statistischen Bundesamtes und der Statistischen Landesämter.

Table 4.2   Government Majorities in _Länder_ Parliaments

Minority	1–5 Seats	5–10 Seats	More than 10 Seats
Schleswig–Holstein 1987	Schleswig–Holstein 1983	Hamburg 1982	Schleswig–Holstein 1988
Hamburg 1986	Schleswig–Holstein 1992	Hamburg 1987	Bremen 1983
Hesse 1982	Hamburg 1991	Bremen 1987	Bremen 1991
	Lower Saxony 1982	North Rhine–Westphalia 1990	North Rhine–Westphalia 1980
	Lower Saxony 1986	Hesse 1983	North Rhine–Westphalia 1985
	Lower Saxony 1990	Rhineland–Palatinate 1987	Rhineland–Palatinate 1983
	Hesse 1987	Rhineland–Palatinate 1991	Baden–Württemberg 1980
	Hesse 1991	Baden–Württemberg 1984	Baden–Württemberg 1992
	Saarland 1980	Baden–Württemberg 1988	Bavaria 1982
	Saarland 1985	Saarland 1990	Bavaria 1986
		Berlin (West) 1989	Bavaria 1990
			Berlin (West) 1981
			Berlin (West) 1990

112

his party to distance himself from his preferences for a 'Grand Coalition' and to try out a 'Red–Green' coalition with the AL.

The FDP's central role in Bonn allowed the party flexibility with regard to coalition arrangements, which even enabled it to form a government with the SPD in Hamburg in 1987 – the first social democratic–liberal coalition since Chancellor Helmut Schmidt's downfall in 1982. The only parties which, in the early 1990s, were still excluded from coalitions with all other parties in *Land* parliaments were the right-wing extremists, even when, as in the case of Baden–Württemberg, a minimum-winning coalition between them and the Conservatives would have been possible. The 1992 post-election period in Baden–Württemberg broke the ice between the CDU and the Green party. For the first time in German history there were serious negotiations with regard to the possibility of a 'Black–Green' coalition. The failure of those negotiations was not due to the CDU's outright rejection of a coalition government with the Greens, but to irreconcilable differences with regard to policy preferences. Previously, ideological distance between the Conservatives and the Greens had ruled out minimum-winning coalitions, although they had been numerically possible (in Hamburg in 1986, in Lower Saxony in 1986, in Hesse in 1987, in Rhineland–Palatinate in 1987 and in Berlin in 1989). The SPD, too, has been reluctant to accept the Green party as a possible coalition partner. Not until the mid-1980s did the general distrust between both parties disappear.

Another factor hindering coalition formation were the coalition commitments which the FDP regularly made during election campaigns in the 1980s, on the rationale that the party was worried about its image. The FDP's readiness to change coalition partners had been interpreted by critics as an expression of unprincipled opportunism and hunger for power. The FDP argued that its main aim was to make absolute majorities of either big party impossible, and that it would only join a government in which the coalition partner had less than the absolute majority in parliament. The latter argument gained importance when, after the 1991 election, the FDP turned down the offer of the SPD in Hamburg to continue the Social Democratic–Liberal coalition there. A more ambivalent case is the FDP's decision to form a coalition with the SPD after the 1991 election in Rhineland–Palatinate, because they had promised to renew the political partnership with the CDU. They also pointed to the alternative of a 'Red–Green' coalition for securing a majority in the *Land* parliament. Of similar ambivalence was the readiness of the FDP to join a 'black traffic–light' coalition (CDU–FDP–Greens) in Baden–Württemberg after the 1992 election, although the CDU and the Greens would have had a parliamentary majority even without the support of the Liberals.

Land Party Systems in Eastern Germany

In the former GDR five elections were held simultaneously on 14 October 1990. Berlin had its first all-Berlin election on 2 December, the day of the Bundestag election. Party politics in the Eastern *Länder* represented a new beginning, with party competition based on a new political 'mixture' composed of rather artificial *Land* branches of new parties with weak organizational infrastructures (the SPD and the Bündnis 90), and organizationally consolidated parties of the former 'socialist bloc', now turned democratic and accepted by their Western counterparts (the CDU and the FDP).

At the time of the *Land* elections the parties were in the forefront of the unification process. The plebiscitary phase of demonstrations in the streets had ended and the political–administrative phase of integration had yet to start 'Infiltration' of the East by West German parties dominated political discourse (Löbler, *et al.*, 1991: 14f). Organizationally this meant integration by bureaucratic and technical rules and standards set in the West and an estrangement of the mobilized party grass roots in the East. The latter were thrown back to a political culture of authoritarianism with the centre of authority now in Bonn. Where West German parties had old socialist bloc parties as partners, they reacted with an efficiency drive in the East German *Länder* entailing the reduction of party personnel. Where they had to support a new party, as in the case of the SPD, they set up an aid programme to give financial and organizational assistance for building up a party organization.

Another aspect of party competition was the transfer of political personnel from West Germany to the East, not only for the election campaign, but also to fill the offices of *Land* government (see Table 4.3). In Saxony both big parties had their top candidate 'imported' from West Germany. When Gerd Gies, the Prime Minister of Saxony-Anhalt, was forced to resign in July 1991 after only nine months in office, because of revelations of manipulation to secure his seat in the parliament, he was succeeded by his former Finance Minister, Werner Münch, a West German from Lower Saxony. In 1992 Josef Duchac, the Prime Minister of Thuringia resigned after revelations of his past career in the Stasi. He was substituted by yet another Westerner, Bernhard Vogel, the ousted Prime Minister of Rhineland–Palatinate.

During the election campaigns, West German public relations professionals, often with little understanding of local political perceptions, competed with each other on the new territory (Grafe, 1991: 72). Another special characteristic of the Eastern *Land* elections was the fact that it was the third round of elections in the former GDR in the year 1990. The same electorate had already voted in the *Volkskammer* (East German parliament)

Table 4.3   Top Candidates in *Länder* Elections in the East

	Know Candidate %	Like Candidate %	Dislike Candidate %
Mecklenburg–West Pomerania			
Alfred Gomolka (CDU) (East)	32	12	3
Klaus Klingner (SPD) (West)	49	16	5
Brandenburg			
Peter-Michael Diestel (CDU) (East)	95	27	51
Manfred Stolpe (SPD) (East)	86	52	7
Saxony–Anhalt			
Gerd Gies (CDU) (East)	12	3	2
Reinhard Höppner (SPD) (East)	55	23	5
Thuringia			
Josef Duchac (CDU) (East)	33	2	2
Friedhelm Fahrtmann (SPD) (West)	51	5	2
Saxony			
Kurt Biedenkopf (CDU) (West)	80	52	5
Anke Fuchs (SPD) (West)	83	43	17

Source: Noelle-Neumann, 1990.

elections on 18 March and the local elections on 6 May. Moreover, there was still no established political record to vote on, so that *Land* issues could not play a role in electoral choice. These factors mean that it is unwise to draw conclusions from the October elections about the future of the party system in the new *Länder*.

It does appear, however, as though personalities mattered relatively little. Three of the five top CDU candidates were not even known to half of the electorate. The name of Gerd Gies of Saxony–Anhalt was recognized in opinion polls in his *Land* by just 12 per cent of those interviewed, and only 3 per cent liked him. The better-known candidates were imports from the West or politicians who played a role in the *Volkskammer* (such as its Vice President, Richard Höppner), the then GDR government (Peter-Michael Diestel, Interior Ministry) or in the Protestant Church (Manfred Stolpe).

None of the better-known candidates won a *Land* election. In the case of Peter-Michael Diestel the strong dislike he engendered by his lenient attitude towards the Stasi certainly contributed to his electoral defeat. However, the same is not true for the rest of the candidates against whom there existed no such strong feelings. On the contrary, in Mecklenburg–West Pomerania the better-liked Social Democrat lost against his CDU rival just as in Saxony–Anhalt and in Thuringia.

The overwhelming influence on the *Land* elections was the hope invested by the electorate in national party programmes (Infas, 1990). To put it more bluntly, the question the voters asked themselves was, 'Which is the party that guarantees my personal well-being in the shortest possible time'? As there was no accumulated experience to guide the electorate, this decision had to be made on the basis of assumptions about the relative competence of the competing parties; it was also made with a clear priority on national issues, as *Land* politics were, at best, embryonic. Moreover, the elections took place in a situation in which the CDU still had the reputation in the East as the most efficient manager of the unification process (see Figure 2.8, page 76). Even in the fields of welfare policies, for which the SPD in the West is regularly attributed a better record than the CDU, the CDU was in the lead. With regard to the central concern of the voters in the East German *Länder*, namely unification, the SPD was only seen in a very minor role.

Expectations of this kind help to explain the fact that, in contrast to other industrialized countries, workers in the East voted in large numbers for the party of the Right, giving the CDU 50 per cent of their votes against 25 per cent for the SPD. The SPD's support, at 22 per cent, was also relatively weak among Protestants, who traditionally support the party. Among them the CDU gained a majority of 55 per cent (Forschungsgruppe Wahlen, 1990a: 4). Psephologists have found no special clientele voting for the SPD at the elections in the new *Länder*. The SPD party organization was dominated by theologists, engineers and other professionals, who had serious problems not only in organizing the party but also in presenting themselves as being sensitive to the burning social problems (Grafe, 1991: 75).

The result of the Berlin election of 2 December was strongly influenced by the general election of the same day. This meant that the voting behaviour in East Berlin remained relatively stable compared to the earlier local election results and that the PDS – the successor to the East German Communist Party (SED) – lost further ground. The electoral triumph of the CDU in Berlin, which in East Berlin was a part of the trend across the Eastern *Länder*, found additional support in West Berlin. Here it reflected *Land*-specific factors such as the disappointment of moderate SPD supporters with the 'Red–Green' coalition government, the decline of the Alterna-

Table 4.4 Berlin Elections, 1989 and 1990 (% of votes)

	Berlin 2.12.90	Berlin-West 2.12.90	Berlin-West 29.1.89	Berlin-East 2.12.90	Berlin-East 6.5.90
SPD	30.4	29.5	37.3	32.1	34.1
CDU	40.4	49.0	37.7	25.0	18.6
PDS	9.2	1.1	–	23.6	30.0
Greens/AL Alliance 90	5.0	6.9	11.8	1.7	–
Greens	4.4	1.3	–	9.7	9.9
FDP	7.1	7.9	3.9	5.6	2.2
Republicans	3.1	3.7	7.5	1.9	–
Others	0.4	0.6	1.8	0.3	5.2

Source: Forschungsgruppe Wahlen, 1990b

tive List and the return to the CDU of right-wing voters who had voted for the Republikaner in 1989. In West Berlin, the Social Democrats were punished for their hesitant attitude to German unity; while in the East of the city they defended their lead over the Conservatives. Whereas in West Berlin the CDU's candidate, Eberhard Diepgen, led his SPD rival, Walter Momper, in opinion polls by 15 per cent, in East Berlin Momper was given a lead of 35 per cent over Diepgen (Forschungsgruppe Wahlen, 1990b). As in the elections in the five new *Länder* the personality factor did not, however, exert a decisive influence, and Momper was unable to convert his personal popularity in East Berlin into a similarly emphatic vote for the SPD.

It is not yet known what the results of the first *Länder* elections in East Germany mean for the future. Much depends on whether these elections can be regarded as 'critical elections' (Key, 1955) which serve to structure long-term party loyalties after events which have fundamentally changed the fabric of society. This process of fundamental change is still in flux. As Schultze (1990a) has pointed out, East Germany contains the preconditions for a long-term political realignment. There has been a complete break with the old political system, and there are political generations with no collective memory of a united Germany. Their political experience had been shaped, on the one hand, by survival and career strategies in a communist dictatorship and, on the other hand, by the media-image of West German capitalist society. Thus the 1990 elections meant a fundamental political reorientation for the electorate in the Eastern *Länder*.

A clearer picture of the strength of party loyalties will not emerge until after the next round of *Land* elections in the East. Indications of volatility were found in the 1991 opinion polls which showed the SPD now clearly in the lead over the CDU, and also in the Berlin local elections of 1992, in which the CDU in East Berlin gained only 14 per cent of the vote. Only after unification is consolidated through national integration and economic equalization will it be possible for each of the smallish East German *Länder* to develop its own political profile and to enjoy the relative policy autonomy which federalism guarantees. With regard to the 1990 elections it is so far only possible to differentiate roughly between the electoral behaviour in the North and the South of the former GDR (Schultze, 1991). The South has, at least temporarily, developed into a Conservative stronghold (above all in Saxony), whereas in the North (Brandenburg, Mecklenburg–West Pomerania) the Social Democrats were more successful. The FDP had a special bonus in Saxony–Anhalt, because of the Halle effect: Hans-Dietrich Genscher, the former very popular Liberal Foreign Minister, secured an overwhelming FDP vote in his home town. Table 4.5 shows the distribution of seats in *Land* parliaments.

Where possible coalition formation in the new *Länder* followed the Bonn pattern (see Table 4.5). Even where majorities were extremely small, (as in Mecklenburg West–Pomerania), 'Grand Coalitions' were avoided. Three other developments can be identified, each with longer-term consequences for party politics in Germany at least at the *Land* level. The first is the ostracizing of the PDS, which is defined by all other parties as the anti-system party, and ruled out as a possible coalition partner. Second, coalition rules, dominated by the Bonn example until the end of 1990 have now become more variable. In Brandenburg the Liberals agreed to their second (after Hamburg) coalition with the SPD, along with the civil rights movement Bündnis 90. This was the first German red–yellow–green 'traffic-light coalition'. In Berlin, after the December election, a Grand Coalition of the CDU and SPD was formed, thus breaking the pattern of the CDU–SPD non-cooperation.

The third remarkable development was the (temporary) disappearance at the *Länder* elections of the DSU (German Social Union), which had the support of the Bavarian CSU. Even in Saxony, its stronghold at the *Volkskammer* election with 13.1 per cent of the vote, it was reduced to 3.6 per cent and failed to overcome the five-per-cent hurdle. In the other *Länder* it was almost completely wiped out. In 1992, however, dissenters from other parties joined forces in the parliament of Saxony–Anhalt to form a DSU parliamentary party. The poor election results for the DSU were all the more surprising, because the CSU in Bavaria fought a *Land* election on the very day of the East German elections and regained its

Table 4.5 Distribution of Seats in *Land* Parliaments

	Mecklenburg–West–Pomerania	Brandenburg	Saxony–Anhalt
CDU	29(G)	27	48(G)
SPD	21	36(G)	27
PDS	12	13	12
FDP	4(G)	6(G)	14(G)
Alliance 90	–	6(G)	5*
Total	66	88	106

	Thuringia	Saxony	Berlin
CDU	44(G)	92(G)	100(G)
SPD	21	32	76(G)
PDS	9	17	23
FDP	9(G)	9	18
Alliance 90	6*	10*	11
Greens/AL	–	–	12
Total	89	160	240

Notes: (G) = parties in government.
* Joint list with the Greens.

absolute majority. For the CSU the failure of the DSU underlines its strategic dilemma. If it wants to retain its national influence in a greater Germany and cannot count on the help of the DSU, the CSU itself may be forced to compete at *Land* elections in East Germany.

New Rules for the Bundesrat?

German unification has changed the federal system by confronting it with new economic challenges, but it has not necessarily altered the logic of party competition. What it has done is to add complexity to the role which *Land* parties play on the federal level via the Bundesrat. Some of this complexity is not new, although in different circumstances and in other historical periods of the Federal Republic it seemed to matter less

(Schüttemeyer, 1990). By mid-1991, the Bonn opposition had a majority in the Bundesrat, with serious consequences for policy-making, especially since a bill needs the consent of the Bundesrat to become law. This meant that SPD *Land* party assumed the role of the opposition, shifting the focus from the parliamentary party. This gives the Social Democrats an opportunity to strengthen their profile via the Bundesrat, but it also poses a threat because it means that they have to agree to compromises and have to shoulder responsibility in quasi-coalitions with the government.

Consensus government via the joint Bundesrat–Bundestag Conference Committee, (*Vermittlungsausschuss*), carries the inherent danger of a lack of transparency in political decisions. This could lead to an increase in electoral abstention as a protest against political 'horse-trading'. In 1992 the CDU-led federal government of Helmut Kohl twice broke up a social democratic majority in the Bundesrat by offering special favours to one of the SPD-led *Land* governments. Brandenburg voted with the Conservatives to secure itself extra income from the VAT increase due in January 1993. As part of a similar bargain SPD-led Rhineland–Palatinate agreed to the slimming down of the planning process for new traffic systems (with reduced citizen participation) when it was offered special infrastructure measures by the federal government.

What remains unclear is whether the logic of party politics will be able to bind together *Länder* ruled by the same party, but with very different economic interests (Sturm, 1992a): for example, smaller *Länder* reliant on federal aid, and more successful bigger ones; or *Länder* in the East and those in the West. This will depend upon the pattern of coalition formation in the *Länder*. German unification has increased the number of possible coalition permutations. The new *Länder*, with the exception of Brandenburg, have not revolutionized coalition rules. Indeed, it appeared initially as if the successes of the Conservatives in the East German *Länder* would enable them to hold their Bundesrat majority with the help of traditional CDU–FDP coalitions. It has been the dramatic changes in the political landscape of the Western *Länder* which has provided the opportunity for trying out new partnerships in the Bundesrat, due to the wide variety of possible coalition arrangements (see Table 4.6). This is not, however, to say that the basic rules have become obsolete. The division of the *Länder* between A-*Länder* (SPD-led) and B-*Länder* (CDU-led) is still the dominant factor in interparty relations in the Bundesrat.

Nevertheless, it is far from clear that the SPD and the CDU, even in their 'safer' coalition arrangements with the Greens and the FDP respectively, can always count on their coalition partner. And it should not be forgotten that the Bavarian CSU sees itself as an independent party, and not as Bavarian branch of the CDU.

Table 4.6   Distribution of Seats in the Bundesrat, 1992

SPD Controlled:		
SPD	16	(Hamburg, North Rhine–Westphalia, Saarland, Schleswig–Holstein)
SPD–Greens	10	(Hesse, Lower Saxony)
Compromises Have to be Found:		
SPD–FDP	4	(Rhineland–Palatinate)
Traffic-light coalition	7	(Brandenburg, Bremen)
Grand Coalition	10	(Berlin, Baden–Württemberg)
CDU Controlled:		
CDU–FDP	11	(Mecklenburg-West Pomerania, Saxony–Anhalt, Thuringia)
CDU	4	(Saxony)
CSU	6	(Bavaria)

The Future of the *Land* Party Systems

It can safely be said that, although in general the same parties compete at the national and the *Land* levels, *Länder* party systems will continue to have individual characteristics. The regional support for different parties varies; specific *Land* problems exert an independent influence on *Land* policies. The relative strength of the political camps constituted on the federal level, (CDU–FDP versus SPD–Greens), extends from near-equilibrium to the clear dominance of one political party or coalition over the other(s). Party competition is both influenced by and exerts an influence upon the organizational capacities of *Land* parties. Parties in government clearly differ in their character from *Land* parties languishing in opposition. Whereas in North Rhine–Westphalia, the SPD has no problem in recruiting top political personnel and is characterized by acute policy pragmatism, the same party in the Diaspora in Bavaria, and (until 1992) Baden–Württemberg, places stronger emphasis on programmes and visions, but its best brains try to make a career in national, rather than *Land*, politics.

Unification has meant the transplantation of the West German party system to the East German *Länder*. One consequence is that the fate of the PDS as a genuine party of the former GDR is now in doubt. The party will probably survive much longer in the East German *Land* parliaments than in the Bundestag, to which it was elected in 1990 only because of an exception to the five-per rule. Without that special provision, it is unlikely that it will be represented in the next parliament.

In 1991 the Greens in East Germany, except those in Saxony, joined the West German Green party and formed *Land* branches. It took the East German civil rights movements a long time to decide how to compete in future elections. In May 1991, New Forum's general assembly voted against a merger with the Bündnis 90 coalition, which it had concluded in some *Land* elections. In Brandenburg, on the other hand, New Forum decided in June 1991 to merge with 'Democracy Now' and, in Saxony, the Greens voted in May 1991 for an alliance with the civil rights movements. In June 1991 Bündnis 90 took the first step to becoming a *Land* party in its own right when it decided to compete in all future elections. Three options for the future of the civil rights movements were debated in 1991: autonomy in the form of new social movements; party organization, for example as Bündnis 90; and a merger with the Greens. After the federal-level decision made in favour of the third option (above all because of the pressures exerted by the five-per-cent hurdle) a merger between Bündnis 90 and the Greens in the Eastern *Länder* has become highly probable. Should the civil rights movements be unable to make clear choices, the result of such an internal quarrel may be counterproductive. If competing civil rights movements (and, also perhaps, the Greens in the East German *Länder*) fail individually to secure 5 per cent of the vote as happened in some of the 1990 *Land* elections, none of them will be represented in the respective *Land* parliaments, even though their combined vote may be much higher than 5 per cent. Of the big parties, the SPD has the greatest organizational problems in East Germany, but the party hopes to have overcome these problems before 1994, the year when new *Land* elections may be due.

With an increase in the number of *Länder* from 11 to 16, it has been argued that the frequency of *Land* and local elections has become an obstacle to the functioning of democracy. Politics, so the pessimists say, will degenerate into a permanent election campaign, and even fewer voters will bother to go to the polls when, as will be the case in 1994 for example, 17 elections are held in one year. Critics have therefore advocated a model of reform which would install one date for all *Land* elections, to coincide with the middle of the Bundestag period. Reforms should at least try to bring about a concentration of the numerous election dates (von Beyme, 1992). However, in addition to constitutional problems (*Land* constitutions would have to be altered to allow such a reform), these suggestions have drawn an adverse reaction from the champions of federalism, who argue that one mid-term election date for all the *Länder* would completely change the character of *Land* elections and transfer them into a quasi-national election at half-time. This change would not only leave no room for *Land* affairs in the election campaign, it would also eliminate the innovative function of *Land* elections with regard to the partisan change discussed above.

Where there is already one common election date for a number of *Länder*, namely in the former GDR, this is seen as being counterproductive, because it prolongs a quasi-GDR identity on the political level and further complicates an integration process which is already proving problematical. The arrangement of common elections in the five new *Länder* may, however, be short-lived. It is as yet undecided which of the new *Länder* will have their *Land* election every four years, and which will adopt a 5-year schedule. In Saxony, for example, the CDU government favoured a 5-year election period to be written into the new *Land* constitution, whereas the SPD preferred a 4-year term (see Entwurf, 1991).

Party competition in the *Länder* in the late 1980s and early 1990s produced some indications for future coalition formation both at *Land* and national level see Table 4.7). The sharp confrontation of two political camps, so typical until the mid-1980s, has been blurred by 'Grand Coalitions' in

Table 4.7   The Political Landscape in the *Länder*

Land	Since	Governing Party/ Coalition	Head of Government Today (Party)
Baden–Württemberg	1992	CDU–SPD	Erwin Teufel (CDU)
Bavaria	1966	CSU	Max Streibl (CSU)
Berlin	1990	CDU–SPD	Eberhard Diepgen (CDU)
Brandenburg	1990	SPD–FDP–Bündnis 90	Manfred Stolpe (SPD)
Bremen	1991	SPD–FDP–Greens	Klaus Wedemeier (SPD)
Hamburg	1991	SPD	Henning Voscherau (SPD)
Hesse	1991	SPD–Greens	Hans Eichel (SPD)
Lover Saxony	1990	SPD–Greens	Gerhard Schröder (SPD)
Mecklenburg-West Pomerania	1990	CDU–FDP	Berndt Seite (CDU)
Northrhine-Westphalia	1980	SPD	Johannes Rau (SPD)
Rhineland-Palatinate	1991	SPD–FDP	Rudolf Scharping (SPD)
Saarland	1985	SPD	Oskar Lafontaine (SPD)
Saxony	1990	CDU	Kurt Biedenkopf (CDU)
Saxony-Anhalt	1990	CDU–FDP	Werner Münch (CDU)
Schleswig-Holstein	1988	SPD	Björn Engholm (SPD)
Thuringia	1990	CDU–FDP	Bernhard Vogel (CDU)
Federal Government	1982	CDU–CSU–FDP	Helmut Kohl (CDU)

Berlin and Baden–Württemberg, and by the increased readiness of the Liberals to join the Social Democrats in coalitions. As a result the SPD has had the greatest variety of coalition options, because of the fact that they dominated the political scene in the *Länder*. Although just a few of the upcoming *Land* elections may change this picture, it is also possible that, as in the past, the pattern of coalition formation in the *Länder* may fore-shadow change in national politics. Far-reaching change in the German party system may be in prospect if tendencies in the *Länder* stabilize and spread to the federal level. One new feature of the national and regional party systems could be the establishment of right-wing extremist parties in parliaments. Another may be coalitions between the CDU and the Greens, perhaps including the Liberals – unthinkable a short time ago.

References

Beyme, K. von (1992), 'Zusammenlegung von Wahlterminen: Entlastung der Wähler – Entlastung der Politiker?' in *Zeitschrift für Parlamentsfragen*, **23**, (2), pp. 339–53.

'Entwurf der Verfassung des Freistaates Sachsen' (1991) in *Leipziger Volkszeitung*, 7 June, pp. 9–14.

Forschungsgruppe Wahlen (1990a), 'Alles dreht sich um die Einheit' in *Die Zeit*, 19 October, p. 4.

Forschungsgruppe Wahlen (1990b), *Wahl in Berlin. Eine Analyse der Wahl zum Abgeordnetenhaus vom 2. Dezember 1990*, Mannheim: FG Wahlen.

Forschungsgruppe Wahlen (1992), *Wahl in Baden–Württemberg. Eine Analyse der Landtagswahl vom 5. April 1992*. Mannheim: FG Wahlen.

Grafe, P. (1991), *Tradition und Konfusion – SPD*, Frankfurt/Main: Eichborn.

Infas-Report Wahlen (1990), *Die fünf neuen Bundesländer 1990*, Bonn-Bad Godesberg: Infas.

Key, V. O. Jr. (1955), 'A Theory of Critical Elections' in *Journal of Politics*, **17**, (1), pp. 3–18.

Löbler, F., Schmid, J. and Tiemann, H. (eds), (1991), *Wiedervereinigung als Organisationsproblem. Gesamtdeutsche Zusammenschlüsse von Parteien und Verbänden*, Bochum: Brockmeyer.

Noelle-Neumann, E. (1990), 'Die heimischen Kandidaten sind kaum bekannt' in *Frankfurter Allgemeine Zeitung*, 10 October, p. 5.

Riker, W. H. (1962), *The Theory of Political Coalitions*, New Haven/London: Yale University Press.

Schmid, J. (1990), *Die CDU. Organisationsstrukturen, Politiken und Funktionsweisen einer Partei im Föderalismus*, Opladen: Leske + Budrich.

Schultze, R-O. (1990a), 'Wählerverhalten und Parteiensystem' in *Der Bürger im Staat*, **40**, (3), pp. 135–44.

Schultze, R-O. (1990b), 'Föderalismus als Alternative? Überlegungen zur territorialen Reorganisation von Herrschaft' in *Zeitschrift für Parlamentsfragen*, **21**, (3), pp. 475–90.

Schultze, R-O. (1991), 'Bekannte Konturen im Westen – ungewisse Zukunft im Osten. Eine Analyse der ersten gesamtdeutschen Bundestagswahl vom 2. Dezember 1990' in *Wahlverhalten*, Stuttgart: Kohlhammer.

Schüttemeyer, S. S. (1990), 'Die Stimmenverteilung im Bundesrat 1949–1990 in *Zeitschrift für Parlamentsfragen*, **21**, (3), pp. 473–4.

Sturm, R. (1991a), *Die Industriepolitik der Bundesländer und die eurpäische Integration*, Baden-Baden: Nomos.

Sturm, R. (1991b), 'Die Zukunft des deutschen Föderalismus' in U. Liebert and W. Merkel (eds), *Die Politik zur deutschen Einheit*, Opladen: Leske and Budrich, pp. 161–82.

Sturm, R. (1992a), 'The Changing Territorial Balance' in G. Smith, W. W. Paterson, P. H. Merkl and S. Padgett (eds), *Developments in German Politics*, London: Macmillan.

Sturm, R. (1992b), 'Regionalisierung der Industriepolitik? Die Suche der Bundesländer nach einer flexiblen Antwort auf den neuen europäischen Wirtschaftsraum? in *Aus Politik und Zeitgeschichte*, (10–11), pp. 25–35.

Sturm, R. (1992c), 'Die Baden–Württembergische Landtagswahl vom 5. April 1992. Rechtsruck oder Protestwahl?' in *Zeitschrift für Parlamentsfragen*, **23**, (4).

Wahlen zu den Landtagen der Länder Mecklenburg-Vorpommern, Brandenburg, Sachsen-Anhalt, Thüringen, Sachsen, (1990), Berlin: Gemeinsames Statistisches Amt.

Part Two
Party Perspectives

5   The Christian Democrats and the Challenge of Unity

William M. Chandler

Unification and its consequences presented challenges for all political parties, but for none has this been more immediate than for the Christian Democrats who, by virtue of being the Chancellor-party and the dominant partner in the governing majority at the time, found themselves well placed to be the popular advocates of rapid unification. They also inherited primary responsibility for the implementation of a policy agenda full of risks. This discussion explores the challenges for German Christian Democracy resulting from political unification.

The Roots of Christian Democracy in Germany

The collapse of the Third Reich in 1945 led to the division of Germany between the victorious Allies. Consequently, the re-creation of constitutional order and the restructuring of party systems proceeded under very special circumstances, with profound consequences for post-war politics.

German parties were re-established under military occupation authorities, first in the Soviet zone where four parties – the Christian Democrats, the Liberals, the Social Democrats and the Communists – were licensed. The same pattern followed soon afterwards in the British, American and French zones. Apart from the Communists whose support quickly dissipated outside the Soviet zone, it is remarkable how the configuration of parties first licensed in the midst of devastation came to provide the vital core of post-war party competition in the Federal Republic. As the three Western zones united in the newly established Federal Republic, a multi-party system took shape. Although the CDU was initially little more than a collection of local–regional notables campaigning under a common umbrella, it emerged from the polls with a slim edge over the organizationally stronger

129

SPD. Crucially for the future of Christian Democracy, it was Konrad Adenauer who seized the opportunity to take power with his election as Chancellor, by just 202 out of 404 Bundestag votes, on 15 September 1949. Thereafter, economic recovery alongside mounting East–West tensions undoubtedly worked to the advantage of the Union parties and reinforced Adenauer's strategy which was designed to appeal to a diverse cross-section of German society. This served to establish the CDU–CSU as the prototypical *Volkspartei* in post-war European politics (Smith, 1982).

In the Soviet zone the evolution of parties was, of course, quite different, as the SPD agreed, under pressure, to merge with the Communists to form the Socialist Unity Party (SED). The CDU and LDP survived by recognizing the 'leading role' of the SED. It is inaccurate to see the Ost-CDU as an opposition force tolerated by a hegemonic SED. In practice, the link between the CDU and Honecker's SED was one of a 'hand-in-hand' relationship. The CDU served as an integral system party – a party of socialism. (Turner, 1987: 16–22; Merkl, 1963: 15–6; Buchstab and Gotto, 1990; von Ditfurth, 1991). Throughout the life of the GDR, the CDU also played an ornamental role as part of the National Front, a multi-party facade for single-party rule. It did provide an opportunity for limited participation and a channel for career advancement outside SED networks, but like the other block-parties whose activists constituted part of the privileged élite, it appeared heavily compromised by its involvement in a repressive regime (Lapp, 1988). For this reason, prior to unification, analysts of German Christian Democracy could easily dismiss the Ost-CDU as an instrument for the legitimization of the SED's effective monopoly of power.

Until 1990 the CDU in the East appeared to have minimal popular appeal or political future, yet, ironically, it not only survived the collapse of the SED state but went on to play a key role in unification. The speed of the unification process, including the re-establishment of the five eastern *Länder* and the immediacy of the *Volkskammer* election, forced upon the CDU in Bonn an urgent need to recruit candidates and mobilize support based largely on existing networks. In preparation for the crucial *Volkskammer* election of March 1990, the Western CDU–CSU hurriedly promoted the formation of a coalition of three parties, the Eastern CDU, the DA (Democratic Awakening) and the DSU (German Social Union) under the 'Alliance for Germany' umbrella. With Chancellor Kohl as the leading advocate of rapid unification and monetary union, the Ost-CDU suddenly emerged as the primary political force in the last days of the GDR, winning 40.8 per cent of the popular vote (with the alliance as a whole capturing 48.1 per cent), and became the principal party in a multi-party coalition with the mandate to achieve unification quickly.

Table 5.1 Two-party Competition, 1949–90

	1949	1953	1957	1961	1965	1969	1972	1976	1980	1983	1987	1990
Vote-share												
CDU–CSU	31.0	45.2	50.2	45.3	47.6	46.1	44.9	48.6	44.5	48.8	44.3	43.8
SPD	29.2	28.2	31.8	36.2	39.2	42.7	45.8	42.6	42.9	38.2	37.0	33.5
Combined	60.2	73.4	82.0	81.5	86.8	88.8	90.7	91.2	87.4	87.0	81.3	77.3
CDU–CSU Advantage	+1.8	+17.0	+18.4	+9.1	+8.4	+3.4	−0.9	+6.0	+2.6	+10.6	+7.3	+10.3

Electoral Relations

The first Bundestag election appeared to presage a return to Weimar-style polarization (Falter, 1981), but while the 1949 vote reflected past divisions, it provided no accurate guide for the future of the party system. By the critical 1953 election the CDU–CSU's broad appeals of recovery, prosperity, and anti-communism had effectively united much of the non-socialist electorate. This confirmed Adenauer's hold on power and substantially simplified the party system. The enactment of a five-per-cent national minimum for the proportional sharing of seats in the 1953 election also facilitated the exclusion of most regional and minor parties from the Bundestag, to the advantage of the Christian Democrats.

From this point until 1969, German party competition could be characterized as an unbalanced struggle between the two 'giants', the CDU–CSU and the SPD. Subsequent to the SPD's new moderate social democracy enunciated in 1959, the gap between the two began to narrow. The 1966–69 'Grand Coalition', in which the CDU–CSU and the SPD shared power, demonstrated to many voters that the Social Democrats could provide an acceptable alternative. The building of the social–liberal coalition forced the Christian Democrats, for the first time, into opposition, a role for which they were unaccustomed and unprepared. However, the collapse of the SPD–FDP coalition in 1982 restored the Christian Democrats to their traditional governing vocation.

The 1983 and 1987 Bundestag elections reconfirmed the Christian Democratic–Liberal majority. However, the 1987 results also contained warning signs, as the CDU–CSU polled its lowest share of the popular vote since 1949 (44.3 per cent). Especially disturbing to Christian Democratic strategists were signs of disaffection within certain core support groups, notably rural voters in traditional CDU–CSU bastions and middle-class voters in major urban centres.

Chancellorship and Party

Of the four Christian Democratic Chancellors, Konrad Adenauer and Helmut Kohl are of special importance not only because of their durability in power but also because they have governed through the two most critical turning-points in post-war German history.

In 1949 essential facets of an emergent parliamentary democracy – in particular, the relationships between the Chancellor and Bundestag and between government and opposition – were still to be defined by practice and custom. As the first post-war Chancellor, Adenauer enjoyed the opportunity to shape the governmental process and set basic policy priorities. His rule provided the model for Chancellor-democracy and meant 20 years of Christian Democratic dominance. During the 14 years of Adenauer's rule, the CDU party organization remained dependent on governmental authority and the popularity of the Chancellor. The party quickly became his electoral arm for the maintenance and exercise of power.

Between the demise of Adenauer in the early 1960s and the ascendency of Kohl to the Chancellorship in 1982–83, Christian Democratic politics was rife with challenges to the leadership. Chancellors Erhard and Kiesinger were neither dominant leaders nor masters over their own party. After falling into opposition in 1969, leadership issues remained unresolved and tended to preoccupy the party from within. The 13 years in the wilderness of opposition must be seen as times of organizational modernization and membership development (Haungs, 1990). Only in the 1970s did an effective party machinery become a stable feature in the success of this party *par excellence* of the post-war consensus. During Kohl's chairmanship, the CDU transformed itself from a primitive machine for re-electing the Chancellor into a mass membership, 'catch-all' party – in other words, a modern *Volkspartei* (Schönbohm, 1985; Haungs, 1990). The Bavarian CSU experienced its own modernization process somewhat earlier than did the CDU (Mintzel, 1978).

In the 1980s, following the return to power, the era of organizational innovation and membership growth came to a halt. A new version of the Chancellor-party was re-established, but the parallels with the Adenauer era were limited. Whereas Adenauer had effectively dominated parliament and had operated in a context of a weak party apparatus serving as his electoral machine, Kohl inherited a modern governmental process, in which executive–legislative and federal intergovernmental relations were firmly in place, and a complex, sophisticated party organization.

Unlike Adenauer, Kohl's success in retaining control has rested neither on leadership image nor personal popularity and, for this reason, his ability to maintain power remains something of an enigma (Smith, 1991: 58). Apart from being in the right place at the right time (in 1982 and again in 1989), Kohl's political endurance has depended on his capacity to manage and balance both the coalition partners and the various interests and factions found within the CDU itself. He has relied on management skills and organizational control, rather than charisma. Even after the 1987–89 period, during which the CDU suffered repeated setbacks in *Land* elections, and despite discontent within the CDU over his leadership, Kohl demonstrated at the 1989 party congress in Bremen that he remained fully in control, as evidenced by the failure to challenge his leadership and his replacement of Heiner Geissler as General Secretary.

Table 5.2   Trends in Christian Democratic Support

Pre-unification

Hesse	April	87	42.1	(+2.7)	
Rhine-Pal	May	87	45.1	(–6.8)	Starting in May 1987
Hamburg	May	87	40.5	(–1.4)	a series of CDU
Bremen	Sept.	87	23.4	(–9.9)	setbacks.
Schl.–Hol.	Sept.	87	42.6	(–6.4)	
B–W	Mar.	88	49.0	(–2.9)	
Schl.–Hol.	May	88	33.3	(–9.3)	
Berlin	Jan.	89	37.7	(–8.7)	

Transition to Unity – 1990

Saar	Jan.	90	33.4	(–3.9)	Lafontaine victory.
L. Saxony	May	90	42.0	(–2.3)	CDU loss of power.
NRW	May	90	36.7	(+0.2)	
Bavaria	Oct.	90	54.9	(–0.9)	CSU stability.

Unity Elections

Mk-v. Pom	Oct.	90	38.3		CDU victories in
Brandbg	Oct.	90	29.4		4 of 5 elections.
Sax-Anh.	Oct.	90	39.0		
Saxony	Oct.	90	53.8		
Thuring.	Oct.	90	45.4		
Bundestag	Dec.	90	43.8	(–0.5)	Majority confirmed.
Berlin	Dec.	90	40.3	(+11.2 W.Ber.)	CDU gains

Post-Unity

Hesse	Jan.	91	40.2	(–1.9)	Reversion to pattern
Rh. Pala	April	91	38.7	(–6.4)	of CDU setbacks.
Hamburg	June	91	35.1	(–5.0)	Electoral disasters
Bremen	Sept.	91	30.7	(+7.3)	in two CDU bastions.
B–W	April	92	39.6	(–9.4)	Revival of extreme
Sch–Hol.	April	92	33.8	(+0.5)	right protest vote.

The Impact of Unification

The almost instant absorption of the former GDR into the Federal Republic, according to Article 23 of the Basic Law, transformed the policy agenda and dynamics of German politics. Although many of the deeper consequences of unification will not be fully ascertainable for years to come, we can identify two general effects that relate concretely to party politics. One involves changing competitive factors in the electorate; the other concerns internal developments.

Although historical parallels are limited, changes in territory, demography and economy have significantly defined the circumstances of political development both post-1945 and post-1989. In the traumatic 1945–49 period, during which the two German states were created, territorial truncation and massive emigration from former eastern territories of the Reich and Soviet occupation zone profoundly altered the prospects for party competition. Millions of expellees and refugees poured into the Western zones and established a portion of the electorate that lacked local roots. This provided a first source of erosion of traditional milieus. At the same time, the loss of predominantly Protestant territory to the East created an even confessional split and strengthened the case for an interconfessional alliance. This provided an essential cornerstone for the 'catch-all' character of the new CDU.

By comparison, population shifts in 1989–90 were miniscule. Yet the exodus of thousands of disillusioned East Germans seeking West German passports in Prague, Budapest and elsewhere, or those who passed directly across the border opened in September 1989 between Hungary and Austria, proved a powerful catalyst to regime collapse. The sudden arrival of tens of thousands of refugees per week also created emergency conditions in West Germany and obliged both Bonn and the *Länder* to respond immediately.

Although the events of 1990 bear no resemblance to the devastation of 1945, economic misery and pessimism certainly encouraged both mass exodus and political protest. As the incorporation of the GDR into the Federal Republic became reality, economic and monetary union quickly exposed a moribund economic structure with long-term policy problems and political pitfalls. In both periods (1949 and 1990), the economic challenges of recovery and reconstruction provide a core of divisive issues for party politics.

Changing Patterns of Party Loyalty

Four decades of voting trends attest to the extraordinary stability and loyalty of the Christian Democratic electorate (see Table 5.2). Since 1953 levels of support have fluctuated within a range of only about 7 per cent. With the exception of 1972, Christian Democracy has maintained its claim to be West Germany's most popular political force. In the 1980s, although the relative dominance of the two major parties has weakened, the balance of forces between the Left and Right has remained steady. Moreover, support for the Christian–Liberal majority persisted at the same level throughout the 1980s and over the unification period (see Table 5.3). Indeed, despite exceptional circumstances, the first Bundestag election in united Germany is notable for its continuity with the past.

Table 5.3   Composition of the Christian–Liberal Coalition, 1983–90

	Electorate (% Vote)	Bundestag (Seats)	Cabinet Ministers
1983			
CDU	38.2	191	9
CSU	10.6	53	4
FDP	7.0	34	4
Total	55.8	278	
CSU Share	19.0	19.1	
1987			
CDU	34.5	174	11
CSU	9.8	49	5
FDP	9.1	46	4
Total	53.4	269	
CSU Share	18.4	18.2	
1990			
CDU	36.7	268	12
CSU	7.1	51	3
FDP	11.0	79	5
Total	54.8	398	
CSU Share	13.0	12.8	

This record is all the more remarkable given evidence of dealignment and increasing volatility within the voting public. (Dalton, 1984). Evolving social and occupational structures, including secularization and social mobility, have weakened traditional party loyalties and have facilitated an increase in issue voting (Veen and Gluchowski, 1988; Schultze, 1990).

The return of free elections in East Germany, combined with *Land* elections scheduled in the West, made 1990 a year of many ballots. The most significant of these elections were those for the *Volkskammer* in March, the Landtage in October and the Bundestag in December.

For all parties, unification brought together two electorates with very different experiences, needs and expectations. At first, Eastern voters constituted a great unknown, but as the 1990 *Volkskammer* election demonstrated, it was an electorate driven by the hopes and fears of unification. By 1990 the rejection of communism was manifest, and a broad consensus in favour of unification spanned most of the new party system. The *Volkskammer* election was, in effect, a popular referendum about how quickly political unification and the restoration of a market economy should be achieved. The significance of this consensus was grasped more quickly by the Chancellor and his advisors than by the SPD opposition. Unification issues divided the SPD between East and West and between Brandt's pro-unity stance and Lafontaine's hesitation, based on anticipated costs and problems. The ambivalence of the SPD on unification destroyed its early advantage in public opinion (see Chapter 2), and handed the Christian Democrats a golden opportunity (Müller-Rommel, 1991). The vote on 18 March swept the remnants of SED rule from power and elected a transitional government with the mandate to bring the division of Germany to an end. Thus, the *Volkskammer* election was formative in setting a pattern of voting that would carry over into the subsequent elections of 1990, which solidified the Christian–Liberal majority (Veen, 1990).

For the CDU, the 1990 *Volkskammer* election signalled a recomposition of its bases of support. The victorious Alliance for Germany represented a conservative–centrist coalition brought together hastily at the urging of the federal CDU–CSU in order to provide both candidates and a party structure to campaign for the positions articulated by Chancellor Kohl in favour of rapid economic and political union. Support for the Alliance had two distinctive components: confessionally-oriented voters and the underprivileged of the old regime – especially disadvantaged workers in the industrial regions of Saxony, Saxony–Anhalt, and Thuringia, where the CDU attracted a portion of the working class that historically had constituted a secure base for the SPD.

CDU strength in the new *Länder* was reinforced by the elections of 14 October. The low intensity of these contests produced a sharp drop in turnout in the October voting (–24.5 per cent compared with the *Volkskammer* election). The results confirmed the breadth of Christian Democratic support in Eastern Germany, where it emerged as the strongest party in four of the five *Länder*. Again, the CDU showed greatest strength in the formerly 'red' bastions of the south, especially in Saxony where Kurt Biedenkopf led his party to an absolute majority. These elections also signalled the demise of the DSU within the Christian Democratic camp, the DA (Democratic Awakening) had already joined the CDU in August of 1990). As in the *Volkskammer* election, these results demonstrated the effective penetration of the Eastern political landscape by the Western party system (Feist and Hoffmann, 1991).

The 1990 Bundestag election convincingly confirmed the existing majority, and halted the erosion of popularity that had plagued the CDU since 1987. However, the results were not entirely comforting for the party. By the autumn of 1990 Chancellor Kohl had reached the zenith of his popularity, yet the anticipated Chancellor-bonus failed to materialize. In fact, the Christian Democratic vote share dropped slightly to its lowest level since 1949.

The downward trend of the Christian Democrats in Landtag elections since 1987 and the corresponding revival of the SPD in the *Länder* forfeited control in the Bundesrat. In the Bundestag the effect has been neglible because, in both 1987 and 1990, the SPD lost an even greater portion of its vote shares and the gap between the the two widened to more than 10 per cent by 1990.

For the Chancellor and his coalition, 1990 was a unique year of political triumphs. After victory in the Bundestag elections, the *Kanzler der Einheit* immediately found himself in a dominant and advantageous position: no alternative majority coalition appeared possible, nor had he to fear any immediate internal challengers. In addition, the opposition SPD was in search of new strategies and new leaders following an ineffective campaign. However, within less than a year the euphoria of national unity had disappeared and the political fortunes of both the Chancellor and the Christian Democrats appeared to have taken a nose dive. There was a sudden return to the negative governing atmosphere that had pervaded West German politics prior to the collapse of the Honecker regime and the opening of the Berlin Wall. What went wrong and why did it happen so quickly?

Part of the answer lies in the fact that unification itself became a basic source of discontent. The realization that the process would be far more costly and difficult and that the time-frames for recovery would be much longer than originally believed gave rise to disillusionment in the East, balanced by impatience and irritation in the West. If Germany was united, Germans were not. The governing coalition's popularity was also damaged by the strategic error of promising no tax increases to finance unification. This backfired with negative consequences in the Landtag elections of 1991–92. Moreover there was a simmering public anxiety over immigration and asylum-seekers, and a growing perception that the government was not addressing these concerns.

The erosion of traditional loyalty networks for both major parties was already evident in the 1980s. However the post-unity elections at *Land* and local levels have demonstrated that this trend toward fragmentation in the German party system has been accentuated by the political tensions and public disenchantment associated with the thorny issues of unification. Generally, the 1991–92 regional elections signify a further breakdown in voter trust and have produced a downward spiral for the *Volksparteien*, which has opened the door for the rise of smaller parties. Such fragmentation makes a shift toward a five-party system increasingly plausible.

The deterioration in the political climate has translated into several electoral disasters for the CDU, with parallels to the dismal record of setbacks in the 1987–89 period. The first of these, in May 1991, came in Rhineland–Palatinate where the CDU suffered substantial losses in one of its traditional bastions and was forced to cede power to an SPD–FDP majority after 43 years of uninterrupted rule. Four months later the election in Bremen, although primarily a concern for the locally dominant Social Democrats, was notable for the revival of right-wing extremism – just after many observers had concluded that any such threat had disappeared. Here a loss for the SPD served as a warning sign for the Christian Democrats.

The election of greatest significance for the Christian Democrats was undoubtedly that of 5 April 1992 in Baden–Württemberg, the only remaining *Land* where CDU still had an absolute majority. Here the CDU slipped badly, losing almost 10 per cent, while the extremist Republikaner grew in strength achieving 10.9 per cent. This was a devastating loss and a national shock. Although the CDU remained the strongest party, it was obliged to form a 'Grand Coalition'.

In Schleswig–Holstein on the same day, the CDU was unable to benefit from SPD losses. As in Bremen, the far-right DVU made substantial inroads. These results indicate that the threat from the far Right is not only to the CDU. Damages have been felt by both major parties. Nor are extremist votes necessarily drawn only from conservative core voters. Young, blue-collar males and vote-switchers seem especially prone to vote for the radical Right (see Chapter 2). Even so, these results exposed a new danger to which the CDU would need to respond.

Electoral developments in the *Länder*, particularly in Rhineland–Palatinate and in Baden–Württemberg, attest to the substantial disappearance of previously secure regions for the CDU, a development with both immediate and long-term consequences.

By 1992 electoral erosion and the rise of extreme right-wing parties had provoked coalition tremors, accentuating tension between the two basic tendencies within German Christian Democracy. The CSU has consistently contended that extremists have benefited because the government missed opportunities to decisively deal with the asylum issue.

Although the task of carefully balancing coalition partners, regions and social bases is hardly new, it has been made more delicate by unification. The CDU's governing ability is increasingly dependent on its capacities for forming coalitions, which by 1992 appeared to be in some doubt. These new circumstances put Helmut Kohl in a more tenuous position, especially as unexpected events intervened to worsen coalition relations, including the scandal over arms deliveries to Turkey, which forced the resignation of CDU veteran Gerhard Stoltenberg, the sudden, but not entirely unexpected, resignation of Foreign Minister Hans-Dietrich Genscher and the subsequent FDP fiasco of intraparty intrigues in selecting his successor (see Chapter 6). This served to further irritate the CSU which felt itself excluded from coalitional bargaining.

A New Confessional Balance

Fusion in 1990, like fission in 1945, readjusted the confessional balance in German society. As a result of unification, the traditional bastions of postwar Christian Democracy, found disporportionaltely in rural regions and among practising Catholics, have been diminished. As in pre-1933 Germany, these primary reservoirs of CDU–CSU support once again constitute a distinct minority. Correspondingly, a northern, predominantly Protestant voice is now stronger within the party. In addition, the active engagement of Protestant church pastors in the protest movements of 1989 suggests a new source of political mobilization within the CDU. Nevertheless, the new nominal Protestant majority is likely to have limited impact because practising Protestants lack partisan cohesion.

From a different perspective some might argue that, despite the long-term trend towards a more secular society, unification could revive religious identities and give new meaning to confessional divisions. Moreover, an intensification of confessionally-sensitive issues, such as abortion, could have effects on the cohesion of the party as a whole.

A New Regional Balance: Prospects for CDU–CSU Relations

Unlike the SPD, Christian Democracy developed initially as a confederation of local notables within *Land*-based party organizations (Smith, 1991: 57; Schmid, 1990). Federalism institutionalized this dispersion of power. The autonomous Bavarian CSU has best demonstrated this factor within Christian Democratic party politics.

Relations in the post-war era between the CDU and CSU have, to an important degree, defined the character of German Christian Democracy as a whole. Their differences reflect, in part, distinctive ideological leanings and policy preferences but have been most evident in the leadership rivalries and strategic debates that have permeated party life over the past few decades. During the years in opposition, especially in the late 1970s, an acute rivalry developed between Helmut Kohl and Franz Josef Strauss. This was defused temporarily by Strauss's candidacy in 1980, which demonstrated the improbability of a majority based on his conservative strategy. Kohl's election as Chancellor served to contain this potential friction, but the rivalry ultimately was ended only by the death of Strauss in 1988.

What does unification mean for the CSU? The first obvious new reality is that Bavaria will be a smaller part in a united Germany. Even if CSU bastions of support within Bavaria remain secure, its position at the federal level has been significantly altered. Furthermore, while the CSU has retained its pre-unification identity, the CDU and the FDP, its coalition partners, have changed both becoming more socially and regionally diverse. Indeed, unification has allowed the CSU's primary rival in power-sharing, the FDP, to become the more powerful partner for the CDU and to become the second party in the coalition. For the FDP, expansion into the Eastern *Länder* was a political windfall, while the CSU was effectively blocked from such expansion once its DSU sister-party collapsed. As a result, the CSU's relative standing among federal coalition partners has diminished (see Table 5.3 page 136). Entering the 1990s the CSU is more regional, and its influence as a coalition partner in Bonn and Berlin is unlikely to regain its pre-unification strength.

There exist two possible scenarios for the future of the CDU–CSU alliance. The first scenario sees the CSU providing the spearhead of a new traditionalist force reliant on rural, predominantly Catholic supporters. The resultant regional and socioeconomic tensions that inevitably will be found within the Christian Democratic camp could open a potential for a split in which the CSU would become the leading force in a new conservative party, based on confession and region, to the right of a centrist CDU. This would suggest competition between two large conservative forces (perhaps not unlike that in France between neo-Gaullists and moderates), and thus a fragmentation of the conservative Christian block that has always held together throughout the post-war era. Whether intensified regional grievances or economic insecurity could prompt a revival of a confessionally-based conservative clientele party seems unlikely. Certainly there is no basis for predicting any immediate split-up of the CDU–CSU.

Alternatively, the CSU could stabilize as a purely regional party with reduced federal influence. In this case the CSU would become essentially the equivalent of other CDU *Landesverbände* (regional organizations), but with a Bavarian accent. When the new CSU leader, Theo Waigel, joined the government as Minister of Finance he signalled a new relationship of cooperation. While in the post-unification era significant policy tensions between the two parties are evident, the CSU cannot regain the political leverage it enjoyed prior to unification.

Viewed broadly, unification involves greater regional diversity, and this may create new tensions between *Länder*, between Bund and *Länder*, and within parties. There can be little doubt that the unification elections of 1990 made the CDU (but not the CSU) a more socially heterogeneous party. Such changes imply potentially new sources of strain and tension as the Christian Democratic umbrella has expanded to cover a population in the East that had little in common with its Western wing. It is reasonable to expect that, for the foreseeable future, the CDU–CSU may be characterized by significantly stronger internal tensions based on divergent economic and cultural priorities. The established north–south divide that has been an integral part of party politics still exists, but it is now overlapped by an east-west divide, which dominates the new policy agenda and which potentially poses more danger for party unity.

Internal Adaptation

The events of 1989–90 have created a need for parties to rethink value positions and develop new orientations. This implies organizational and programmatic adaptation. Ideology for the CDU–CSU has always defied simple description in that it has drawn its values from Catholic social thought, from conservative and liberal economic views, and from anti-communism (von Beyme, 1985). As such, party programmes have comprised flexible ideas with moderate tendencies. Indeed, it is often argued that the CDU–CSU's post-war formula for governing has been built on a broad electoral coalition based on a mix of values that gave the Union parties their pragmatic centrism. Will unification reshape this tradition of the middle way?

While the *Volkspartei* character of the CDU–CSU may not be endangered, the strains of unification politics may make it increasingly difficult to work out consensus positions on basic values and policy priorities. If so, one may see an intensification of programmatic debates within the party, perhaps more akin to those characteristic of the SPD in recent years. The primary dilemma is that the lack of clear policy direction for the CDU–CSU will risk further erosion of once loyal support groups. On the other hand, too sharp a programmatic profile may limit the social diversity of Christian Democratic support, which will be increasingly essential to long-term, post-unification, political survival. The new difficulties of defining a politically successful programmatic content provide a basic challenge for the CDU–CSU but, even so, the principles found in the 1978 party programme are not about to be scuttled. Renewal will proceed carefully and slowly, with a new programme only appearing in preparation for the 1994 Bundestag elections.

Prior to unification two strategic alternatives shaped Christian Democratic thinking. The first assumed that political ascendancy could best be maximized through the mobilization of a conservative majority from a Christian–bourgeois popular base. The second conceived of a wider Christian–Liberal alliance as the preferred route to realizing a viable parliamentary majority. This strategic debate now must be recast. The former strategy relied heavily on a stable electoral core within traditional milieus located predominantly in the south and west of Western Germany. Unification necessarily erodes the viability of this strategy because such bastions of past success will henceforth carry less weight in electoral competition. Whether the alternative strategy, which strives for a broad centrist alliance based on 'the politics of the middle way', still retains its plausibility is also open to question. At first glance, the inclusion of the new *Länder* appears to renew credence in a diverse interconfessional strategy. However, the expanded socioeconomic diversity of a united German electorate raises doubts as to how this strategy could be translated into issue stances that will allow for programmatic consistency while avoiding schisms.

Beyond programmatic and strategic considerations, the CDU also faces new challenges of organizational adaptation. There are, in fact, two overlapping organizational issues. First, well before unification, repeated losses in Landtag elections from 1987 through 1989 had raised concern about organizational weaknesses. After 1982, critics contended, the CDU reverted to organizational modes more typical of a Chancellor-party and neglected to adapt to changes in society and politics. This critique was at the heart of the struggle over Geissler's role as General Secretary. Stagnation in membership, an accentuation of the generation gap and lack of a programmatic profile, it was argued, had resulted in sagging support. Subsequent to unification these organizational concerns have intensified.

The CDU's crumbling power base is evident in the series of *Land* elections since 1990. While Helmut Kohl has often been portrayed as a master of organization, the party apparatus appears to be increasingly in disarray. The CDU has failed to attract younger members and a new generation of future leaders, and this failure is especially acute in the new *Länder* where organizational problems pose the greatest challenge. Nationally there has been a membership decline of about 80,000 since 1984: in the former DDR, from a reported membership of some 130,000 CDU members, only some 60,000 remain and, more importantly, few new members have been recruited. The desolate situation of the CDU was reflected in the May 1992 municipal elections in former East Berlin where the CDU emerged as a party of 10 per cent in many districts.

The broad organizational issue, a direct consequence of unification, centres on the problem of integrating the western and eastern wings of the party. As a natural and inevitable counterpart to national unity, the two branches of the CDU quickly moved towards building a single party. However, integration has brought together two quite different political traditions and memberships.

The membership core of the CDU in the West has always been rooted in the previous strongholds of the pre-1933 Catholic Centre Party, especially the Rhine–Ruhr and much of southern Germany. Yet the new Eastern membership has little in common with this traditional core of the Western CDU. This translates into a new internal diversity with new tensions based on economics, confession, region and generation.

Although the Eastern CDU has undergone substantial internal changes, including removal of some of the old leadership and the transformation of basic principles and goals, there remains a residue of conflict based on ingrained value differences that are likely to cause misunderstanding for some time to come. Following unification, the CDU remained filled with office-holders from the old regime. The record of close links between the Ost-CDU and the SED system of control – especially the Stasi – left a negative residue and made grass-roots renewal very difficult as competitive party politics were installed in the new *Länder*. For the newly integrated CDU, disillusionment on the part of younger potential members has limited recruitment.

The burdens of past involvements have also provoked crises of confidence within governing coalitions and in party organizations. Allegations of past complicity in the DDR regime led to the dismissal of leading CDU notables, including Lothar De Maizière, the last Prime Minister of the DDR, who resigned as the CDU Deputy Chairman on evidence of past involvement as an 'unofficial operative' of the Stasi. Similarly, both Gerhard Gies, Minister-President in Saxony–Anhalt, and Josef Duchac, Minister-President in Thuringia, were forced to resign on the basis of prior Stasi links. By 1992, three out of four CDU Minister-Presidents in the new *Länder* were Western imports.

It is clear that problems of indigenous leadership have profoundly affected East–West relationships inside the CDU and have resulted in a penetration of leadership positions by Western politicians and political bureaucrats. At the federal level there also exists the corresponding dilemma of adequately representing Eastern interests with few credible Eastern élites available for promotion to key offices.

Christian Democracy in Evolution

From the founding of the Federal Republic to unification, West Germany's Christian Democrats have benefited from being the party that has best articulated the post-war consensus. This consensus was built on three pillars: the success of the social market economy; the integration of West Germany into the Western Alliance; and a commitment to an emergent goal of European unity. Although that consensus has been given a symbolic boost by the collapse of communism throughout the former Soviet bloc, it has also been challenged by unification. With the disappearance of the GDR, the once solid underpinnings of post-war German politics, as practised for over 40 years in the Federal Republic, have been substantially altered. A new consensus must be defined, and this poses major challenges for all parties.

Germany is once again united. In less than a year the population of the former GDR has been absorbed into the constitutional rules of parliamentary democracy. Similarly, the act of economic union prepared the way for a return to a market economy – although the achievement of a healthy economic system in the East may take some years. However, although political unification is an accomplished fact, in important ways two Germanies will persist. Perhaps the most difficult transition will involve closing the gap between two value systems and their emotional legacies that have been ingrained over more than 40 years (see Chapter 9). Clearly, the treaties of economic and political union cannot serve to eliminate basic differences of mentality built up over decades of socioeconomic experiences and political socialization. A transition period full of new conflicts, tensions and uncertainties, will place the long-standing centrist style of conflict resolution in doubt. This poses a most basic challenge to all parties, but for none is this more compelling than for the Christian Democrats, who, by virtue of governing at the time of unification, have inherited the primary responsibility for guiding the course of unified German politics into a new age.

References

Beyme, K. von (1985), *Political Parties in Western Democracies*, Aldershot: Gower.

Buchstab, G. and Gotto, K. (eds) (1990), *Die Grundung der Union*, Munich: Olzog.

Dalton, R. (1984), 'The West German Party System Between Two Ages' in R. Dalton, S. C. Flanagan and P. A. Beck (eds), *Electoral Change in Advanced Democracies*, Princeton: Princeton University Press, pp. 104–33.

Ditfurth, C. Von (1991), *Blockflöten wie die CDU ihre realsozialistische Vergangenheit verdrängt*, Cologne: Kiepenheuer and Witsch.

Falter, J. W. (1981), 'Kontinuität und Neubeginn, die Bundestagswhl 1949 zwischen Weimar and Bonn', *Politische Vierteljahreschrift*, **22**, (3) pp. 236–63.

Feist, U. and Hoffmann, H-J. (1991), 'Landtagswahlen in der ehemaligen DDR am 14. Oktober 1990', *Zeitschrift für Parlamentsfragen*, March, pp. 5–33.

Haungs, P. (1990), 'Die CDU: Krise einer moderisierten Volkspartei?' in H-G. Wehling (ed.), *Parteien in der Bundesrepublik*, Bürger im Staat, Stuttgart: Kohlhammer.

Lapp, P. J. (1988), *Die Block-parteien im System der DDR*, Melle: Verlag Ernst Knoth.

Merkl, P. (1963), *The Origin of the West German Republic*, New York: Oxford.

Mintzel, A. (1978), 'The Christian Social Union in Bavaria' in M. Kaase and K. von Beyme (eds), *Elections and Parties*, London: Sage.

Müller-Rommel, F. (1991), 'The Beginning of a New Germany? The GDR Elections of 18 March 1990, *West European Politics*, **14**, (1), pp. 39–44.

Schmid, J. (1990), *Die CDU*, (eds), Opladen: Leske and Budrich.

Schultze, R-O. (1990), 'Wählerverhalten und Parteiensystem', *Der Bürger im Staat*, **40**, (3), pp. 135–44.

Smith, G. (1982), 'The Career of the Catch-all Concept' in H. Döring, and G. Smith (eds), *Party Government and Political Culture in Western Germany*, New York: St Martins.

Smith, G. (1991), 'The Resources of a German Chancellor', *West European Politics*, **14**, (2), pp. 48–61.

Turner, H. A. (1987), *The Two Germanies Since 1945*, New Haven: Yale University Press.

Veen, H-J. (1990), 'The GDR Election of March 1990', *German Comments*, **19**, June.

Veen, H-J. and Gluchowski, P. (1988), 'Sozialstructurelle Nivellierung bei politischer Polarisierung – Wandlungen und Konstanten in den Wählerstrukturen der Parteien 1953–1987', *Zeitschrift für Parlamentsfragen*, **2**, pp. 1–24.

6 The Free Democratic Party and the New Germany

Geoffrey K. Roberts*

The events of 1989 and 1990 which culminated in the unification of Germany and the first all-German Bundestag elections were, of course, welcomed enthusiastically by the Free Democratic Party (FDP). The party had always given prominence and priority to unification in its programmes (see below). Hans-Dietrich Genscher, then FDP Foreign Minister, had himself made a series of very significant contributions to the unification process. Firstly, it was 'Genscherism' – emphasizing detente and security simultaneously – which opened up the very possibility of peaceful unification. Second, Genscher played a key role in negotiations in the summer of 1989 regarding East German refugees in Western embassies. Third, it was his invention of, and participation in, the 'Two plus Four' talks which created the external conditions for unification. Finally his imaginative proposals in West German–Soviet negotiations allowed Gorbachev to accept the right of a unified Germany to belong to NATO. In more general terms, the FDP observed how its fundamental political orientations became precisely the goals of the 'GDR revolution': the market economy, as free as possible from state-policed distortions and controls, and the liberty of the individual. Although the East German voters did not initially reward the Liberals with their electoral support, by December 1990 they gave the FDP a

* I acknowledge with gratitude: the generous financial assistance provided by the Nuffield Foundation and the University of Manchester (1990) and the Deutscher Akademischer Austauschdienst (1991) which enabled me to spend periods of sabbatical leave in Germany; the hospitality of the Forschungsstelle für gesellschaftliche Entwicklungen, University of Mannheim, and Professor Rudolf Wildnenmann; and the provision of information and assistance by staff of the Friedrich-Naumann-Stiftung, Königswinter, the Friedrich Naumann Archive, Gummersbach, the FDP Bundesgeschäftsstelle, Bonn and staff of the *Länder* offices of the FDP. I am also grateful to the many colleagues in Germany who gave me information and advice concerning my research into the FDP.

147

level of voting support in the five new *Länder*, which exceeded even the record 1961 vote-share of the West German party. Rarely has the FDP been so strong, so confident, so united and regionally so efficient (by mid-1992, it was represented in all the *Land* parliaments for the first time since the mid-1970s). It can now hope to continue to play its role – so effectively developed in the West German political system since the 1960s – as a 'pivotal party' and 'creator of governing majorities' in the 'New Germany' (although the decline of the Christian Democrats and the rise of radical right-wing parties may complicate this role over the next few years).

The ability of the FDP to fulfil this role will depend on a number of factors. It will be affected by the way in which the party system develops, and on the way in which other parties (especially the Christian Democrats and the SPD) adapt themselves to the 'New Germany'. It will depend on the political agenda, on the state of the economy, on social conditions and on international affairs – all of which the FDP itself can only partially and occasionally influence. However, it will depend also upon what the FDP itself can do to strengthen its organizational structure (especially in the five new *Länder*), to develop appropriate and imaginative policy programmes, and to attract and retain party members and party voters. In particular, it will very much depend on how swiftly the FDP can integrate the disparate component elements of the GDR Liberal parties which formally merged with the FDP at the Hanover congress in August 1990.

The series of elections scheduled for 1994 leaves the FDP little time in which to consolidate and reinforce its organization in the five new *Länder*, although a special project to modernize and improve organization is now underway. Much depends on the success of the FDP in doing this. Like the *Wende* (change of direction) of 1982–3, the *Wende* in East Germany has presented the party with a challenge and an opportunity. If it meets the challenge, it can be as potent a political force as it was in the pre-unification Federal Republic.

The FDP in the Federal Republic

The FDP was established at a congress of *Länder* liberal parties from the Western zones, held at Heppenheim in December 1948. It thus became the first German Liberal party successfully to include, within a single organization, the various versions of political liberalism which had had separate organizational structures since the formation of the National Liberal party in 1867 as a breakaway from the Progressive party. However, the creation of a single organization did not eliminate the divisions within post-war liberalism. These divisions not surprisingly reflected the divisions between the two Liberal parties: the German Democratic party and the national–liberal German People's party in the Weimar Republic which had collapsed only 15 years before the Heppenheim congress, and members and supporters of which had participated in creating local liberal parties after the Second World War came to an end. So the FDP included within it a more progressive, liberal–democratic wing (represented especially by the Liberal parties of the south-west *Länder* and the Hansa city-states), and a more national–liberal wing, strongest in the *Land* parties of Hesse, Lower Saxony and North Rhine–Westphalia. These divisions became particularly important once the immediate matters of the drafting of the Basic Law, the creation of the Federal Republic and the campaigning for the first *Bundestag* elections had been dealt with. By the mid-1950s, internal party conflicts constituted a very real threat to the unity of the FDP – a threat which reached a climax at the Bad Ems party congress in 1952, when two competing programmatic manifestoes were presented by the national-liberals and by the liberal-democratic wing (though neither was adopted). A crisis within the ruling Christian Democrat–Liberal coalition in 1956, caused by the attitudes of Adenauer and the Christian Democrats to the Saar issue and to changes to the electoral system which would have limited severely the Bundestag representation of the Free Democratic party, led to a breakaway of the 'ministerial wing', consisting chiefly of sympathizers with the 'national–liberal' position. The FDP managed to survive this loss, as indeed it has survived the less significant loss of members and voters as a result of its change of coalition partner in 1969 and 1982.

These divisions within the party have continued up to the present, though in modified form and rarely of such virulence as to threaten the organizational integrity of the FDP. In very general terms, on the left there remains a liberal–democratic wing, more sympathetic to coalition with the Social Democrats, emphasizing particularly issues of civil liberties, detente and social liberalism. On the right is the market-economy wing, identified with a high-income clientele of managers, the self-employed and members of the professions, which is more comfortable in coalition with the Christian Democrats. Although the *Land* parties retain distinctive characteristics and although they still possess considerable autonomy, it would be an oversimplification to identify particular *Land* parties with either of these tendencies. However, even though the FDP has survived despite these inbuilt tensions, there has been an effect on the party's identity, in that it has frequently given the impression of being divided, able and willing to be a partner to either the SPD or the Christian Democrats. This syndrome is accentuated by conflicting coalition alignments in the *Länder*. Moreover, internal party life is often riven by disputes about policy and coalition strategy. During the short periods when the party has appeared to be more homogeneous and integrated, its identity has been unclear and vague. Such identity problems have inevitably had an effect on the party's electoral and coalition behaviour.

Despite its very limited levels of electoral support, membership and financial resources, the role of the FDP in the party system has been one of great influence and importance. It has benefited from two related properties of the West German political system: first, the two-vote system used for federal and some *Land* elections has enabled the FDP to garner 'split' votes from supporters of other parties (Roberts, 1988); second, the inability of either of the two major parties to obtain a governing majority (except in the 1957 election) has given the FDP an indispensable coalition role. Thus the FDP has survived not just as a Bundestag party, with between 5.5 and 12.5 per cent of second votes, but also as *the* ever-present party of government, with the exceptions of 1956–61 and 1966–69. It owes its pivotal role in government formation to its central location in the party system.

The pivotal role of the FDP is now endangered by two recent developments in the party system. First, the presence of the Greens as a fourth party in the Bundestag between 1983 and 1990, was a complicating factor, providing an alternative coalition partner for the Social Democrats should they be in a position to form a government. Second, reunification meant an enlarged Bundestag and an increase in the number of parties, making coalition arithmetic still more complex and uncertain. The conclusion to this chapter will take up this theme of coalition arithmetic in the changing post-unification party system.

The FDP and Government

Despite sometimes protesting to the contrary, the FDP leadership has seemed to require that the party should be in government on a more-or-less permanent basis, in order to survive. In each of the two periods when it was not a partner in coalitions in Bonn, (through its own decision to withdraw from Christian Democratic-led coalitions), the FDP failed to prosper. The party lost votes in the 1957 election (7.7 per cent, its worst result until 1969) and came near to electoral shipwreck in 1969, polling only 5.8 per cent, its lowest share of the vote in any federal election. In neither of these elections was the party able to announce in advance which party it would wish to see as its coalition partner. In government, on the other hand, the FDP is able to demonstrate its significance as the 'creator of government majorities', its political influence in terms of cabinet decisions and parliamentary legislation, and its importance through media publicity for its ministers. It is thus able to campaign in elections on its record in government, as it did in 1953, 1965, and in every election since 1972.

The FDP has always been able to benefit disproportionately in terms of the allocation of ministries which it receives from coalition negotiations, not only in terms of its share of cabinet ministers (and parliamentary state secretaryships) but also in the importance of those portfolios. It has held the Foreign Minister post since 1969 (and with it the Deputy Chancellorship); since then, it has also held either the Interior Ministry or Justice Ministry, provided the Minister of Economics since 1972, and has also held the portfolios for Agriculture (1969–82) and Education (since 1987). In the cabinet resulting from the 1990 Bundestag election it has added the Minister for Housing Construction to the Foreign, Economics, Justice and Education ministries. It is no wonder the CSU has complained stridently about the FDP's coalition 'pay-offs' compared to their own under Kohl's chancellorship.

These ministries have provided the FDP with three political advantages. By their very nature they confer media prominence on the party (especially the Foreign Ministry). Moreover, their significance has often been heightened by political developments – for instance, crises in the European Community, detente, unification and its economic consequences, the Gulf War. Finally, they are often ministries dealing with policies of special importance for FDP 'target voters' – especially those in the free professions, the self-employed and the intelligentsia. Other ministries – such as Labour, Defence or Transport – would not have these advantages for the FDP.

On the one hand the FDP is sometimes accused of not having clear policies; on the other, a survey of its electoral manifestoes, its Freiburg and Kiel programmes, its policy declarations on everything from abortion law to environmental pollution, from tax reform to the development of the European Community suggest rather that it has a superfluity of policy. Its election campaigns, coalition-negotiation demands, and policy proposals when in office provide a clearer view of the FDP's priorities in policy terms (Hofferbert and Klingemann, 1990; 277–304). Three themes are dominant in FDP programmes, and may be regarded collectively as the special policy 'flavour' which the FDP brings to government, irrespective of its choice of coalition partner:

1   Free-market economics, especially through reductions in taxes, removal of regulatory barriers to trade and production, and elimination of subsidies.
2   The protection of individual rights and civil liberties against intrusion by the state or other large organizations, especially over issues like abortion, data protection, and the right to demonstrate.

3   'Genscherism': the mixture of security and detente developed by
    Genscher during his long reign as Foreign Minister, and associated
    especially with the NATO 'twin-track' strategy of seeking arms reduc-
    tions and the lowering of international tensions, but from a basis of
    strong collective security. 'Genscherism' appears to have received its
    greatest possible justification by the course of events in Eastern Europe
    in 1989–90, and more generally by progress on arms reduction talks
    between the Western powers and the USSR.

The FDP manifesto for the 1990 Bundestag election (*Das liberale
Deutschland*) illustrated the priority the party gives to these themes. The
first section, entitled 'Peace', dealt with foreign and defence policy issues
and occupied 14 pages out of a total of 90. The next two sections on the
market economy and taxation ran to 13 pages. The following section,
dealing with legal and civil rights issues, filled 11 pages. Only then followed sections on social policy, women's rights, education, culture, science
and research, environmental protection, energy and transport, and agricultural
policy (a total of 28 pages).

Although often accused of putting office before policy or principle, the
FDP can point with some justification to its continuity of policy in what-
ever coalition it has been a junior partner, especially since 1969. Indeed, in
the 1983 election campaign, Genscher and the FDP used with great effect
the claim that votes for the FDP would secure continuity especially of
foreign policy, and that it had changed coalitions in part to maintain the
opportunity to promote its liberal policies.

The FDP and the German Question

The FDP has always given great prominence to the 'German question' in
its programmatic statements and political activity. Indeed, the extent to
which the FDP should be a 'nationalist' party and give priority to the
question of rapid reunification was a major issue of inner-party controversy
in the 1950s. The emphasis on the 'German question' was also a cause of
conflicts within the Adenauer coalition, clashing, as it did from time to
time, with Adenauer's policy of Western integration for the Federal Republic. The uncompromising stance taken by the FDP on the Saar question was
a contributory factor to the termination of the coalition by the FDP in 1956.
The Berlin Programme (1957), the FDP's first general programme, concluded with the firm statement that unification was the priority goal of the
FDP, and that all domestic and foreign policy had to serve that goal (Kaack,
1976: 87). In 1963, Mende, joining Erhard's coalition following the depar-

ture of Adenauer, took the post of Minister for All-German Affairs, (in preference to the science ministry he was initially offered) and was responsible for several improvements in relations between the two German states (Mende, 1986: 101–2).

By the mid-1960s, the ideas of some in the FDP, concerning an alternative approach to Adenauer's negative stance regarding relations with the German Democratic Republic, had gained ground, deriving in part from the famous 'Schollwer papers' on German–German relations (Baring, 1982: 212–14). A seminal article in a party journal opened up the question of the most suitable policy for dealing with the GDR (Rubin, 1967), and was associated with internal party debate which was especially strident at the 1967 Hanover party congress (Koerfer, 1981: 63–9). This congress began the process of leadership change, completed a year later when Mende was replaced by Scheel – a change which made possible both the 1969 federal election campaign, with its emphasis on new approaches to *Ostpolitik*, and the formation of the Brandt–Scheel coalition after the election.

That coalition implemented its *Ostpolitik*, including a treaty-like agreement between the two German states, signed in 1972, which laid the basis for improved future relations. This agreement seemed to mark an end to any realistic hopes of unification in the foreseeable future. This 'new realism' was confirmed at the FDP Mainz congress of 1975, which ratified a policy document on German–German relations: *Perspektiven Liberaler Deutschland Politik*. This set out a number of improvements in German–German relations which the FDP wished to see implemented, but emphasized the *Realpolitik* of the international context within which such improvements could be made. The whole document stressed a policy of 'small steps' within a broader situation of detente and European cooperation. On unification, it stated: 'Unity at any price is not a goal of liberal policy …. The German policy of the Liberals orientates itself not in relation to a nation-state concept of unity, but to the unalterable basic right of self-determination' (Kaack, 1978: 206–9).

Thus the policy of the FDP was one of encouraging contact between the peoples of the two German states, fostering of inter-German trade for its economic and political benefits, offering subsidies for GDR infrastructure projects whilst at the same time maintaining the ultimate goal of unification and condemning the fortified border that divided Germany. At the Hanover party congress in August 1990, Lambsdorff referred explicitly to these principles as having contributed to the events of 1989: 'What many saw as a mistaken recognition of eastern dictatorships was in reality the foundation for vanquishing them' (*Das Parlament*, 17/24 August 1990).

The events of summer and autumn 1989 posed a challenge to the FDP, as it did in different ways to all the parties of the Federal Republic. However, the FDP did not equivocate in its attitude to unification: it upheld the right of the citizens of the GDR to make a free decision whether or not to link with the Federal Republic. In an important letter to the chairmen of constituency parties at the beginning of November 1989, Lambsdorff warned against illusions concerning policy towards the GDR. He said that, while the FDP had always supported the idea that the East Germans themselves should decide on their own future relationship to the Federal Republic, support (including economic support) should be given to reform groups in the GDR. However, the impression should not be given that the Federal Republic was somehow 'purchasing' reform. The overcoming of the division of Germany, he concluded, must occur with the support of Germany's European neighbours (*Frankfurter Allgemeine Zeitung*, 2 November 1989).

In the *Volkskammer* elections in March 1990, all three liberal parties which constituted the electoral alliance, 'Bund Freier Demokraten' (Association of Free Democrats) stated their support for unification. While the two 'new' parties (the German Forum Party and the Free Democratic Party of the GDR) were unequivocal in their demand for speedy unification, the Liberal Democrats made a more qualified statement, involving the creation of a confederal arrangement as a preliminary to unification (*Das Parlament*, 9 March 1990). Following the elections to the *Volkskammer*, the FDP in the Federal Republic gave its full support to swift unification, differing from the Christian Democrats only in terms of detail concerning the timing and modalities of the process.

The Creation of an All-German FDP

Parallel to the process of German unification in 1990, the FDP underwent its own process of merger. In a two-step process, an electoral alliance was created between the three GDR Liberal parties; the LDP (Liberal Democratic Party), the German Forum party, and the FDP of the GDR. Subsequently these parties were merged with the West German FDP.

The FDP had been the only one of the three main parties in the Western zones during the occupation period which had made a serious attempt to form an all-German party, linking the Western and Eastern liberal parties. The SPD had lost its East German partner in the fusion of the SPD and the Communist party to create the SED; Adenauer's CDU was uninterested in the creation of an all-German party – Adenauer himself distrusted Berlin, and even within the Federal Republic the CDU left the Bavarian Christian Democrats their own separate party organization (Richter, 1980). However, the Liberals of the Western zones and the Liberal Democratic Party of the Soviet zone (LDP) did create a loose organizational structure which provided for periodic meetings of an all-German party executive, with alternating chairmen from West and East Germany. This body met twice in 1947 to discuss policy matters and proposals for a constitution for a new party (Grundmann, 1978: 73–7). However, by early 1948 it had become clear that the LDP was no longer autonomous in terms of its political action, and reluctantly the Western Liberals abandoned the experiment. By 1950 the party leadership of the LDP had changed, so that only those prepared to cooperate closely with the SED remained; others were expelled or resigned. In 1952 the LDPD (having by then added the word 'Germany' to its title) had consented to recognize 'the leading role of the working class' and of the SED. Along with the other so-called 'block parties' it thus contented itself with the secondary role allocated to it by the SED (Itzevott, 1982: 182–4; Koch, 1984: 3–14). The FDP occasionally attempted to revive contacts with the LDPD, but never with much success (Juling, 1973: 446–9).

The 'revolution' in the GDR therefore found the LDPD at first regarded very much as part of the old, and now rejected, group of 'block parties' associated with the *ancien regime*. So when it became clear by January 1990 that there was to be a new democratic order based on free elections, the FDP in the Federal Republic was in a dilemma. On the one hand, it was ready to welcome representatives from the LDPD to joint party activity, since their presence represented the democratic breakthrough in the GDR. On the other hand, it was likely that a new Liberal party might be founded, and it was feared that an association with the old 'block party' could be used by the SPD and the Greens as an electoral weapon against the FDP The rescheduling of the date of the *Volkskammer* election from May to mid-March forced the issue, because the FDP would have to decide on where to direct its assistance during that campaign, and prepare the delivery of that assistance.

Meanwhile two other Liberal parties had been formed. The German Forum Party (DFP) held its founding congress in Chemnitz on 27 January 1990, having formed in December 1989 on the basis of an appeal by some of the members of New Forum, which had been so prominent during the events of autumn 1989. By February it had a self-estimated 50,000 members, but had problems in terms of resources and communication within the GDR (the poor telephone service being a particular factor). An East German version of the FDP ('FDP in the GDR') had also been founded, and had about 8,000 members by the time of its founding congress on 4 February in East Berlin. At that congress, Otto von Lambsdorff made it clear that the FDP wanted a united front from the GDR Liberals for the coming election, and that the FDP would only assist the LDPD. With about 110,000 members and the financial, technical and property resources associated with its role in the old regime, this was by far the strongest of the three Liberal parties. Assistance would be conditional upon a purge of LDPD leadership and a reformed programme which abandoned all traces of socialism. 'It's a political risk to be associated with a party which shares responsibility for the policy of the GDR over the past forty years,' said Lambsdorff (*Frankfurter Allgemeine Zeitung*, 5 February 1990). All would depend on the Dresden congress of the LDPD, scheduled for 9 and 10 February.

In fact at that congress everything went well for the Liberals. The LDPD changed its name back to the pre-1952 version (LDP) and elected a new chairman, Rainer Ortleb. It produced a new programme, stressing the market economy, speedy unification and liberal principles in terms of human rights and the role of the state. And it made clear that it was prepared to cooperate in an electoral alliance with the other Liberal parties. They had sent representatives to that congress, and aided by the efforts of Lambsdorff and other senior FDP figures who came to Dresden, arrangements were made for the three Liberal parties to form the 'Association of Free Democrats' (BFD) as an electoral alliance for the *Volkskammer* elections. This was to an extent modelled on the 'Alliance for Germany' which the Christian Democrats had put together for the election, but the BFD would campaign collectively, whereas the 'Alliance for Germany' would campaign under separate party labels.

The election results were not very heartening for the Liberals, with 5.3 per cent of the vote giving them 21 seats. Results ranged from 10 per cent in the Halle district to only 3 per cent in Berlin and New Brandenburg. Pressure grew for a fusion, not just of these three parties but of the three with the FDP in the Federal Republic also. Just as the proximity of the first Bundestag elections in 1949 put pressure on the Western-zone Liberal parties to form the FDP in 1948, so the increased likelihood of unification and all-German elections in 1990 gave impetus to the idea of the creation of a single all-German Liberal party. However, rivalries between the 'new' Liberal parties and the LDP both before and after the *Volkskammer* elections prevented a fusion within the GDR liberal camp alone. The LDP changed its name on 27 March to '*Bund Freier Demokraten* – Die Liberalen', and the next day the NDPD (National Democratic Party of the GDR) announced its fusion with the *Bund Freier Demokraten*. In April a meeting of the chairmen of all four parties in Hanover agreed to try to create a single all-German party during the course of 1990. A special unification committee (*Vereinigungsausschuss*) was created to examine the modalities of fusion. The committee divided into three working groups (with parity representation for each of the four parties) to consider respectively the statute, programme and organizational structure of the new party.

Plans for a congress to join the various Liberal parties together had to be speeded up, because of the pace of unification. The FDP Praesidium on 12

June prepared for a congress in September; a week later, the date had become 25–26 August; one week after that, the date was fixed for 11–12 August (*Frankfurter Allgemeine Zeitung*, 13, 19 and 26 June 1990). The delegate allocation for the congress, based on the existing mode of delegate allocation for the FDP (a mixture reflecting both membership strength and electoral success of the party units), produced 402 delegates from the FDP of the Federal Republic, and 260 shared among the DDR Liberal parties. Lambsdorff was elected chairman of the enlarged party unopposed (with 524 votes, but 72 votes against). The enlarged list of deputy chairmen included both Ortleb and the DDR-FDP chairman, Mentzel. The party executive was also expanded, to give DDR liberals adequate representation. Exceptionally, the officers of the party elected at the Hanover Congress were given only one-year terms, instead of the usual two years, to allow the new party to hold another election after the elections for the Bundestag had been taken into account for the allocation of delegates for the next party elections. The new party – the first from the Federal Republic to become an all-German party – had about 200,000 members, of which 67,000 were in the Federal Republic.

Already structured on the basis of *Länder* parties, in the GDR as well as in the Federal Republic, the FDP was able to obtain improved results in the *Land* elections in the former DDR on 14 October 1990, shortly after unification. In Sachsen–Anhalt it won 13.5 per cent of the vote, in Thuringen 9.3 per cent, and managed not to fall below 5 per cent in any *Land*. However, fusion also brought its problems. After the elections of 1990, tensions and divisions which had existed between the numerically-dominant, wealthier and experienced LDP and the smaller, impoverished, politically-inexperienced East German FDP and German Forum Party resurfaced within the enlarged, all-German FDP. These arose out of jealousies and mistrust relating to the past record of many of the East German Liberals who had made careers in the 'block-party' system before the *Wende*. The need to cede illegitimately acquired wealth and property of the LDP and NDPD to the *Treuhandanstalt* (and to produce proper accounts relating to the capital holdings, income and expenditure of those parties from unreliable and incomplete records) has been a time-consuming task. The FDP declared bravely that it would not hold on to such property and wealth, and would pass over to the *Treuhand* trustee agency the land, buildings and businesses which the LDP possessed. However, the difficulties of assessing the value of such holdings, determining the legal position concerning ownership, and deciding which were needed anyway for the work of the FDP in the new *Länder*, meant that, even by April 1992, the situation had not been clarified (*Der Spiegel*, 10 June 1990: 29–31; 27 April 1992: 125). The need to redeploy or make redundant large numbers of salaried party employees in the former GDR (mainly from the LDP), and the consequent disappearance of much of the former service-oriented superstructure of the party at district (*Kreis*) and local levels, also had a negative effect on the FDP in the new *Länder*. Membership has declined, party income has been reduced, morale has fallen, and the lack of members willing or able to take on the unpaid duties of party posts in local branches has harmed the operation of the FDP in East Germany.

The 1990 Bundestag Election

The FDP was doubly fortunate in the context in which it campaigned for the 1990 Bundestag election. First, it benefited generally from the pro-government mood associated with unification, reducing the likelihood of otherwise dissatisfied FDP voters moving to the SPD. Second, the developments which led to unification could be exploited to the benefit of the party's two leading personalities. Genscher, who had played such a prominent role in the external negotiations associated with unification was consistently regarded as Germany's most popular politician (*Der Spiegel*, 29 October 1990: 40); Lambsdorff, the party chairman, was regarded as 'the Pope of the market economy, (*Die Zeit*, 16 November 1990) – the economic system offered to the former GDR as substitute for its failed socialist economy and as the prescription for a 'happy-ever-after' prosperity.

The prospects for the FDP were thus favourable. The party had supported the unamended adoption of the FDR's electoral system for the all-German election, but was not expected to be negatively affected by operation of a dual calculation of the five-per cent requirement adopted after a decision of the Constitutional Court. It had obtained encouraging results in *Land* elections in the East in October. Opinion polls suggested that the FDP would win around 9–10 per cent of the vote (*Der Spiegel*, 29 October 1990: 41; *Frankfurter Allgemeine Zeitung*, 1 December 1990). Moreover the party was unusually internally harmonious during the run-up to the election, and its general organizational and financial situation was sound. The unification of the West and East German Liberal parties had proved to be a positive factor in this respect.

The FDP's campaign strategy was broadly similar to that for is previous Bundestag elections since the *Wende* in 1982. There had been no real doubt about its coalition decision (always a potentially crucial factor in FDP election campaigns at federal and *Land* levels). The decision to seek a continuation of the existing coalition with the Christian Democrats was confirmed by the election congress held on 30 September in Nürnberg. The party decided to adopt a central expenditure budget of 12.8 million DM (approximately 6 million DM in 1987), in the hope that the relatively high outlay would be profitable financially in terms of extra votes each worth an electoral subsidy in excess of 5 DM. Whilst strategic aspects of the campaign would be handled by the Praesidium, and, less frequently, by the party's Executive, tactical decisions were the responsibility of FDP campaign staff at party headquarters in Bonn, under the leadership of Frau Schmalz-Jacobsen (the General Secretary). Technical and practical matters relating to publicity were the responsibility of Ogilvie, Mather and Partners, the public relations agency selected by the FDP for this campaign. The agency met at least weekly with party staff to coordinate their responsibilities for publicity. Campaign planning in fact began in September 1989, was interrupted by the developments in the GDR from November to March (including diversion of attention and resources to the *Volkskammer* election campaign), but then resumed, so there had been a long lead-time.

The campaign itself focused on Genscher and Lambsdorff, especially in terms of speeches at major rallies, television and radio party-political broadcasts (each had semi-biographical broadcasts relating their backgrounds and achievements), leaflets, posters and press advertising. The campaign was to be the same in both parts of Germany, although particular problems of the former GDR (such as the need for tax concessions) were the subject of regional campaigning. As it became obvious that the opposition had no real chance of winning the election, the FDP's strategy increasingly emphasized its differentiation from the Christian Democrats and the need to avoid an absolute majority for the CDU–CSU. The CDU campaign emphasized its need for both votes ('The second vote is the vote for the Chancellor'), but, as usual in campaigns since 1972, the FDP deliberately sought to attract second votes from supporters of the CDU–CSU and, with smaller hopes of success, the SPD. Ultimately, it was helped, rather than disadvantaged, by the attention which the larger parties gave to the issue of split-voting in their attempt to prevent it. The FDP identified its target groups – the self-employed, and the professions – and produced special publicity material to send to them.

The FDP manifesto was the result of a long process of discussion, beginning in autumn 1989 in the committees of experts (*Fachausschusse*), and involving every level of party organization from grass-roots membership (via publication of the draft manifesto in the membership magazine, *Neue Bonner Depesche*), to the party executive. Final approval was bestowed by the party congress in September. Problems of coordinating the campaign from Bonn arose because of the impracticability of communicating by telephone with East Germany, and the difficulties of motivating members and potential voters after three elections in less than a year in the former GDR. Moreover, it was hard to persuade members to perform voluntarily tasks such as pasting up posters, delivering leaflets and manning information stands, for which in the old regime they had often been remunerated. In addition, the East German roots of leading politicians, such as Genscher in Halle and Mischnick in Dresden, were a bonus exploited effectively by the party.

The result delighted even the most optimistic in the FDP. Firstly, the overall result of 11 per cent and over 5 million votes exceeded expectations; second, the party won a constituency seat (in Halle) for the first time since 1957; third, the result increased the relative strength of the party within the coalition, both in relation to the CDU and to the CSU. The results were almost equally good in the West (10.6 per cent) and the East (12.9 per cent). The second-vote strategy had again paid-off handsomely: only 7.8 per cent of voters voted in constituencies for the FDP, although the difference in the Eastern area (11.7 per cent of first votes) was much smaller, perhaps because voters there had not yet acquired the electoral sophistication needed to engage in split-voting. The party obtained over 9 per cent of second votes in every *Land* except Saarland (6 per cent, representing the only FDP *Land* result lower than for the previous federal election) and Bavaria (8.7 per cent). However, in one electoral aim there was failure: the electoral arithmetic denied the FDP their 'golden scenario' of being able, theoretically, to switch coalition partners, since the SPD and FDP lacked a Bundestag majority.

Coalition Bargaining

For the FDP, coalition strategies in relation to elections, and coalition negotiations after elections, are of very special significance. Wrong decisions in either case can mean electoral losses which can endanger the very survival of the party. The decisions to leave the coalition with the Christian Democrats in 1956 and 1966, to contest the 1957 and 1969 federal elections without a clear coalition statement to guide the voter, and the *Wende* in 1982, all demonstrate this assertion. The consequences (a decline in electoral support in 1957, 1969 and 1983, and a period in opposition to the 'Grand Coalition' in 1966) have been near-calamitous. The situation is very simple. The party must try to remain in government and to profile itself in government. It must then normally make a coalition statement in advance of the federal election giving reasons why the governing coalition should continue. From time to time, however, and after subtly preparing the ground through rumour, coalition strategies at *Land* level and carefully chosen issues for coalition conflicts, the party must position itself for a change of coalition. There is no rule which the FDP can follow concerning the timing of such a coalition change. The *Wende* in mid-term in 1982 was criticized because it seemed to breach promises to both the electorate and the SPD that the FDP would remain a loyal partner for a full legislative period. On the other hand, it is difficult for the party to remain in office with a partner-party until a few days before it starts fighting an election with a coalition strategy to change partners after the election.

The changes in both major parties in the period prior to the Grand Coalition meant that by the mid-1960s both the SPD and CDU could credibly be considered as coalition partners for the FDP. Although in the mid-1950s some party members advocated a change of coalition partner (Mende, 1984: 388–9), the programme of the pre-Godesberg SPD was incompatible at federal level with that of a free market-oriented FDP. By 1961, though, the FDP could conceivably have entered into a coalition with the SPD in terms of policy, and did seek to use the availability of the SPD as a threat against the Christian Democrats (Mende, 1984: 454–5). In 1969, after three years in opposition had enabled the FDP to change its leader, become more reformist in its policies and become more attractive to a younger and broader electoral clientele, the party campaigned without a formal statement of coalition preference. However, its support for Heinemann in the presidential election earlier in 1969, the generally iconoclastic tone of its manifesto, and the political speeches of its leaders, all indicated an openness to a coalition with the SPD. Party leader, Walter Scheel virtually confirmed his own preference for such a coalition in the televised question-and-answer session with all the party chairmen three days before the election (Baring, 1982: 166–83; Bermbach, 1970: 5–23).

Leaving the coalition with the SPD was almost as difficult an experience as its formation had been. Suggestions that the FDP should at least consider the timing and modalities of coalition change were being expressed well in advance of the 1980 federal election. Indeed that election might have seen such a change had the CDU–CSU not chosen Franz-Josef Strauss (arch-enemy of the FDP) as its Chancellor-candidate. However, in August 1981 Genscher, as party chairman, wrote a letter to party members identifying problems which existed in the coalition, and suggesting that the time might be arriving for a change of coalition partner. The following year, a paper from Lambsdorff (Economics Minister) to Chancellor Schmidt demanding changes in economic policy was used as an excuse to terminate the coalition, and the FDP entered into a new government with the Christian Democrats under Chancellor Kohl (Jäger, 1988: 63–8; Merck, 1989: 246–81; Filmer and Schwan, 1988: 209–66; *Der Spiegel*, 28 February 1983: 44–75). The consequences for the FDP were grave indeed. Many leading personalities left the party, some for the SPD (among them Verheugen, the former General Secretary; Matthäus-Maier, the finance expert; von Schoeler, a former Parliamentary Secretary of State), others to try to form a new Liberal party, and yet others to leave active politics altogether. Many who left were among the younger and more active of grass-roots supporters. A challenge was mounted against Genscher as party chairman at the party congress later that year, and in the opinion polls FDP support fell well below the vital five-per-cent level. Only the postponement until March 1983 of the election called to legitimate the change of government enabled the FDP to obtain a respectable 7 per cent.

There were no great problems in connection with the 1987 Bundestag election. The FDP confirmed that it would remain in coalition with the Christian Democrats, in line with the views of its supporters. One survey reported 79 per cent of FDP supporters as favouring that coalition, and only 14 per cent a coalition with the SPD (*Der Spiegel*, 19 January 1987: 61). The improved result for the FDP (9.1 per cent) enabled it to obtain an additional ministerial post, the Education Ministry, alongside those of the Foreign, Economics and Justice Ministries which it retained from the previous administration.

Coalition negotiations in 1990–91 were also not particularly dramatic. Lambsdorff made clear that his own strategy was to negotiate about policy first, then the overall structure of the government (given the changes which might be necessary for post-unification Germany). Only after that would the FDP agree nominations for particular posts (*Frankfurter Allgemeine Zeitung*, 5 December 1990). This schedule allowed Lambsdorff and the FDP to finesse an otherwise embarrassing problem: the resignation of Haussmann immediately after the Bundestag election had left the Economics Ministry vacant. Mischnick was expected to confirm his decision, taken months earlier, not to stand for the *Fraktion* leadership, but had not yet done so. The personal ambitions of several younger members of the FDP 'élite', especially Möllemann, Adam-Schwaetzer and Solms, were tied in with this situation. The omission of a replacement for Mischnick (who would be elected by the Fraktion only in mid-January) from the ministerial team could only happen if it was clear that Mischnick would, in fact, leave such a vacancy. In addition, Lambsdorff had his own preferred disposition of posts in mind, but this was not congruent with the wishes of Möllemann in particular. As it happened, Mischnick announced his decision not to remain as *Fraktion* chairman before Christmas, and the FDP could then work out a suitable set of appointments. The result was that Solms became *Fraktion* leader (he had acted as Mischnick's deputy for some time past); Möllemann, despite a lack of economic expertise, was appointed as Economics Minister; Adam-Schwaetzer became Minister of Housing Construction (having been persuaded not to compete against Solms for the *Fraktion* leadership); and Kinkel, formerly Secretary of State in the Justice Ministry, became

Minister of Justice easily beating Hirsch of the 'liberal-democrat' wing of the party. The former leader of the East German LDP, Ortleb, became Education Minister (*Frankfurter Allgemeine Zeitung*, 16 January 1991).

Policy negotiations were carried out partly by working groups, and there were few really serious issues of contention among the three parties involved (the CDU, CSU and FDP). The main problem was the seemingly uncompromising announcement by the FDP that there would be no election of a Chancellor without agreement on provision of 'low-tax area' status for the former GDR (*Frankfurter Allgemeine Zeitung*, 11 December 1990). Theo Waigel, CSU Minister of Finance and his party were opposed to such concessions. Eventually a face-saving formula was found, and a coalition agreement satisfactory to all the parties was reached (*Frankfurter Allgemeine Zeitung*, 17 and 25 January 1991).

The FDP Today

There is little evidence to suggest that the new FDP is very different from the old. With regard to the sources of voting support in the 1990 election there were more female than male FDP voters in both the Western and the Eastern electoral areas – but only in line with the differences in the population as a whole. The younger age groups provided disproportionately fewer FDP voters; those in the 40–60 year groups disproportionately more FDP voters than in the general population. In terms of occupation, the party did relatively poorly among blue-collar workers (*Arbeiter*), better among white-collar workers, managers and civil servants (*Angestellte, leitende Angestellte und Beamte*), and best, in relative terms, among the self-employed. Fewer Catholics and relatively more Protestants than in the population as a whole supported the FDP (Forschungsgruppe Wahlen, 1990: 30–1, 34–5).

These trends are in line with evidence concerning the structure of the FDP vote in previous elections over the past 20 or 30 years: it is a party supported by those in the better-paid occupations, with high academic qualifications and twenty or more years of career development. They are attracted to the party because of its concerns for their interests (including tax reform, reduction of official regulations, and so on) and because it presents itself as the guardian of the market economy and of civil liberties. Data on party membership, on those holding office within the party, and on its leadership group suggest that the social composition of the FDP electorate are reflected, in exaggerated form, at higher levels of the party 'pyramid'. For example, a study of middle-level party élites showed that 89 per cent of delegates to the FDP federal party congress were male, and that 64 per cent (higher than the CDU, SPD or CSU) had university qualifications

(Niedermayer and Schmitt, 1983: 299–300). The FDP's own 'Women's Report' (FDP, 1989) demonstrated the progress being made within the party to bring the representation of women in party institutions to at least the proportion (about 25 per cent) which they constitute of the total membership. In 1989 women occupied three seats of nine elected on the party praesidium, seven of 33 elected posts in the party executive, seven of 48 FDP Bundestag seats, 13 of 126 members of the federal grand committee and 67 of 402 delegates at the federal party congress. Similar levels of representation were reached in several of the *Land* party organizations, where female membership of *Land* executive committees ranged between 11 and 36 per cent). The lists of Liberal-party candidates elected in Eastern Germany to local and regional offices suggests that, despite the different historical development, economic structure and political agenda in the GDR, the Liberals (as in West Germany) have attracted particularly the self-employed and professional people to the ranks of its activists.

The membership of the LDP, though now declining, remains a significant component of the total membership of the FDP. Indeed, the FDP is the only party of the former West German party system now to have more members in the new *Länder* than in the old: 67,000 in the West as against 90,500 in the East as of October 1991. At the end of 1989, LDPD statistics stated an official membership of 111,278; a month later this had declined to about 108,000, partly because of emigration to West Germany. Using East German social classifications, 32.5 per cent of the 1989 membership were *Angestellte* (white-collar employees); 23.7 per cent were *Handwerker* and *Gewerbetreibende* (craftsmen and those engaged in small businesses); and 21.3 per cent were in 'intellectual' occupations (teachers, scientific workers, and so on). In addition, 64 per cent of members were male, and nearly half the members were in the 31–50 age group. A third had higher education qualifications. The main difference, compared to membership in the West German FDR, remains the relatively large number of teachers in the East German *Land* party organizations. With the further development of a centralized membership register and data processing facilities in all *Land* headquarters, a more precise membership profile is expected to be obtained by the party in the future.

However, two warnings must be given against trying to interpret or compare any quantitative data for FDP membership. The numbers are usually very small (so percentages may be affected greatly by small changes in the composition of party groups – for example, the party praesidium. Moreover the electorate and membership of the FDP are especially volatile, so an accurate statistical summary may lose its value over the course of one or two years. The rapid turnover of party membership and electorate can mean sudden changes in the social structural composition of the party.

The FDP has always had a somewhat chequered history of leadership elections, leadership succession and changes in attitudes within the party towards its leaders. Following the contested re-election in 1982 during the *Wende* crisis, Genscher announced his intention of not standing again for the office of party chairman. The failure of the FDP to win 5 per cent of the votes in the elections for the European Parliament in June 1984 meant that Martin Bangemann, a former general secretary of the party and a former chairman of the Baden–Württemberg *Land* party organization, became available as Genscher's chosen successor. He was elected unopposed in February 1985 at the Saarbrücken congress. Bangemann's much criticized performance as party leader and his undisguised ambition to go to Brussels as a member of the Commission of the European Community, led to a rather drawn-out campaign for the leadership between Lambsdorff and Adam-Schwaetzer, with Lambsdorff winning the election at the party congress in 1988. He was subsequently elected as the first leader of the all-German FDP in August 1990, and was very successful campaigning on behalf of the party in the 1990 Bundestag election. Finding a suitable sucessor to Lambsdorff – who has said that he will retire in 1993 – was made more controversial than might have been expected. In the course of the jostling within the party for ministerial and other positions during coalition negotiations, Möllemann announced that he would be a candidate for the leadership when it became vacant, and that Lambsdorff had given his support in that ambition (*Frankfurter Allgemeine Zeitung*, 17 December 1990). This pre-emptive strike by Möllemann produced reactions from other members of the FDP élite: in particular the chairman of the Hessen FDP, Gerhardt, indicated that a Möllemann candidacy would not necessarily go unchallenged (*Der Spiegel*, 14 January 1991: 22). Lambsdorff was re-elected at the Suhl party congress in November 1991, by 433 votes against 184, having made it clear that he would not continue beyond the end of that two-year term.

Hans-Dietrich Genscher's surprise resignation as Foreign Minister in April 1992 plunged the party leadership in considerable disarray. Initially an announcement was made that Irmgard Schwaetzer (formerly Adam-Schwaetzer) would be appointed. Annoyed at not having been consulted, however, the parliamentary group of the FDP insisted on a vote. They elected as their nominee for the post, the Justice Minister, Klaus Kinkel, who subsequently defeated Schwaetzer in a ballot. Sabine Leutheusser-Schnarrenberger, a relatively unknown backbench member of the FDP *Fraktion*, elected to the Bundestag only in 1990 on the Bavarian list, was elected as the nominee of the party to be Kinkel's successor as Justice Minister. The embarrassing mishandling of the Genscher succession aroused increasing concern about Lambsdorff's leadership, focussing attention once again on the issues of who was to succeed him and whether the party could afford to wait until 1993 before putting a new leader in place. Apparent resentment in the party at Möllemann's assumption of his role as heir-apparent encouraged a search for alternatives. In particular, the popularity of Kinkel and his able handling of his role as Justice Minister made his the most frequently-mentioned name as a potential challenger to Möllemann. A survey (*Der Spiegel* 11 May 1992: 51) showed a preference for Schwaetzer as Lambsdorff's successor (48 per cent) rather than Kinkel (31 per cent) or Möllemann (14 per cent). Kinkel apparently now has Lambsdorff's support, although Genscher prefers Möllemann (*Süddeutsche Zeitung*, 10 June 1992). Kinkel himself has only reluctantly agreed to be regarded as a candidate if 'massive resistance' in the party to Möllemann makes him unelectable. (*Der Spiegel*, 30 March 1992: 33). There is also concern that the party may suffer if its leader had his time and attention taken up by the demands of the Foreign Ministry. One advantage which Kinkel would enjoy is that he is not from North Rhine–Westphalia (unlike Möllemann or Schwaetzer), which would perhaps give him support from other *Land* party delegations, and would dilute the domination of that powerful *Land* party. Of the FDP's leaders, only Heuss, Dehler, Maier and Bangemann have become party chairman from other *Länder*, compared to Blücher, Mende, Scheel, Genscher and Lambsdorff, who were in office for nearly three-quarters of the period since 1948.

A potential unknown factor in terms of the FDP's future is the extent to which the party in the five new *Länder* fuse reasonably homogeneously with the West German party. Initial suspicions that merger might lead to a revival of 'social-liberalism' because of left-wing tendencies in the parties of the former GDR seem not to have been confirmed. The autonomy of the *Land* organizations remains quite powerful within the party, however: on matters of coalition strategy, for instance. 'The political backbone of the party are the *Länder* parties, which both politically and organisationally are extremely autonomous' (Verheugen, 1984: 80), and this autonomy could be a factor if developments in the GDR cause the FDP to lose voter support, and tempt the FDP in Saxony–Anhalt, Thuringia or Saxony to strike out on a more independent course in local or *Land* elections. Certainly the 1991 party congress in Suhl, at which the party organizations in the new *Länder* showed increasing influence in terms of representation on party organs (the new General Secretary, Uwe Lühr, comes from Sachsen–Anhalt) and in policy debate, demonstrated that fusion was working reasonably well. However, some critics regret that fusion has not been used more positively as a chance for programmatic renewal by the FDP:

So it relies principally on the tried and tested and attempts to cover up its internal frictions with an unpolitical and unadventurous technocratic pragmatism. In this, it seems, the inner-party unification process matches that of the all-German unification process. (Vorländer, 1992: 15)

One of the most significant factors for the FDP in the 'New Germany' will be the range of coalition opportunities available to the party. Such opportunities – at federal and at *Land* levels – will depend upon three factors. Firstly, they will be shaped by the political, economic and social developments which occur especially (but by no means exclusively) in the new *Länder*. These will include the question of economic reconstruction in the East, the controversy concerning the increasing numbers of asylum-seekers, and the debate about reform of the Basic Law. Second, and connected to the above, the future of the FDP will depend upon changing electoral relations in the party system, not only among the established Bundestag parties, but also the PDS, the Greens–Bündnis 90, right-wing radical parties, and perhaps even some yet-to-be-created East German 'resentment' party (Roberts, 1991: 386–7). In turn, this will be crucial in shaping the readiness and the ability of the FDP to contemplate new coalitions, in Bonn or in the *Länder*.

Even before unification, the question of when, and under what conditions, a change of coalition in Bonn could occur was discreetly raised within the FDP. The first 'incongruent' coalition since the *Wende* of 1982–83 was established in Hamburg in 1987. Another has been formed in Rhineland–Palatine in 1991. 'Traffic-light' coalitions, involving the FDP in coalition with the SPD and the Greens, exist in Brandenburg and Bremen (see Chapter 4). Current opinion-poll indications suggest that, on present levels of support, the existing coalition in Bonn is unlikely to retain an overall majority in 1994 (though much can change by then, of course). Tensions within the coalition are increasing, suggesting that its continuation, in any case, might be problematic.

Certainly the party system – and thus the coalition options for the FDP – in post-unification Germany has become more complex. This may even, in some scenarios, make the FDP redundant, if it is unable on its own to create a majority coalition with the CDU–CSU or the SPD. Indeed, in some multi-party *Länder* legislatures or in the Bundestag, the much discussed possibility of a 'Grand Coalition' could rob the FDP of its place in government. Policies, organization, leadership, coalition strategies: by 1994 the FDP must get all four right, if it is to thrive in the 'New Germany' and continue to be a small, but essential, partner in government.

References

Baring, A. (1982), *Machtwechsel*, Stuttgart: Deutsche Verlags-Anstalt.
Bermbach, U. (1970), 'Stationen der Regierungsbildung 1969', *Zeitschrift für Parlamentsfragen*, **1**, (1), pp. 5–23.
FDP (1989), *Frauenanteil in der FDP*, Bonn: FDP Bundesvorstand.
Filmer W. and Schwan, H. (1988), *Hans-Dietrich Genscher*, Düsseldorf: Econ. Verlag.
Forschungsgruppe Wahlen, (1990), *Bundestagswahl 1990*, Mannheim: Forschungsgruppe Wahlen.
Grundmann, K-H. (1978), *Zwischen Verständigungsbereitschaft, Anpassung und Widerstand: Die LDP in Berlin und in der Sowjetischen Besatzungszone 1945–1949*, Bonn: FDP.
Hofferbert R. and Klingemann, H-D. (1990), 'The Policy Impact of Party Programmes and Government Declarations in the Federal Republic of Germany', *European Journal of Political Research*, **18**, (3), pp. 277–304.
Itzerott, B. (1982), 'Die Liberale-Demokratische Partei Deutschlands (LDPD)' in H. Weber, *Parteiensystem zwischen Demokratie und Volksdemokratie*, Mannheimer Untersuchungen zu Politik und Geschichte der DDR, Bd. I. Cologne: Verlag Wissenschaft und Politik, pp. 179–84.
Jäger, W. (1988), 'Die "Wende" 1982. Schuldzuweisungen für das Ende der sozial-liberalen Koalition', *Politische Meinung*, (241), pp. 63–68.
Juling, P. (1973) 'FDP und LDP: Dialog zum Mehr-Jahres Rythmus', *Liberal*, **15**, (6), pp. 442–9.
Kaack, H. (1976), *Zur Geschichte und Programmatik der Freien Demokratischen Partei*, Meisenheim-am-Glan: Anton Hain.
Kaack, H. (1978), *Die FDP*, (2nd enlgd. edn), Meisenheim-am-Glan: Anton Hain.
Koch, M. (1984), 'Blockpolitik und Parteiensystem in der SBZ/DDR, 1945–50', *Aus Politik und Zeitgeschichte*, (Beilage, *Das Parlament*), (37), pp. 3–14.
Koerfer, D. (1981), *Die FDP in der Identitätskrise. Die Jahre 1966–69 im Spiegel der Zeitschrift 'Liberal'*, Stuttgart: Klett-Cotta.
Mende, E. (1984), *Der neue Freiheit*, Munich: Herbig.
Mende, E. (1986), *Von Wende zu Wende: 1962–1982*, Munich: Herbig.
Merck, J. (1989), 'Von der sozial-liberalen zur bürgerlichen-liberalen Koalition' in W. Mischnick (ed.), *Verantwortung für die Freiheit. 40 Jahre FDP*, Stuttgart: Deutsche Verlags-Anstalt, pp. 246–81.
Niedermayer, O. and Schmitt, H. (1983), 'Sozialstruktur, Partizipation und politischer Status in Parteienorganisationen', *Politische Vierteljahresschrift*, **24**, (3), pp. 293–310.
Richter, M. (1980), 'Parteien für ganz Deutschland?' *Deutschland Archiv*, **13**, (10), pp. 1144–53.
Roberts, G. (1988), 'The "Second-Vote" Strategy of the West German Free Democratic Party', *European Journal of Political Research*, **16**, (3), pp. 317–37.
Roberts, G. (1991), '"Emigrants in their own Country": German Reunification and its Political Consequences', *Parliamentary Affairs*, **44**, (3), pp. 373–88.

Rubin, H. (1967), 'Stunde der Wahrheit', *Liberal*, **9**, (3), pp. 161–4.

Verheugen, G. (1984), *Der Ausverkauf. Macht und Verfall der FDP*, Reinbek bei Hamburg: Speigel Buch, Rowohlt.

Vorländer, H. (1992). 'Die FDP nach der deutschen Vereinigiung', *Aus Politik und Zeitgeschichte* (Beilage, *Das Parlament*), (5), pp. 14–20.

7 'Loosely Coupled Anarchy': the Fragmentation of the Left

Stephen J. Silvia

In the spring of 1992, Otto Count Lambsdorff, head of the liberal Free Democratic party (FDP), described today's German Social Democratic Party (SPD) as the most 'pleasant' opposition party that 'we have ever had' (Lösche, 1992: 531). Lambsdorff's remark is justified, for German society has become increasingly culturally and politically fragmented over the past 25 years, and this social fragmentation has hampered the ability of the Left to preserve the unity of its collective political organizations and to offer a credible alternative to the governing conservative coalition led by Helmut Kohl. This chapter analyses political developments within the German Left since the early 1980s, focusing on the activities of the Social Democratic Parties and the Greens both before and after German unification.

The Crisis of Social Democracy

Despite a recent influx of competitors on the left of the German political spectrum, the Social Democratic Party remains the leading political party of the German Left. The past decade has been difficult, electorally, for the Social Democratic Party. The high-water mark for the SPD came in 1972 when the party received 45.8 per cent of the vote, and, in the two subsequent elections of 1976 and 1980, the Social Democrats were able to maintain a strong position at just under 43 per cent of the vote. Since then, however, the SPD's performance has declined substantially. In 1983 they garnered only 38.2 per cent of the ballot, losing 750,000 votes to the Greens and over two million to the Christian Democratic Union (CDU) and its Bavarian sister party, the Christian Social Union (CSU). In the 1987 and 1990 federal elections, the Social Democratic Party's share of the vote fell again, first to 37 and then to 33.5 per cent. The 1990 results represent the weakest showing for the SPD since the mid-1950s (Koelble, 1991: 22–3).

The SPD's 20-year electoral slide manifests the deep institutional, ideological, and tactical divisions within the party. Social Democracy originally rose to power as a junior coalition partner to the CDU–CSU in 1966 and as the senior partner to the FDP in 1969 on a Keynesian contract that offered the working class, public servants and professional employees a programme of economic modernization that would provide a rising standard of living, full employment and a more open, tolerant and professional society which would reward individuals on the basis of merit rather than on custom and tradition. The fruits of this contract were indeed a period of unprecedented growth and affluence under 13 years of Social Democratic rule. The collapse of the Social Democratic Party's governing coalition with the Free Democratic Party on 1 October 1982 under the weight of both economic and security crises marked the end of the SPD's 'prosperous, and in many ways quite glorious, Bad Godesberg era' and the beginning of an as of yet unresolved era of crisis within German Social Democracy (Markovits, 1986: 428–32).

German society changed dramatically during the Social Democratic years. Service and public-sector employees increased their proportion in the workforce, the welfare state expanded rapidly, and the government reformed the education system to open the way for greater social advancement. Politically, 'new social issues', such as ecology and women's rights, became continually more prominent. These trends all served to dissolve the social constellation upon which the SPD had constructed its Bad Godesberg Basic Programme in the late 1950s (Lösche, 1992: 535–6; Padgett and Paterson, 1991: 54: Sozialdemokratische Partei Deutschlands, 1959).

These disaggregating trends have remoulded not only the SPD's external environment but also its internal configuration from one which was, at times, overly disciplined into what has been described by one observer as a 'loosely coupled anarchy' (Lösche, 1992: 532). This transformation has occurred because the party has changed in two related ways. First, it has become far more heterogeneous. Until the 1960s, skilled, male, blue-collar workers predominated in its membership, and the SPD's principal social ally was the trade union movement. In 1958, blue-collar workers comprised 55 per cent of the SPD's membership, while white-collar employees accounted for only 21 per cent. By 1982, however, the percentage of blue-collar SPD members had fallen to 21.1 per cent that is, approximately half the percentage of blue-collar workers found in the adult population at that time, whereas the combined share of student and white-collar employees in the party had reached 45.9 per cent. Furthermore, by the mid-1970s, current and former public-sector employees held more positions within the SPD than any other group (Michal, 1988a: 278; Padgett and Patterson 1991: 49). Second, the SPD has become more decentralized as a direct result of its increasing heterogeneity.

Increasing party heterogeneity and decentralization have weakened the SPD in several ways. First, they have opened up the party to new social groups. Although this was an explicit goal of the Bad Godesberg programme it has bifurcated the SPD into a traditional workers' party and a 'New Left' party of teachers, students, and public servants. In the past two decades, these two 'sub-parties' have often disagreed vociferously over many of the major issues of the day (for example, economic growth, ecology, security and women's rights), fragmenting and dissipating the SPD's energy. Although the influx of individuals from beyond the working class greatly expanded the talent pool available to the party and made it far more attractive to white-collar voters, it also had its drawbacks. Academics and others with advanced degrees reintroduced a utopian dimension to the SPD that had been more characteristic of the late nineteenth and early twentieth centuries than in the immediate post-war period. Moreover, the addition of these new social groups made the SPD far less flexible because much less business could be concluded on the basis of an informal mutual understanding among like-minded individuals, but instead had to be argued out in public and put to paper (Weege, 1992: 211–13).

Throughout the 1970s the leadership of the SPD ignored the issues raised by the 'New Left'. Consequently, the youth wing of the party, known as the Young Socialists (JUSOs), attempted to take over the party. The SPD's top officials responded to this challenge by centralizing their authority and stifling democracy within the party. Although this short-sighted strategy was successful, the costs were ultimately high. The SPD became increasingly sterile and immobile internally, while some of the party's young left-wing outcasts eventually formed the first serious left-wing alternative to the SPD in the post-war era, namely the Greens (Braunthal, 1983: 289–97).

Second, decentralization has progressed to such an extent that 'the SPD risks deteriorating into a confederation of largely autonomous interest groups' that resembles a 'grand coalition of local and regional party organizations, various party interest groups, ... traditional party wings (left, right, centre), patronage machines, and ad hoc citizens' initiatives' (Lösche, 1992: 532–3). The role of the specialized 'working groups' within the SPD – that is, the Young Socialists, the Working Group of Socialist Women (ASF) and the Working Group for Employee Affairs (AFA) – in determining party policy has grown dramatically over the past decade. For example, during the 1980s the ASF pushed successfully for the implementation of a system of quotas for women within the party, with the result that, by 1994, 40 per cent of all SPD offices and mandates must be filled by women. In the next few years these party working groups will continue to accumulate power as party reforms granting working groups the right to submit resolutions and to call for votes at future party conventions come into effect. The SPD has also recently permitted the groups to accept members who are not already in the SPD. It is important to note, however, that these reforms will only fragment the SPD further by enhancing the capacity of the working groups to build independent centres of influence within the party (*Die Zeit*, 9 October 1992: Lösche, 1992: 533).

Third, the new emphasis on open discourse within the SPD as a means to promote communication between the party's divergent constituencies has exposed the party to manipulation by political opponents, reduced the speed of party decision-making, and allowed party sub-groups to wage unrelated internal battles at the expense of the SPD as a whole (*Die Zeit*, 9 October 1992).

Fourth, the expansion of the working groups' role within the SPD has not achieved the hoped-for expansion of contact between the party and the average member, but rather has widened the gap between the rank and file and the leadership by adding another layer to the party structure. This increased distance has aggravated the feeling of alienation at the grassroots level, further reducing inner-party participation (Lösche, 1992: 533–4).

Fifth, party heterogeneity and decentralization have contributed toward many SPD members pursuing what SPD official Norbert Gansel has called 'the politics of self-actualization' (*Der Spiegel*, 14 September 1992). By this, Gansel is referring to those party members who propose and defend rigid utopian and ideological positions primarily in order to feel pure and superior as individuals, rather than to promote the shaping of concrete policy.

No single development better illustrates the practical difficulties generated by increasing party heterogeneity and decentralization within the SPD over the past 20 years than the drafting of a new party programme during the 1980s. This process, which began in the final days of the Schmidt chancellorship in 1982 and ended at a special Berlin party convention in December 1989, was unprecedented in its openness and its length. It included innumerable party gatherings to discern the concerns of the membership and to develop various sections of the text, discussions at five federal party conventions, and the circulation of two draft proposals. Yet the final document proved to be politically obsolete before it was even issued (Sozialdemokratische Partei Deutschlands, 1990).

Party fragmentation made the development of a programme that would be a clear, coherent, and concise statement of the SPD's plans for the future virtually impossible. Unlike its predecessor, the Berlin Basic Programme contains no underlying strategy. The need to satisfy all of the constituencies within the party turned the Berlin Programme into a 'department store catalogue' of more than 60 pages, 'contradictory in style and argumentation'. Internal party interest groups quickly began to use the drafting process for the programme less to shape policy than to measure their relative strength vis-à-vis each other on the basis of their ability to insert language into the document. Thus, the Programme became more of an internal party scorecard than a statement of policy for the general public (Lösche, 1992: 535).

The economic section of the Programme, which was by far the most important and controversial portion of the document, is the least satisfying. The intense battle within the SPD over the appropriate form and extent of government intervention in the economy could only be settled by parroting the phrase from the Bad Godesberg Programme calling for 'as much competition as possible, as much planning as necessary', but the Berlin Programme does not state clearly how the SPD of today interprets this phrase differently. Whereas the Berlin Programme abandons the Bad Godesberg document's embrace of growth and Keynesian demand management, it fails to replace these elements with a credible alternative. As a result, the economic section of the new SPD programme simply looks hollow and inadequate (Müller, 1990: 63–4; Potthoff, 1991: 355). The rest of the Berlin Programme is a 'post-materialist' document that clashes violently with its economic section. The section on ecology appears to be lifted virtually verbatim from the Greens, and issues such as gender equality, multiculturalism, participation, common European security, the Third World and the relationship between Man and Nature figure prominently (Müller-Rommel and Poguntke, 1992: 338; Schmidt, 1992: 149–59).

In summary, the SPD's Berlin Basic Programme is an uninspiring patchwork text with no coherent vision. It promises a little to a wide range of Social Democratic constituencies, but only in a superficial and unconvincing fashion. As a result, the Programme proved wholly ineffective as an electoral tool in the first election after its approval – namely the first postwar pan-German federal election of 3 December 1990.

The failure of the Berlin Programme to resonate among the electorate was in part because of its failure to take account of the dramatic changes that unification has brought to the German political landscape. The SPD completed the preliminary version of the final draft before the events of autumn 1989 unfolded. Once the East German communist regime collapsed, however, SPD officials merely inserted some superficial references to unification into the text. In an effort to capitalize on the events, the congress appointed to approve the new Programme was moved from its original location in Bremen to Berlin. Nevertheless, the last-minute additions to the Programme looked completely out of place within the otherwise post-material original text, and the additions gave no clear indication of SPD's policy on unification (Padgett and Patterson, 1991: 58; von Winter, 1990: 350–8).

Thus the trends toward increasing heterogeneity and decentralization led the SPD to craft, in the words of former parliamentary party leader, Hans-Jochen Vogel, a 'somewhat stillborn' post-materialist party platform just at the moment when the most significant problems facing Germany had suddenly reverted to the classic materialist concerns of production and wealth distribution. The SPD was caught flat-footed, but there was no going back. Diverse groups, task forces, and committees within the SPD had worked for five years to produce the Berlin Programme. Given the numerous divisions still within the party, writing another programme would take at least as long (*Handelsblatt*, 29 May 1991).

The Rise and Decline of the Greens

No other party in the history of post-war German politics has grown so quickly or changed so fast as the Green party. It began in 1979 as a distinctively West German phenomenon, and was described by one of its founders, the late Petra Kelly, as the 'anti-party party', alternative to the 'established' West German parties. Just four years after its birth, the Green party obtained slightly more than 5 per cent of the vote in the 1983 federal election and entered the Bundestag. The party has elected representatives to 15 of the 16 German *Länder* and remains a force in German politics, despite the failure of the Western Greens to return to the Bundestag after the 1990 election (Hermann, 1992: 295). Broadly speaking, the Greens are a product of the SPD's fragmentation and 'could only have come into being out of an acute integrative weakness of the governing SPD' during the late 1970s. The vast majority of Green supporters are to some degree 'frustrated' Social Democrats (Lösche, 1992: 136).

Heterogeneity and decentralization have caused far bigger problems within the Green party, given that it is largely made up of political outcasts and gadflies. The remnants of the milieu created by the 'New Left' in the 1960s have served as a social anchor for the party. Most Green voters and party officials were born between 1945 and 1965, come from the middle and upper-middle class, and are either students, teachers, public servants or white-collar service employees. Few blue-collar workers have ever been party members or supporters. More women than men tend to vote Green, although less than 10 per cent of German female voters have ever supported the Greens in any federal election (Müller-Rommel and Poguntke, 1992: 351–6; Hermann, 1992: 307).

Given the Greens well-deserved reputation for in-fighting, there is a surprising amount of agreement over the party's ideology and programme: the keenest debates have been over tactics and organization rather than substance. Furthermore, although, taken in isolation, few Green themes are original, it is the combination of ideas and the different emphases that make the Green political programme unique.

The most distinctive and original contribution of the Greens to the German political debate is their emphasis on ecology over economy, including a willingness to sacrifice economic growth and material comfort in favour of environmental preservation, although most Greens will quickly assert that the relationship between the economy and the environment is not necessarily zero-sum. Second, the Greens emphasize an anti-hierarchical *Basisdemokratie* (grass-roots democracy) as their central organizing principle. This has included the principle of 'rotation', which is a strict form of term limitation for both party offices and electoral mandates; a ban against holding more than one party and/or elected position simultaneously; the division of executive authority among a collective; and close ties to citizens' initiatives. Recently, however, the Greens have curtailed many of these reforms and have even dropped some altogether because they have proved inefficient and cumbersome while not noticeably enhancing democratic practice.

Third, the Greens emphasize a non-violent approach both to national and international politics. This has included a call for unilateral and multilateral disarmament, and the dissolution of all military blocs. However, a few isolated Greens have called for exceptions to this uncompromising policy. Anarchists on the fringe of the party for example have argued that the use of violence against the police should at times be permissible and, during the Gulf War, a few Greens reluctantly supported the use of military force in defence against aggression. In general, though, the Greens have rarely deviated from unconditional support for non-violence.

Finally, the Greens support a strong social welfare state, and their social policy is actually quite eclectic. The 'alternative party' has called for the decentralized, egalitarian control of all public- and private-sector organizations, akin to the Christian Democratic notion of subsidiarity and the Social Democrats' emphasis on participatory democracy. The Greens also share the Social Democrats' belief in government intervention to redistribute income, protect the environment, and create equal opportunity for disadvantaged groups. Lastly, the Greens are fervent supporters of civil liberties, which is a traditional strongpoint of the FDP (Muller-Rommel and Poguntke, 1992: 333).

The Green party's entrance into the Bundestag and several state parliaments in the early 1980s provoked a tumultuous decade-long, internal debate over the role of the party in the German political system. This controversy was reminiscent of the famous debate within the *fin de siècle* SPD over whether it should strive for 'reform or revolution'. In practical terms, however, Green party's debate was over the advisability of forming a coalition with the SPD under any circumstances.

The 'fundamentalist', or 'Fundi', wing asserted that the Green party was not merely a political party, but a broadly-based movement with parliamentary and extraparliamentary components. The party should therefore never compromise or form alliances with the established political parties, otherwise the alternative movement would inevitably lose its distinctiveness and hence its power. On the other hand, the 'realist', or Realo Greens argued that at least the parliamentary portion of the alternative movement is in fact a political party and that it would be foolish to pretend otherwise. They judged the fundamentalists' position to be self-defeating because the voters would soon abandon a party that accomplished nothing owing to its pretensions to purity. Moreover, the Realos argued, the Fundis' maximalist stance excluded the possibility of making immediate concrete gains by influencing the policies of the established parties through cooperation and even a coalition. The Realos also maintained that the Fundis' approach put the entire German Left at a structural disadvantage by reducing the possibilities for a majority, left-of-centre coalition.

It is important to note that the debate between the Fundis and Realos over the nature of the Green party was as much a clash of personalities as it was of tactics. By the mid-1980s, rank-and-file party members cynically referred to the unending strife as 'the battle among the mullahs', the chiefs of whom were Joschka Fischer for the Realos and Jutta Ditfurth for the Fundis.

Party in-fighting came to an abrupt and largely anticlimactic finish at the end of the 1980s. In 1988, a third, centrist faction called Aufbruch (Fresh Start), arose within the party around the Lutheran minister, Antje Vollmer, with the explicit aim of putting an end to intraparty quarrels. The group soon found that it could work far more easily with the Realos than with the Fundis. Thus, an alliance between Aufbruch and the Realos at the December 1988 federal party convention in Karlsruhe voted out the existing members of the federal party's executive committee, who were overwhelmingly fundamentalists, and replaced them with representatives from all three party factions. Thereafter, a coalition of Aufbruch and Realo executive committee members gained control of the federal party.

Events within two state-level Green parties at the close of the decade also helped to end the tactical debate within the party. In-fighting within the Hamburg Greens – AL (which had always been a fundamentalist stronghold), and a rigid refusal to participate in any coalition split the local party and brought it a disastrous defeat at the polls. In Berlin, the success of the extreme right-wing Republikaner in the January 1989 city elections convinced the predominantly fundamentalist local Greens, the AL, to change their position and form a coalition with the Social Democrats rather than risk destabilizing Berlin politics further.

Despite the abrupt acceptance of coalitions by most Greens at the end of the 1980s, the decade of party in-fighting left its scars. Several talented individuals were forced out of prominent positions, and others abandoned the party altogether. The Greens predilection toward political self-mutilation also dissipated the party's original optimistic spirit and dissuaded many from joining or voting for it.

The Left and Unification

The response of the West German Left to unification represented a collective political failure. Since the 1960s, the Left's attitude toward German unity and the GDR had been ambivalent. Virtually the entire Western Left saw the division of Germany as an appropriate historical punishment for the country's transgressions of the first half of the twentieth century. This view, however, neglected the reality that East Germans bore the brunt of this punishment. Some Western leftists took solace in regarding the GDR as an example of the first socialist state on German soil, and as a Germany that – at least in its public pronouncements – had made a solid break with its Nazi past. The majority of Social Democrats and Greens simply put great faith in the SPD's *Ostpolitik* as an instrument that would bring about the eventual mellowing of the GDR state apparatus until it became a truly democratic socialist state that would be superior to the then existing regimes in both Eastern and Western Germany (*FES–Informationen*, March–April 1991: 24; Lösche and Walter, 1992: 384; Padgett and Patterson, 1991: 72–3).

Although the Eastern citizens' movements that brought down the Honecker regime at the end of 1989 briefly captured the imagination of the West German Left, this did not last. Once it became clear in the first free East German election on 18 March 1990 that *Mitteldeutschland* was no longer the left-wing bastion it had been before the Nazi era and that its people were far more interested in catching up materially with the West than in pursuing an experimental 'third way' of organizing society, large segments of the German Left rejected the East (*Frankfurter Rundschau*, 23 May 1991). Erhard Eppler, a prominent SPD leftist, has pointed out that 'many leftists have not accepted the democratic decision of the people in the GDR, namely to dissolve their state'. Several leftists both inside and outside the SPD have continuously dismissed the political choices of Easterners in a patronizing fashion, characterizing them as an expression of false consciousness (*Frankfurter Rundschau*, 31 May 1991).

The SPD in the New Germany

The latter half of the 1980s was a period of generational change for the Social Democratic Party. Despite the common criticism that the old guard of the SPD has been far too reluctant to relinquish power (see, for example, Michal, 1988b), recent analyses of the SPD federal executive board show that by the end of the 1980s, the 'post-war' generation (that is, those born between 1930 and 1944) had largely displaced the Second World War generation of Brandt and Schmidt from power. Nevertheless, this criticism is not without foundation, since there are no prominent SPD officials younger than forty-five (Schmidt, 1992: 163–6; Weege, 1992: 196). This highly westernized, affluent post-war generation of political leaders within the SPD, of which Oskar Lafontaine, Gerhard Schröder, and Björn Engholm, prime ministers of the Saar, Lower Saxony, and Schleswig-Holstein respectively, are the most prominent members, is commonly referred to as the *Enkel* (grandchildren) The *Enkel* were young politicians at the time of the student upheavals of the 1960s and have been heavily influenced by the rise of the 'new social movements' of ecology and feminism in the 1970s. Today, this generation exudes the post-modern, antinomic ideology that has become increasingly common within the SPD. Members of the *Enkel* milieu comfortably combine calls for a post-materialist society with luxurious personal lifestyles, and find any form of nationalism – unless of course it is a Third World struggle for 'national liberation' – hopelessly antiquated (Padgett and Patterson, 1991: 54; Seebacher-Brandt, 1991).

When party officials selected Oskar Lafontaine as the SPD's candidate for Chancellor in the spring of 1989, they hoped that his post-modern/post-material approach would make Helmut Kohl appear old-fashioned and out-of-step to West German voters. Unification, however, completely transformed the campaign, because it made traditional material concerns paramount. During 1990 voters became increasingly disenchanted with Oskar Lafontaine. Easterners, for instance, wanted to hear Lafontaine congratulate them for throwing off the yoke of communism. Instead, he gave them admonishing lectures on the excessive costs and social hardship generated by unity which, by implication, faulted the Easterners for freeing themselves. This message understandably repulsed and angered Eastern voters (von Beyme, 1991: 181; Fetscher, 1991: 218).

Lafontaine also managed to alienate traditional SPD supporters in the West. Several months before the election and before the events in East Germany began to unfold, Lafontaine deliberately instigated a dispute with the trade union movement over a reduction in working hours in a bid to demonstrate his political independence. West German trade unionists responded to the dispute by lending Lafontaine the bare minimum of indirect support during his campaign, making it clear to all that he was by no means labour's ideal candidate (Silvia, forthcoming). Moreover, Lafontaine's smug, imperious and combative personality exacerbated antipathy towards Saarlander and his party throughout Germany.

Lafontaine was not the sole cause of the SPD's disastrous performance in the election of December 1990. The grave structural and organizational weaknesses of the SPD's Eastern wing severely damaged the party's electoral effort in the five new *Länder*. In many ways, the re-establishment of the SPD in the East parallels that of Eastern Germany as a whole since 1989. Originally, the Eastern SPD was founded in autumn 1989 as an independent party, but ties quickly developed between the fledgling party and the much larger and more affluent Western SPD. Within a year, the two Social Democratic parties merged into one. After an auspicious start, the Eastern SPD 'experienced all the childhood diseases that can afflict a young party', as the SPD federal deputy chairman and former chairman of the Eastern SPD Wolfgang Thierse has aptly put it. These disorders, rooted in the difficult circumstances surrounding the formation of the party in the East, continued to retard the development of Social Democracy east of the Elbe. The 'Social Democratic Party in the German Democratic Republic' was formed on 7 October 1989, at a clandestine meeting in a Lutheran rectory in the village of Schwante, north of Berlin, (*Die Welt*, 12 January 1990; Elmer, 1991: 140). The Eastern SPD grew relatively rapidly at the outset, attaining approximately 20,000 to 25,000 members by the end of 1989. The vast majority of these new members were Lutheran clerics who had been involved in anti-government efforts to varying degrees. After some hesitation, the Western SPD began to provide substantial financial and material support to the Eastern SPD (Silvia, 1993). This aid helped the new party attract members because it greatly expanded the eastern SPD's resources and served as an imprimatur for the fledgling party (*Rheinischer Merkur*, 3 November 1989; Barbe, 1989: 779–81; and Jesse, 1992: 75).

During the winter of 1989–90, the new Eastern SPD seemed to be the only viable political force in the East. The former ruling Communist Party, the Socialist Unity Party of Germany (SED) remained discredited among

most citizens. Its support was restricted to government and party bureaucrats and a few younger people. Despite its numerous reform efforts, the
installation of a new leadership 'unburdened' (*unbelastet*) by the past, and
even a change of name to the Party of Democratic Socialism (PDS), it
remained politically isolated. The Eastern CDU and the other established
secondary parties in the former GDR appeared to be too tainted by their 40
years of cooperation with the SED, whereas the grass-roots movements that
led the peaceful November revolution and eventually combined to form
Bündis 90 were too amorphous and unsophisticated to be politically successful in a standard electoral campaign. Furthermore, the common wisdom was that the citizens of Eastern Germany would be unwilling to
embrace the market unconditionally, but instead would look for an interme-
diate alternative between centrally planned socialism and free-market capitalism; something that most closely resembled social democracy (*Der
Spiegel*, 26 March 1990).

The common wisdom proved wrong, however. The Eastern SPD received only 21.9 per cent of the vote in the 18 March 1990 *Volkskammer*
elections. The CDU, in contrast, garnered 40.9 per cent, as most Easterners
opted for the party that promised them the fastest and easiest road to
material security and that had the better public reputation for managing a
capitalist economy. The Eastern SPD's electoral failure was in part a product of underestimating the capacity of Helmut Kohl's Christian Democratic Union to intervene effectively in Eastern politics. Even more debilitating in the election, however, were the serious structural anomalies that
began to manifest themselves within the Eastern SPD at the start of 1990
(*Frankfurter Allgemeine Zeitung*, 20 March 1990).

Since its creation, the Eastern SPD has had the reputation of being a
'Pastor's party' because virtually all of its founders and its leadership have
been clerics who were active within the dissident Lutheran movement in
the GDR. This is hardly surprising, given that when the SPD was reconsti-
tuted, the SED still dominated all working-class organizations, and the
Lutheran Church was the major autonomous sanctuary for political organization within the GDR. Still, even in the post-GDR Eastern Germany, the
SPD membership has failed to branch out beyond ministers, Lutheran
peace activists and a few intellectuals. In fact, since 1990, many have
accused the Eastern SPD of actually being hostile to new members because
the original members have tended to dismiss any latecomers as opportun-
ists and eleventh-hour converts (*Der Spiegel*, 13 July 1992: *Die Welt*, 15
January 1990; Ammer and Kuppe, 1990: 15–16; Elmer, 1991: 138).

Ironically, the membership of the eastern wing of the SPD in many ways
resembles the Western Greens far more than it does the SPD's western
wing. The Eastern SPD, like the Green party, is a milieu party rather than a

mass one. Ideologically, the Eastern SPD and the Greens both have a fervent interest in grass-roots democracy and purely ethical issues to a far greater degree than does the Western SPD (Böhme, 1989: 8). Unfortunately for both portions of the SPD, the resemblance of the Eastern SPD to the Greens extends beyond demographics, structure and ideology to include party disunity.

Intense in-fighting began at the Eastern SPD's founding conference in October 1989 and has remained a debilitating problem within the party ever since. The earliest debates were over the party's position on unification and the content of economic reform. After the *Volkskammer* election of March 1990, the Eastern SPD became embroiled in a fierce argument over participating in a Grand Coalition government. The Eastern SPD leadership's decisions in April 1990 to join the coalition, then a few months later to support without any revision the two *Staatsverträge* (state treaties) that laid the groundwork for unification deeply split the party. The collapse of the Grand Coalition after four months did not produce an end to the internecine struggles within the Eastern SPD (*Frankfurter Allgemeine Zeitung*, 20 April 1990; *Frankfurter Rundschau*, 20 April 1990, 22 August 1990).

As is true for the Western Greens, many disputes within the Eastern SPD have been the product either of personality clashes or of party leaders playing political games with one another. Ideological positions and policies have typically served as means rather than ends in these disputes, much to the detriment of the party. The members' deep-seated fear of bureaucratic domination has led them to employ a particularly pernicious version of the Green's rotation principle. Eastern SPD members have routinely voted out of office anyone who attained a modicum of prominence and have regularly rejected the personnel recommendations of the party's executive committee, simply because they came from above. This behaviour has prompted many to leave the Eastern SPD and has dissuaded many others from joining the party (*Der Spiegel*, 5 March 1990, 25 March 1991).

The Eastern SPD's birth was also comparatively disadvantaged because the party did not possess physical resources comparable to its main rival. Organizationally, the CDU in the East benefited from its status as one of the 'bloc parties' in the previous regime. It had in place scores of offices throughout the former GDR, hundreds of thousands of members, a modest but useful treasury and a solid party infrastructure. Once the Western CDU followed the Western SPD's lead and established formal links with its opposite number in the East, these material assets proved quite helpful during the Eastern electoral campaigns of 1990.

The SPD, in contrast, had no material resources in the East since these had been seized by the communists in 1946. Although the electoral impact of the SPD's organizational disadvantage should not be overstated, it was nevertheless significant. The Western SPD tried to compensate by transferring substantial amounts of money and personnel to its Eastern ally, but the party was unable to make good the organizational deficit. At the time of writing the Eastern SPD was still having trouble finding suitable office space in several cities. Conditions were so bad in mid-1991 that then SPD federal treasurer (now SPD parliamentary party chief) Hans-Ulrich Klose called the Eastern SPD a 'Potemkin village' (von Beyme, 1991: 172; *Frankfurter Rundschau*, 25 May 1991).

Despite the formidable problems facing the SPD in the East, the Social Democrats were extremely slow in developing a long-term assistance programme for the eastern wing of the party. This was in part because party officials on both sides of the Elbe were caught up in purist beliefs regarding the superiority of 'indigenous action', but also because few party officials from the West were interested in entering the Eastern party maelstrom. By the time preparations began for the SPD's first all-German party convention in Bremen at the end of May 1991, however, it became clear that the SPD leadership had to draft some sort of plan for the strengthening of the party's position in the East.

Before the Bremen party congress opened, Klose proposed spending DM 40 million to support a four-year recruitment and infrastructure programme exclusively for the five new *Länder*, with the goal of increasing the size of the eastern wing of the party tenfold. To meet the costs, Klose called for a special levy on all party members. Several Western party officials disagreed vehemently with Klose's plan, arguing that they would never be able to get their members to support the levy if the funds went exclusively to develop the East. Instead, they countered by proposing that the fund be devoted to recruitment and organizational renewal throughout the Federal Republic. Thus the five new *Länder* would only receive a portion of the proceeds. At the congress itself, the Western SPD officials won out, much to the consternation of Wolfgang Thierse and the Eastern delegates. Widely outnumbered at the congress, there was little that the Easterners could do.

The SPD's programme to increase Eastern membership has had no impact. By the end of 1992, despite months of strong Eastern support for the Social Democrats in opinion polls, membership in the East has continued to stagnate at roughly 25,000. In the West, on the other hand, the SPD reports that thousands of members have left the party because of the special levy. (*Frankfurter Rundschau*, 25 May 1991; *Handelsblatt*, 29 May 1991; *Der Spiegel*, 14 September 1992).

Despite its difficulties at federal level, the SPD has flourished in the *Länder*. By 1991, it was a coalition partner in 11 out of 16 *Länder* and held the prime minister's office in nine of those 11 governments. This 'splendid parade of state princes' has given the SPD control of the German upper

house, the Bundesrat. However, policy differences among the various Social Democratic prime ministers have prevented the SPD from making
effective use of this asset (Silvia, 1993).

In recent years, the Social Democrats have turned increasingly to the
Land level as a source for candidates for federal Chancellor. This has the
advantage of drawing on individuals who already have proven executive
experience, but it also has drawbacks because of fragmentation between
the federal party leadership and prominent *Land* prime ministers.

The Bremen party congress of 1991 named Björn Engholm, prime minister of Schleswig–Holstein, as the party's new chairman, making him the
SPD's most likely candidate for Chancellor in the 1994 federal election.
Since Engholm was the only SPD *Land* prime minister who had held an
absolute majority in his *Land* parliament and who had not already run as
the federal candidate for Chancellor, he was the obvious, and for many the
only, choice the party had. Although Engholm shares many of the 'post-
Left' attributes of the previous candidate for Chancellor, Oskar Lafontaine
– in particular, a lavish lifestyle – the two differ in several respects. First,
Engholm practises a style of leadership that his supporters describe as
inclusive and deliberate, but that his detractors denounce as non-existent
and 'Engholm light'. Second, Engholm is by no means ambitious or a
workaholic. It took several months of arm-twisting by prominent SPD
officials to convince him to take the post of chairman. Third, in terms of
economic and social policy, Engholm represents a shift of the party toward
more traditional liberal, free-market values (Leif, 1992: 223–8).

Engholm has already shown that he has learned a great deal from the
errors of Oskar Lafontaine. One of Engholm's first moves was to appoint
Karlheinz Blessing (35) as business manager of the federal SPD. Previously Blessing had been the top aide of the metalworkers' union president, Franz Steinkühler. This step both helped to assuage tensions between
labour and the Social Democrats and allowed Engholm to draw on Blessing's organizational experience to initiate a thorough reform of the party.
Blessing has established a working group, 'SPD 2000', to draft proposals
for reforming the party. Blessing's ideas revolve around the desire to make
the SPD more open and responsive to the party rank and file and to the
public at large. Among his proposals are the establishment of primary
elections to select party candidates, including the candidate for Chancellor;
drawing on experts from outside of the SPD to undertake specific tasks, to
assume top party offices, and even to serve in the Bundestag; and building
a network of discussion groups, cultural activities, clubs and working groups
that resemble the extra-parliamentary citizens' initiatives that have supported the Greens (*Frankfurter Allgemeine Sonntagszeitung*, 16 August
1992; Engholm, 1991: 224–30; Fetscher, 1991: 224).

Although Blessing's proposals are designed to increase the access of the rank and file to the leadership, they might also serve to intensify the fragmentation of internal party life. Furthermore, neither Engholm nor Blessing have ever addressed whether the SPD would be able to pursue a consistent political line if it subcontracts much of its policy-making out to sub-groups and experts, or how bringing in people from outside would affect career officials already deeply mired in the party's infamous 'ox slog'. The initial signs are not encouraging. Blessing's practice of placing SPD critics, such as the former editor of the New Left *Tageszeitung*, Peter Grafe (Grafe, 1991), in prominent party positions has been particularly controversial. Indeed, long-standing party officials brought an action against Blessing in the Labour Court, publicly demanding the creation of a 'Blessing-free zone' within the party (Leif, 1992: 232–3). Thus the Engholm–Blessing reforms may only further disrupt the party, alienating its members rather than attracting the general public. Moreover the rancorous debate within the SPD in late 1992 over changing the laws regulating political asylum and migration (in the wake of attacks against foreigners and the rioting in Rostock) demonstrates the continuing inability of the Social Democrats to develop viable policies or to present their party as a real alternative to the Kohl government.

Green Politics in the New Germany

In the early 1980s the West German Greens supported the principle of German unification as part of a larger utopian vision that included the dissolution of the North Atlantic Treaty Organization and the Warsaw Pact as well as the total disarmament of Europe. In 1987, however, the Greens' electoral programme changed course and came out in favour of full recognition of the GDR, once Mikhail Gorbachev's policy of perestroika made the earlier programme obsolete.

As the events that culminated in the collapse of the SED regime unfolded, the West German Greens always seemed to be one step behind. The cumbersome party decision-making process made it difficult for them to respond to the fast pace of change and, when they did respond, they consistently chose policies that generated little support among the voters. The Greens were the only Western party to oppose unification. They instead favoured a loose confederation between East and West Germany within the context of an expanded European Community that would allow the Eastern Germans to develop a market socialist economy. The unpopularity of this stance on German unity, general disillusionment with the party's record of internal strife, and a minor exodus of Marxists and some fundamentalists from the party to join the PDS, reduced the party's share of the Western vote in the December 1990 federal election to just below the five-per-cent hurdle, thereby eliminating the Western Greens from the Bundestag.

The Greens did not entirely disappear from the Bundestag, however. A legal action brought by the Greens to the Federal Constitutional Court in summer 1990 ruled that the five-per-cent barrier had to be applied to Eastern and Western Germany *separately* in order to ensure fairness to smaller parties. An alliance between Bündnis '90 and the fledgling Eastern German Greens managed to obtain six per cent of the Eastern vote and enter the Bundestag. Ironically, if the five-per-cent barrier had been applied to Germany as a whole, as had been originally planned, the Greens in an alliance with Bündnis '90 would have received just five per cent of the vote and thus would have been eligible for substantially more seats in the new Bundestag.

Since the 1990 election, the Eastern and Western Greens have merged and the party has held a series of unification talks with Bündnis '90. An alliance is essential if the Greens and Bündnis '90 are to stand any chance of overcoming the five-per-cent hurdle in the 1994 Bundestag elections. True to form, however, these talks have verged on the edge of collapse for months and have been filled with mutual recriminations, largely based on clashes of ego and personality (*Tageszeitung*, 12 October 1992).

Conclusion

Despite the tremendous long-term social, economic, and political problems facing Germany and the errors committed by the Kohl government in managing German unification, the destructive trends of party fragmentation and self-indulgence continue to plague the parties of the German Left. In consequence they are unable to pose a viable challenge to the conservative coalition. The 'loosely coupled anarchy' that reigns within the SPD today makes it an unreliable, and hence unattractive, coalition partner for the FDP. A formal Grand Coalition is also unlikely because it would merely leave the political field open for an extreme right-wing party to make substantial gains in the 1994 federal elections. Thus, unless the left-wing parties undergo an abrupt transformation, or the current governing coalition commits a truly monumental error, the SPD and the Greens are likely to remain in opposition for the foreseeable future.

References

Ammer, T. and Kuppe, J. (1990), 'Politische Zielvorstellungen wichtiger Oppositionsgruppen in der DDR' in Gesamtdeutsches Institut, Bundesanstalt für gesamtdeutsche Aufgaben (ed.), *Analysen, Dokumentationen und Chronik zur Entwicklung in der DDR von September bis Dezember 1990*, Bonn: Gesamtdeutsches Institut, Bundesanstalt für gesamtdeutsche Aufgaben.

Barbe, A. (1989), 'Sozial Demokratische Partei (SDP)' Interview, *Gewerkschaftliche Monatshefte*, **40**, (12), December.

Beyme, K. von (1991), 'Electoral Unification: the First German Elections in December 1990', *Government and Opposition*, **26**, (2), Spring.

Böhme, I. (1989), 'Trügnerische Hoffnungen. Interview with SPD-Geschäftsführer Ibrahim Böhme', *Vorwärts-SM*, November.

Braunthal, G. (1983), *The West German Social Democrats, 1969–1982: Profile of a Party in Power*, Boulder, Col.: Westview Press.

Elmer, K. (1991), 'Dokumentation. Auf den Anfang kommt es an!' *Neue Gesellschaft/Frankfurter Hefte*, **38**, (2), February.

Engholm, B. (1991), 'Sozialdemokratie und Gewerkschaften – ein neuer Frühling für ein altes Paar', *Gewerkschaftliche Monatshefte*, **42**, (4), April.

Fetscher, I. (1991), 'Die Politischen Parteien im vereinigten Deutschland', *Gewerkschaftliche Monatshefte*, **42**, (4), April.

Grafe, P. (1991), *Tradition und Konfusion-SPD. Alle Macht den Profis*, Frankfurt/Main: Eichborn.

Hermann, W. (1992), 'Grüne Elitenbildung? in T. Leif, H-J. Legrand and A. Klein (eds), *Die politische Klasse in Deutschland. Eliten auf dem Prüfstand*, Bonn: Bouvier.

Jesse, E. (1992), 'Parteien in Deutschland. Ein Abriss der historischen Entwicklung' in A. Mintzel and H. Oberreuter (eds), *Parteien in der Bundesrepublik Deutschland*, Opladen: Leske + Budrich.

Koelble, T. A. (1991), *The Left Unraveled: Social Democracy and the New Left Challenge in Britain and West Germany*, Durham, North Carolina: Duke.

Leif, T. 'Personalrekrutierung der SPD: kopf- und konzeptionslos' in T. Leif, H-J. Legrand and A. Klein (eds), *Die politische Klasse in Deutschland. Eliten auf dem Prufstand*, Bonn: Bouvier.

Lösche, P. (1992), 'Zur Metamorphose der politischen Parteien in Deutschland', *Gewerkschaftliche Monatshefte*, **43**, (9), September.

Lösche, P. and Walter, F. (1992), *Klassenpartei–Volkspartei–Quotenpartei. Zur Entwicklung der Sozialdemokratie von Weimar bis zur deutschen Vereinigung*, Darmstadt: Wissenschaftliche Buchgesellschaft.

Markovits, A. S. (1986), *The Politics of the West German Trade Unions: Strategies of Class and Interest Representation in Growth and Crisis*, Cambridge: Cambridge University Press.

Michal, W. (1988a), 'Die SPD – die altmodische Variante der Volkspartei?', *Gewerkschaftliche Monatshefte*, **39**, (5), May.

Michal, W. (1988b), *Die SPD–Staatstreu und jugendfrei*, Reinbek: Rowohlt.

Müller, E-P. (1990), *Das Berliner Programm der SPD*, Cologne; Deutscher Instituts-Verlag.

Müller-Rommel, F. and Poguntke, T. (1992), 'Die Grünen' in A. Mintzel and H. Oberreuter (eds), *Parteien in der Bundesrepublik Deutschland*, Opladen: Leske + Budrich.

Padgett, S. and Patterson, W. (1991), 'The Rise and Fall of the West German Left', *New Left Review*, (186), March–April.

Potthoff, H. (1991), 'Aufstieg und Niedergang der SPD', *Neue Gesellschaft/ Frankfurter Hefte*, **38**, (4), April.

Schmidt, H. (1992), 'Die Sozialdemokratische Partei Deutschlands' in A. Mintzel and H. Oberreuter (eds), *Parteien in der Bundesrepublik Deutschland*, Opladen: Leske + Budrich.

Seebacher-Brandt, B. (1991), *Die Linke und die Einheit*. Berlin: Siedler.

Silvia, S. J. (1993), 'Left Behind: The Social Democratic Party in Eastern Germany after Unification', *West European Politics*, **16**, (2), April.

Silvia, S. J. (forthcoming), 'The Forward Retreat: Labor and Social Democracy in Germany, 1982–1992', *International Journal of Political Economy*.

Sozialdemokratische Partei Deutschlands (1959), *Basic Programme of the Social Democratic Party of Germany*, adopted in Bad Godesberg, 13–15 November 1959, Bonn: Bonn-Druck, Storbeck & Co.

Sozialdemokratische Partei Deutschlands (1990), *Basic Programme of the Social Democratic Party of Germany*, adopted in Berlin, 20 December 1989, Bonn: Courir.

Weege, W. (1992), 'Zwei Generationen im SPD-Parteivorstand. Eine empirische Analyse' in T. Leif, H-J. Legrand and A. Klein (eds), *Die politische Klasse in Deutschland, Eliten auf dem Prüfstand*, Bonn: Bouvier.

Winter, T. von (1990), 'Die Parteien und die Zukunft der Arbeit. Arbeitsgesellschaftliche Probleme in der Programmatik von SPD und CDU', *Leviathan*, special issue 11.

Part Three
East German Dimensions

8 The Vanishing Opposition; the Decline of the East German Citizen Movements

Mike Dennis

In those exhilarating days in the autumn of 1989 before the fall of the Berlin Wall, citizens' movements appeared to be in the vanguard of the revolution and the moral leaders of the resistance to the *ancien regime*. As the SED disintegrated, the citizens' movements and proto-political parties – New Forum in particular but also Democratic Awakening, Democracy Now, the United Left and the Social Democratic Party – cherished the notion of a democratic, independent GDR located at a point along the political spectrum somewhere between sclerotic state socialism and the 'elbow society' of West German capitalism. The cultural intelligentsia eagerly participated in the process of democratic renewal. Christa Wolf and Stefan Heym, two famous GDR writers, articulated their idea of a 'third way' before half a million demonstrators on East Berlin's Alexanderplatz on 4 November: they rejoiced that the people had recovered their power of speech and that they could now proceed with the construction of a genuine socialism in place of degenerate neo-Stalinism. Nobody, they averred, would need to leave the GDR. Elsewhere in the Republic, on Leipzig's Karl Marx Square, thousands chanted 'New Forum into power'. People, opposition, intellectuals appeared, at long last, to have emerged from their isolation united by the goal of a reformed, democratic GDR with socialist underpinnings.

A few months later, intellectuals and opposition groups were lamenting the crumbling of their dreams. In the elections to the People's Chamber in March 1990, the electorate had returned the citizens' movements to the periphery of society, and the Alliance for Germany, patched together by West German Chancellor Helmut Kohl, had obtained a resounding vote for its policy of rapid unification. Opposition leaders such as Jens Reich – the

St Francis of Assisi of New Forum – were left deploring the failure of the citizens of the GDR to take advantage of the opportunity to develop their own political culture, preferring instead to imbibe 'the shallow outpouring of the West German political party system' (*Süddeutsche Zeitung*, 24–25 March 1990: 12). The more combative Heym castigated his fellow citizens on their capitulation to the allures of capitalism:

> The very same people who had risen up after decades of kowtowing and fleeing, the people who had only recently been marching nobly into a promising future became suddenly a horde of frenzied shoppers, backs pressed into stomachs, marching only to the Hertie and Bilka department stores and on the hunt for glitzy trash. What expressions on their faces as, with cannibalistic lust, they rooted like pigs through display tables intentionally placed in their paths by Western shopkeepers .... (Heym, 1991: 31. This was written soon after the opening of the Wall)

This chapter examines the role of the opposition forces in the fall of the GDR and then considers the allegation that the politically immature East Germans exchanged their socialist tutelage for a capitalist one instead of developing their own political identity, as desired by the pedagogues of New Forum. It also examines the extent to which the self-styled revolutionaries of the first hour – the citizens' movements – constituted the authentic voice of the autumn revolution and the real driving force behind the political upheavals or whether, as Rolf Schneider has argued, they were little more than dilettantes legitimized by no one but themselves (Schneider, 1990a: 29); '"nice young people" who instead of seizing the reins of power agonized over whether the time was ripe for slaughtering the cows on the agricultural cooperative' (Schneider, 1990b: 26).

The Contours of Opposition

Opposition was not even supposed to exist in the GDR for, as one former authoritative source asserted,

> No objective political or social basis exists for the existence of an opposition in socialist states, for the working class – in alliance with all other working people – is the class which not only exercises power but is also the main productive force in society. (*Kleines politisches Wörterbuch*, 1978: 652)

Opposition to socialism, it was concluded, would therefore be tantamount to a rejection of progress and a self-inflicted wound.

SED dogma notwithstanding, opposition proved endemic to GDR society. The highly ambitious experiment in constructing a socialist system in the Stalinist mode – involving the recasting of the social structure, the nationalization of vast tracts of the economy and the destruction of independent political and social actors – provoked widespread opposition in the early years of the Republic: the traumatic Workers' Uprising in June 1953; the fundamental rejection of the new society by broad sections of the middle class and their political representatives, particularly the CDU and the LDPD; and revisionist attempts in the later 1950s to modify the harsher aspects of the system.

Although the ruling party, the SED, and its dogmatic Stalinist leader Walter Ulbricht managed to survive these challenges, it was unable to stem the outflow of a discontented population. Emigration was a highly sensitive social and political barometer. In the crisis years of 1953, 1956 and 1960, 331,390, 279,189, and 199,188 citizens emigrated to the West; a further 155,402 did so in 1960 before the closure of the border on 13 August.

After the erection of the Berlin Wall, the population, unable to move freely to the West and conscious, too, of the acquiesence of the Western powers in the division of Germany, was forced to adjust to a life within socialism. In the new political conjuncture the SED deployed a variety of consensual instruments, in particular the extension of social welfare measures, to woo various groups in society. A kind of social compact eventually emerged in the later 1960s based on the population's conditional tolerance of the regime in accordance with their perceptions of the benefits and costs of accommodation.

Despite the consolidation of the social compact by 'the unity of economic and social policy' of the early 1970s, the new SED leader, Erich Honecker, was confronted by three major forms of opposition: intellectual dissent, emigration and the highly variegated alternative political culture of peace, ecology and human rights groups.

Honecker inherited from his predecessor several well known dissidents – Heym, Havemann and Biermann – and acquired another notable one, Bahro, in the late 1970s, Heym and Biermann belonged to the cultural intelligentsia, which also included in its ranks, with varying degrees of criticality, Christa Wolf, Volker Braun, Reiner Kunze and Christoph Hein. The clumsily handled expatriation of Biermann in 1976 provoked open clashes between the writers and the SED cultural functionaries and a crackdown by the regime. Controls were subsequently relaxed in the 1980s, and writers like Wolf, Braun and de Bruyn were able to publish on controversial matters such as the dangers of nuclear energy and weaponry, pollution and corruption among lesser party officials.

The arm of benevolent paternalism was not extended to Havemann and Bahro: their critiques of 'real existing socialism' touched upon too many sensitive political nerves among the high priests of Marxist–Leninist dogma. So despite their claim to be renewing socialism, Havemann was put under house arrest and Bahro was imprisoned before being deported to the West in 1978. During the 1980s, no individual of comparable stature emerged to inherit the mantle of prominent intellectual dissident; instead, the main source of ideas for the renewal of socialism was the marginalized and small autonomous groups within the alternative political culture.

From the regime's point of view, a more worrying feature than the dissent of the intellectuals was the continuing pressure for emigration, a clear sign that in certain sections of the population the SED had failed to implement a belief in the superiority of the socialist way of life over that in capitalism. Partly in order to defuse the social and political pressures which had built up by 1983 behind the logjam of an estimated 200,000 to 500,000 exit applications, the SED authorized a sharp increase in emigration and short-term visits to the West. In 1984, over 40,000 GDR citizens received permission to emigrate and by 1987 1.2 million non-pensioners were visiting West Germany under the more generous official interpretation of 'urgent family business'.

One West German analysis of the motives for emigration among a representative sample of the 1984 emigrés (See Table 8.1) discovered that political motives – the lack of freedom of expression and political pressure – were ranked marginally higher than material motives. The over-representation of younger East Germans in the emigration wave in 1984

Table 8.1   Motives for Leaving the GDR, 1984 and 1989

	1984	1989
Lack of freedom to express one's opinion	71	74
Political pressure	66	65
To be able to shape one's own life	–	72
Limited opportunities for travel to other countries	56	74
Supply situation	46	56
Lack of/or unpromising prospects	45	69
Relatives in FRG (reuniting family)	36	28
Making a fresh start	28	–
Unfavourable career opportunities	21	26

Sources: *Köhler and Ronge*, 1984: 1282; *Hilmer and Köhler*, 1989: 1385.

(37.7 per cent were aged 18–30 compared to the GDR average of 23.5 per cent) underlined the declining appeal among young people of the GDR's brand of socialism as well as the appreciable loss of dynamic human potential.

The carefully calibrated policy to appease the population by relaxing restrictions on short visits to the FRG proved to be a palpable failure. Personal experience of conditions in the West undermined official claims about the advantages of the socialist way of life; the continuation of the arbitrary nature of the process of dealing with applications for travel and emigration underpinned popular perceptions of being held under the tutelage of an insensitive bureaucracy. Furthermore, disagreements arose between those who sought to emigrate and those who thought it preferable to stay and improve conditions at home. The whole emigration issue was symptomatic of the deep political and social divisions running through society. The cleavages ran through individuals too. As was attested at the ecunemical meeting in Dresden in April 1989, people's public statements and actions did not reflect their true convictions but what they believed was expected of them (Rein, 1989: 207).

The most significant new form of critical dissent (rather than a fundamental rejection of the GDR and socialism) to materialize in the late 1970s was located within 'the alternative political culture': that is, the articulation outside official channels of a series of peace, ecological, human rights, women's, gay and Second–Third World issues. New Forum, and the other citizens' movements, which were key actors in the revolution of 1989, had their ideological roots in this milieu. Peace and the other issues were propagated by individuals and small groups who, due to the restrictions imposed by the SED on autonomous activities in the public domain, were largely confined to the protective space afforded by the evangelical churches, the only major public institution with a significant measure of control over its own affairs after the conclusion of an asymmetrical 'concordat' with the regime in 1978.

The autonomous groups exhibited some ideological similarities with the new social movements in the West in that they expressed, across the political and military divide, concerns about individual liberty, scientific–technical progress, the militarization of society and environmental degradation. Reflecting a shift in values and a new type of traditional thinking, they did not fit easily into the traditional pattern of 'socialist' versus 'capitalist' (*Lemke*, 1986: 354). They tended, in Hubertus Knabe's view, to have a cultural rather than a power–political orientation, to be reactive rather than pro-active and to favour grass-roots democracy rather than parliamentary forms (*Knabe* 1990: 23). This orientation, inherited by the citizens' movements, proved to be a serious handicap in the power struggle to fill the political vacuum created by the crumbling of SED power during the autumn of 1989.

The activities of the autonomous groups together with popular discontent over restrictions on travel were all aspects of a common theme: the denial of human rights in the GDR. From about the mid-1980s, the issue of human rights came to occupy a more prominent place within the alternative political culture and to attain a political dynamic and quality lacked by the single issue movements. The accession to power of Gorbachev and efforts in Hungary and Poland to establish the roots of a civil society encouraged human rights activists in the GDR. However, unlike their Hungarian and Polish counterparts, the would-be reformers in the GDR were more intent on purging socialism of its Stalinist perversions than decoupling social analysis from traditional Marxism. The East German dissidents within the alternative political culture did not regard themselves as enemies of the system; they desired, according to the Wittenberg pastor Friedrich Schorlemmer, to give socialism a human face, not to decapitate it. In his opinion, if the SED had pursued a policy of dialogue with the autonomous groups instead of treating them as hostile forces, then events might well have taken a different course, (*Zur Person*, 1990: 25).

A key role in human rights issues was played by the Initiative for Peace and Human Rights (IFM) founded in early 1986 and numbering no more than about 30 members before autumn 1989. Not only did it cultivate contacts with dissidents elsewhere in the Soviet bloc but it also deliberately pursued its activities outside what it, and several other groups, regarded as the attempts by many Church leaders and congregations to confine dissent within certain limits for fear of disrupting the Churches' compact with the state.

Throughout much of the 1980s, the SED leadership deliberately loosened party controls in certain areas in order to broaden its political support. Travel restrictions were relaxed, writers, artists and academics were allowed more space for the exploration of critical issues, and a more progressive image was cultivated in relations with the West. However, the SED leaders were allergic to the more fundamental reform impulses within the GDR and in late 1987 and early 1988 they delivered warning shots across the bows of the peace and human rights activists. About 200 activists were arrested after some 100 had intervened in the annual official rally in January 1988 commemorating the deaths of Rosa Luxemburg and Karl Liebknecht. The actions of the security force caused a wave of protests by the Church authorities, and large attendances were recorded at services of intercession for those arrested and deported. Cutting off the heads of the Hydra was, as Joachim Nawrocki observed in *Die Zeit*, self-defeating as there were no heads, only symbolic figures.

By the late 1980s, hardly a Church synod took place without a debate on the democratization of political life. Characteristic of the debate were the proposals in the 'Twenty Theses for Social Renewal' submitted by Schorlemmer to the Church meeting in Halle in June 1988. Reformers like Schorlemmer envisaged renewal through secret elections, the division of powers between executive, judiciary and legislature, freedom of association and travel, and greater independence for the political parties in the SED-controlled Democratic Bloc. The replacement of the practice of internal delimitation by a climate in society conducive to dialogue and tolerance was the target of the group 'Rejection of the Practice and Principle of Delimitation'. These ideas on the creation of a civil society entered the public domain during the GDR's existential crisis in the summer and autumn of 1989.

Despite the higher profile of the autonomous groups and Church intellectuals in the reform process and despite their significance as a moral force and source of creative ideas, the groups were still very much confined to the periphery of society. Stasi data confirm their low level of popular support. In June 1989, it was estimated in one Stasi report that there were only about 150 autonomous groups associated with the Evangelical Churches plus a handful of groups who performed a coordinating function: for example, the IFM and the four regional groups of the 'Church from Below'. The total number of activists engaged in these groups was reckoned be in the region of 2,500. Among the 60 activists designated by the Stasi as the hardcore 'fanatical' enemies of socialism were Eppelmann, Bärbel Bohley, Gerd and Ulrike Poppe, Fischer and Schult (Mitter and Wolle, 1990: 47–8). Pollack (1990: 1217) maintains that the number of activists might have been slightly higher, between 10,000 and 15,000, and the total number of groups about 320.

The limited appeal of the autonomous groups can, of course, be partly attributed to their relatively underdeveloped institutional and communication networks within a system where the public domain was controlled by the SED, the allied parties and the mass organizations. Coercion, too, played a part: the regime subjected its 'unpalatable' dissidents to regular surveillance, occasional detainment or finally 'exported' them, sometimes forcibly, to the West. As for most ordinary citizens, the potential psychological, physical and career costs were too high a price to pay for the risks inherent in direct involvement in civil rights and other politically sensitive issues.

Force, repressive tolerance and differentiated political justice were thus all elements in the SED's system-maintenance strategy. The favourite technique throughout the Honecker era, however, was pacification through consent: that is, on the basis of heavy subsidies for certain consumer staples and public transport, a generous social welfare system, better and cheap housing, a guaranteed job for women as well as men, and some relaxation of the state's intrusion into the private sphere of family and home, the regime was able to maintain a tacit social compact (Dennis, 1988: 126–7). By the summer of 1989, this policy was in need of urgent reappraisal as it was apparent that the GDR had become inextricably enmeshed in the general crisis of the system of 'real existing socialism'. In the Soviet Union, perestroika and glasnost were deployed by Gorbachev in a vain attempt to overcome the systemic obstacles to change; in Hungary and Poland, on the other hand, the reform process in the late 1980s threatened to sweep away the system itself (see Reissig, 1991: 395–8).

The SED leadership sought to keep the reform waves at bay by belittling Gorbachev's reconstruction programme as wallpapering, by warning of the dangers of anarchy inherent in the reform process and by insisting that the GDR, thanks to having commenced its own restructuring process in the early 1970s, was achieving respectable rates of economic growth and a high level of consumer satisfaction.

The negative reaction of the SED old guard to the reforms initiated by the new generation of Soviet politicians was partly determined by their own close association with what Gorbachev disparaged as the Brezhnev 'era of stagnation'. Not only did Honecker owe his appointment as First Secretary to Brezhnev but the Politburo gerontocracy remained wedded to the fundamental aspects of 'real existing socialism' – that is, the neo-Stalinist compromise which had evolved in the Brezhnev years. For the older SED leaders, who had also been schooled in the iron discipline and mentalities of the pre-war communist movement, internal political stability was predicted on the Communist party's retention of its leading role in society, the elimination of party factions, the rigorous application of the principle of democratic centralism, the nationalization of the economy and a controlled socioeconomic modernization within the terms of the scientific–technical revolution. Gorbachev's experimentation, a high-risk policy in the eyes of the SED leaders, therefore threatened not only their own political survival but also their cautious 'perfecting', as they called it, of the system of 'real existing socialism'. Isolated from criticism under their neo-Stalinist carapace, the aged SED leaders were unable to grasp the opportunity afforded by Gorbachev to redress their legitimacy deficit. The inability to understand the process of change and the burgeoning crisis is well illustrated in the official communiqué approved by Honecker, in which the 1989 emigrés were attacked as people 'who through their conduct trampled on moral values and shut themselves out of our society. One should therefore shed no tears over them' (cited Pond, 1990: 41).

Yet the basic reason for the obduracy of the old guard is to be located in their fear that reform would so destabilize the GDR – particularly in view of its acute problem of national identity – that not only would SED rule be endangered but also the survival of the GDR as a separate political entity. Their fear was openly admitted in August 1989 by Otto Reinhold, the influential rector of the SED's Academy of Social Sciences. The GDR, in his opinion, was 'conceivable only as an anti-fascist and socialist state, as a socialist alternative to the FRG' (cited Rheinhold, 1989: 1175).

Although the SED propaganda machine was for a long time successful in concealing the true extent of the GDR's economic problems (the alleged success of the GDR economy was part of the strategy of keeping the reform waves at bay), it became apparent, soon after the overthrow of Honecker, that the country had been experiencing the symptoms of decay affecting the other socialist countries. Produced national income, the major, albeit crude, indicator of the economy's general performance, had been in decline since the mid-1970s, with the fall being particularly marked in the later 1980s. Despite the development of industrial robots and the megabit chip, much plant and equipment was obsolete, thus leading to low rates of productivity and high levels of wastage. Outdated production methods, the wasteful consumption of energy and raw materials and the promotion of the lignite and carbochemical industries, partly for reasons of economic autarchy, created a pollution nightmare, especially in the industrialized regions of the south. Furthermore, the declining competitiveness of the country's exports meant that ever more GDR Marks had to be pumped into the economy in order to earn hard currency abroad, and the GDR's hard debt problem was so serious that it had become heavily dependent on West German, Japanese and other foreign bankers. In 1989, GDR economic experts nervously anticipated IMF involvement in the GDR's internal affairs as part of a debt rescheduling process (Dennis, 1992).

Faltering economic performance made it increasingly difficult to sustain the high level of state subsidies for basic consumer items and the other props of the social contract. The subsidies for rents, basic foodstuffs and public transport, which had rocketed from 16.9 billion Marks in 1980 to 49.8 billion Marks in 1988, also diverted scarce resources from urgently needed investment in industry and infrastructure. The whole system of subsidies and social policy was urgently in need of reappraisal, but as it was fundamental to the SED's claim for the superiority of the socialist way of life and thus for the purpose of regime maintenance, the leaders were reluctant to grasp the nettle of reform. According to Reinhold, the removal of rents and basic foodstuffs subsidies would precipitate a wages and price spiral which would be dangerous both politically and socially (Dennis, 1991: 25).

Serious though the internal situation had become by the beginning of 1989, the survival of the Honecker regime and even of the GDR itself was still highly dependent on developments in the international environment. And here dramatic changes were taking place during the Gorbachev administration which resulted in the GDR becoming a dwindling political, economic, military and ideological asset for the Soviet Union. From about early 1987 onwards, the network of trading, ideological and security interests and instruments of the Soviet bloc, within which the GDR had for so long been safely secured, began to disintegrate as the Kremlin gradually shifted from the 'Brezhnev Doctrine' to the 'Sinatra Doctrine', grew more tolerant of radical political change in Eastern Europe and pursued closer economic and technological ties with Western Europe. Better relations with the West were, of course, part of the overall strategy to relieve the Soviet Union of 'imperial overstretch' and to transform it into a modern, prosperous and efficient state. Relations with West Germany grew considerably warmer after Kohl's visit to Moscow in October 1988 and reflected a growing body of opinion among influential Soviet politicians and their advisors that the FRG could render vital assistance in the modernization process. Yet, although the significance of the GDR within the Soviet bloc was being eroded as a result of the Kremlin's reassessment of its global and European policy, Gorbachev, initially, had no wish to preside over German unification. His preference clearly lay in a reformed version of socialism within an independent GDR. However, one question nagged uncomfortably at the edges of political consciousness: how would the Soviet Union react if the East Germans spurned a new socialist experiment in favour of the West German model?

The Autumn Revolution

Although several cracks had already appeared in the SED monolith (the rigging of the local election results in May 1989 and the SED's support for the repression in China had sparked off public protests), the decisive precipitant of change was the Hungarian dismantling of its fortifications on the border with Austria. The trickle of East Germans fleeing to the West after the barbed wire of the Iron Curtain was cut in May 1989 turned into a flood when, on 10 September, the Hungarian government suspended its bilateral visa agreement with the GDR. Within three days of the decision as many as 15,000 East Germans fled to the West. By the time the Berlin Wall came down on 9–10 November, over a quarter of a million East Germans had left their country, either illegally or with official permission.

The motives propelling tens of thousands to leave their home at considerable personal risk were, according to West German researchers, similar to those in 1984, with political considerations still narrowly outweighing material factors (see Table 8.1, page 196). In a document dated 9 September 1989, the Ministry of State Security identified what it regarded as the major factors behind emigration: widespread dissatisfaction with the quality, range and quantity of consumer goods; the inadequacies of the service sector; the deficiencies in the health service; limited opportunities for foreign travel; unsatisfactory working conditions and discontinuities in the production process; inadequate material incentives to improve work performance, particularly at a time of rising prices; the bureaucratic obstructionism of managers and functionaries; and the artificiality and monotony of reporting in the mass media. Other factors mentioned in the report were people's serious doubts about the future of the socialist system and the desire to rejoin family members in the West. Escaping to the West, it was hoped, would lead to a higher wage, a higher standard of living and greater opportunities to achieve personal goals (Mitter and Wolle, 1990: 141–7). In other words, although the GDR had managed to provide its citizens with a reasonable standard of living, it could not fulfil expectations raised by comparisons with West Germany.

The sheer volume of emigration not only gave the lie to Honecker's fatuous claim during the GDR's macabre fortieth anniversary celebrations that socialism was a 'beacon of hope' for the people of the GDR but it also drove many SED members and officials to despair at the old guard's eerie silence on the issue. Within the Politburo, the mass exodus convinced Egon Krenz and Günter Schabowski that Honecker must be ousted. For the Berlin regional party chief, Schabowski, it was both depressing and humiliating to discover that, despite having a secure job and a home, so many East Germans were willing to leave everything behind (Sieren and Koehne, 1990: 62).

But more significant than the stirring of belated reform sentiments among Politburo members, the mass defections catalysed opposition within the GDR whether as popular demonstrations on the streets of Leipzig, Dresden and Berlin or as organized opposition movements such as New Forum and Democracy Now (Donovan, 1989: 9). This catalyst function of the emigrés entitles them, in the opinion of erstwhile GDR writers, to the title of 'first children of the revolution' (Maron, 1991: 40) and to the claim to be 'the actual motors of all societal change in the GDR' (Schneider, 1990a: 9). While this argument underplays the contribution of the citizens' movements to the undermining of the SED system, it does nevertheless highlight the crucial importance of the mass exodus for the creation of what Jens Reich called 'the emotional frenzy which gripped the country' (Prins,

1990: 71), encouraging people like Reich to come out into the open. No less significantly, in 'voting with their feet' for West German political pluralism and consumerism, the emigrés were swelling the political current which would not only sweep away the citizens' movements' idea of a 'third way' but would also generate powerful pressures against the border barricades. Seen in this light, the desire of many East Germans for a personal form of unification, albeit on the territory of the FRG, not merely in 1989 but throughout the chequered history of the GDR was a major, though obviously not the sole, factor in the crumbling of the Wall. Indeed, between 1949 and June 1990, 5.2 million people left the GDR for the West, with only 470,000 travelling in the other direction (Wendt, 1991: 387). Unification, therefore, was both a cause and consequence of the removal of the Wall.

Demonstrations in the towns and cities of the GDR, notably in Leipzig, constituted another significant form of opposition to the party-controlled system. Sporadic public protests had taken place in East Berlin, Leipzig and Dresden in the late 1980s. Some demonstrators demanded the right to leave the country, others aspired to reform the GDR from within. Relations between the two tendencies were often strained: the radicalization of the would-be emigrés and their use of the space afforded by the Churches aroused considerable antipathy among civil rights activists intent upon internal change (Spittmann, 1988: 230). This cleavage was discernible in Leipzig on 4 September 1989: while pastor Schorlemmer was addressing about 300 people in the Nikolai church on the need for a renewal of socialism, several hundred were demonstrating in the city centre for the right to emigrate (Bornhöft in 'Die Taz', nda: 8).

The number of demonstrators escalated after the pressures generated by the emigration wave began to weaken the security forces' iron grip. In Leipzig the number of demonstrators rose from 5,000 on 25 September to 70,000 on the fateful night of 9 October (Opp, 1991: 303). The demonstration virus soon spread to the other towns and cities, among them Plauen, Jena, Potsdam, Erfurt, Magdeburg, Halle and Karl-Marx-Stadt. The security forces were responsible for much gratuitous brutality, particularly against the demonstrators, during the GDR's fortieth anniversary celebrations in East Berlin on 7 and 8 October. At this moment of crisis for the old regime, Gorbachev, while attending the GDR anniversary, gave it a substantial push when he expressed his impatience with Honecker's obduracy in his famous phrase 'Whoever comes too late is punished by life itself'. And with rumours abounding of his refusal to authorize the Soviet troops to assist in the work of repression, the SED appeared to be losing the ultimate guarantee of its power – the Soviet forces.

A turning-point in the course of the 'gentle revolution' occurred in Leipzig on 9 October. It was suspected before the Monday demonstration that preparations had been made for riot police, army units and factory combat groups to disperse the demonstrators in a GDR version of Tiananmen Square (Pond, 1990: 43–4; Sieren and Koehne, 1990: 79–80). Although it is still not clear to what extent Krenz and other central party and state officials contributed to the peaceful outcome, there can be no doubt that much of the credit must be shared between local party officials and dignitaries such as the conductor Kurt Masur and the 70,000 demonstrators themselves. The demonstrators, with their cries of 'We are the people – no violence', made every effort to avoid provoking the security forces. With the sword in its sheath and the shield badly cracked, Honecker had run out of options; on 18 October he was replaced as General Secretary by Egon Krenz, the Central Committee Secretary responsible for security, in a belated effort by the SED to regain control over events.

With the threat of reprisals subsiding, the demonstrators openly articulated their political demands on a sea of banners and in pithy and often humorous chants: 'We are the people', 'We are staying here', 'The street is the tribune of the people' and 'Democracy now' (Die Taz,' nda: 72–5). In short, the goal of the rapidly evolving political culture of the streets was for the renewal of GDR society on the basis of traditional liberal values: freedom of speech, travel, assembly and association. The many demonstrations before the breaching of the Berlin Wall were not organized by any specific groups or individuals but were rather a spontaneous gathering to express popular dissatisfaction with the regime. The large squares in Leipzig and other towns provided suitable meeting places where protesters could expect to meet like-minded people at a given time (Opp, 1991: 315–16).

The demonstrations reached their climax shortly before the opening of the Wall. On 6 November, about 500,000 braved pouring rain in Leipzig to demand a new travel law and an end to the SED's leading role in society. Two days earlier, an even larger number had gathered in East Berlin for a demonstration organized by the artists' federations. In the heady atmosphere, it appeared that the people and the cultural intelligentsia had at long last come together to renew the GDR, Stefan Heym rejoiced that people had recovered the power of speech and could now proceed with the construction of socialism. Christa Wolf, another GDR author much respected in the West, shared Heym's dream and expressed the hope that one would be able to say 'Imagine, it is socialism, and nobody leaves' (Hahn *et al.*, 1990: 163–4, 172). Unfortunately for these idealists, East Germans were pouring across the open Czech border into West Germany: 15,000 did so on 5 and 6 November alone (Links and Bahrmann, 1990: 84–5).

A third and crucial form of opposition to the SED emerged from the chrysalis of the alternative political culture in the shape of small citizens' movements and proto-political parties. These groups would later claim to have been the revolutionaries of the first hour. In June, the initiative group Democratic Awakening (DA) was launched, principally by Church workers engaged in human rights and peace activities. Its initiators included the Rostock lawyer Wolfgang Schnur, the sociologist and director of studies at the Evangelical Churches Federation in East Berlin, Erhart Neubert, the Wittenberg pastor Friedrich Schorlemmer, the Weimar theologian Edelbert Richter and the East Berlin pastor and peace activist Rainer Eppelmann. The high level of participation by Church ministers and workers was, at this early stage, typical of the DA and the other movements. Although security forces frustrated a founding meeting on 2 October, the group did at least manage to issue a manifesto. A few weeks later, on 30 October, it constituted itself officially as a political party. Members were drawn from a variety of sources: Christians, communists, social democrats, church workers, intellectuals, craftsmen and small businessmen (Süss, 1990: 17; *Junge Welt*, 9–10 November 1989: 6).

In July an appeal was launched by another initiative group, which included Ibrahim Böhme and pastors Meckel, Gutzeit and Noack, with the aim of re-establishing a Social Democratic party in the GDR. The founding of the SDP (later SPD) took place in the ministry house of the village of Schwante on 7 October.

A third group, Democracy Now (Demokratie Jetzt – DJ), had its roots in the circle 'Rejection of the Practice and Principle of Delimitation'. At a meeting in East Berlin on 13 August, Dr Hans-Jürgen Fischbeck called for the formation of an opposition movement which would provide people with a positive alternative to flight to the West. There followed, one month later, the drafting of the 'Appeal for Intervening in our own Affairs', signed by, among others, Fischbeck, Ulrike Poppe, the Church historian and lawyer Wolfgang Ullmann, the mathematician Ludwig Mehlhorn and the film director Konrad Weiss. The Appeal was issued on behalf of the citizens' movement, Democracy Now. The early activists were recruited mainly from intellectuals, scientists, artists and pastors (Rein, 1989: 59–61; Krüger 1990a, 17).

At the beginning of September, a meeting was held in Böhlen to launch the United Left, after an earlier attempt in June had miscarried. A programme was announced under the heading of the Böhlen Platform 'For a United Left in the GDR'. The United Left had its origins in a group called *Gegenstimmen* which had been founded in East Berlin in 1986 by left-wing and Marxist-oriented members of various Church and autonomous groups. A coordinating committee staged a further meeting in the Environmental

Library in East Berlin on 2 October; this can be regarded as the actual founding date of the United Left. Within the next few weeks, more members attached themselves to the movement: factory work groups intent on forming independent trade union organizations; student groups, mainly from Halle and Leipzig; members of the Church from Below, the Friedrichsfelde peace circle and *Gegenstimmen*; women from *Lilo-offensiv*; and ex-SED members. Another group, the Nelken, enjoyed associate membership for several weeks but severed its formal connection before the elections to the People's Chamber in March 1990 (Wielgohs, 1991: 285–7; Rein, 1989: 105–6).

New Forum soon emerged as the most significant group among the new political formations. On 9 September, about 30 representatives of different groups from all parts of the GDR, including Bärbel Bohley, Katja Havemann, Jens Reich, Sebastian Pflugbeil, Rolf Henrich and Reinhard Schult, signed the manifesto *Aufruf 89 – NEUES FORUM*. In plain and simple language it called for the establishment of a broad political platform which would enable people to take part in a widespread discussion on reform and give them an alternative to emigration. In order to realize its goals, on 19 September, New Forum applied for official recognition as an association in accordance with article 29 of the Constitution. A receptive chord was struck among many East Germans by this bold act as well as by the manifesto's deliberate avoidance of the term 'socialism' and by the absence of precise programmatic details. By the beginning of October, 10,000 people, at considerable personal risk, had signed the manifesto. New Forum's support was much greater than that of the other opposition groups; whereas its manifesto attracted about 200,000 signatories within two months, the membership of Democratic Awakening and the SDP lay between 10,000 and 15,000. Support for the other movements was considerably less; Democracy Now, for example, never exceeded 4,000 supporters (Schulz, 1991: 14 Rein, 1989: 13–14; Wielgohs and Schulz, 1990: 18).

One already well established group, the IFM, played a key role in the emergence of the new opposition movements. Many of their founding members – Ulrike Poppe (DJ), Ibrahim Böhme (SDP), Bärbel Bohley (New Forum – had been active in the IFM for several years before the *Wende*. The IFM deliberately avoided becoming a political party, preferring to remain a grass-roots movement dedicated to the creation from below of a democratic political and social order.

As the new movements began to take shape, they sought to define a common set of principles. On 2 October, representatives of the SDP, DA, DJ, the IFM, New Forum, Democratic Socialists and the Pankow Peace Circle issued a short Joint Declaration calling for the democratic restructuring of state and society and for free and secret elections under the auspices of the United Nations (Rein, 1989: 122).

The Joint Declaration embodied the basic goal of the new opposition groups in the period before the opening of the Wall: the establishment of a democratic sovereign GDR encompassing the separation of SED and state, political pluralism, freedom of association and assembly, freedom of travel, an independent judiciary, the removal of censorship and the introduction of an ecologically responsible policy. All of these ideas had, as we have seen, developed within the niches of the alternative political culture and in late 1989 constituted an effective lever for mobilizing popular resistance to the SED regime. There were, however, important differences between the groups. The most left-oriented group, the United Left, advocated public ownership of the main means of production underpinned by democratic forms of worker codetermination and self-management. It proposed an 'uncompromising implementation of the principles of social security and justice for all members of society' (Rein, 1989: 110). The United Left's programme, whilst rejecting SED-style state socialism, was a mixture of traditional Marxist elements and modern left-wing ideas on the environment. The SDP, on the other hand, turned its back on traditional Marxism: it favoured an ecologically-oriented social market economy with democratic controls over economic activity, codetermination in the enterprises and different forms of ownership. In general, its economic programme was much closer to the West German model than that of the other groups.

But was the 'new' GDR to be attired in the colours of a reformed socialism? The United Left was the most trenchant advocate of the construction of a democratic socialist state. Others were more circumspect: it was generally recognized that the term 'socialism' had been contaminated by its semantic association with the SED version, 'real existing socialism'. New Forum, as indicated earlier, avoided the term in its original manifesto, although one of its spokespersons, the physicist, Sebastian Pflugbeil, averred that the movement aspired to embrace positive socialist traditions and was against copying the West German system (Rein, 1989: 26). Democracy Now also ruled out the FRG as an alternative model for the GDR. One of its leading figures, Konrad Weiss, spoke warmly of the new and just society which would be created on the basis of socialist and Christian values. The GDR, in his opinion, was not to be reduced to the level of a mere *Land* of the Federal Republic. And, ironically, in view of later developments, Democratic Awakening, in its provisional Basic Declaration, stated that 'the critical attitude of DA to real existing socialism does not signify a rejection of the vision of a socialist order' (Süss, 1990: 17). Edelbert Richter, one of the group's co-founders underpinned this sentiment one week after the opening of the Wall: 'not only the word socialism but also certain social principles of socialism possess for us, as before, a good ring' (Wielgohs and Schulz, 1990: 18–19).

The adherence to a socialist future, though as yet ill-defined, is perhaps not surprising as the democratic discussion within the alternative political culture had been framed by socialist intellectual traditions. A second factor was that, while the SED remained the most influential political force in the country, it was sound tactics to retain socialism as the political compass for change. Not until the SED's decay became palpable from late November onwards was it no longer imperative to remain within the framework of socialism.

In order to promote dialogue throughout society and grass-roots participation in the process of internal change, movements such as New Forum, the IFM, Democracy Now and the United Left sought to construct the appropriate organizational structures. New Forum erected two organizational tiers. The communal and regional level encompassed relatively autonomous basic groups in factories and residential areas, regional centres and a spokespersons' council elected by regional representatives. The second level comprised thematic working groups. These groups, which were open to anyone with an interest in a particular theme, were expected to put forward both theoretical and practical solutions to problems in areas such as education, the media and the economy (Schult, 1990: 167; Kühnel *et al.*, 1990: 27–8). According to one estimate, New Forum had established at least 80 thematic groups but only 26 territorial groups in East Berlin by the end of November (Schulz, 1991: 20–1). The relatively low number of territorial groups can be attributed to the overrepresentation of the intelligentsia in New Forum and the low participation of the working class. The resulting emphasis on intelligentsia-specific issues in the thematic groups curtailed feedback from the residential groups and impeded a widening of the social base of its membership.

Like New Forum, Democracy Now was subdivided into autonomous territorial basic groups and the more specialized thematic working groups. The basic groups – at communal, regional and, more rarely, at factory level – were organized initially, as in New Forum, through contact addresses. In keeping with its commitment to grass-roots democracy, DJ saw itself as galvanizing democratic participation not as a political party but as an open citizens' movement without a fixed membership; this entailed the organization of campaigns, appeals and widespread discussion on the reform process (Kühnel *el al.*, 1990: 29–30; Poppe, 1990: 162). The United Left did not differ fundamentally from New Forum and DJ in its conception of grass-roots democracy, except that it placed greater emphasis on organizational work in the factories – for example, the formation of independent factory councils. However, it failed to mobilize much popular support: by the end of 1989, its membership had risen to only 1,500 to 2,000 from the 500–600 in the autumn (Kühne *et al.*, 1990: 32; Wielgohs, 1991: 289).

Sooner than could have been anticipated, the embryonic political parties and citizens' movements – especially New Forum as the flagship of the opposition – had to face several difficult questions: would the informal alliance between the masses, the citizens' movements and the cultural intelligentsia in the struggle against the SED and the Stasi endure once the *ancien régime* went into its unexpectedly rapid terminal decline; would democratic socialism within an independent GDR have much appeal for the East German populace?

The answer to these questions was probably 'no' even before the Wall was opened for, despite the courage of New Forum and the other movements in confronting the party–state apparatus, their idealistic notions of grass-roots democracy and many aspects of their economic and ecological policies lacked a popular resonance, whilst the continuing demographic haemorrhage testified to the powerful appeal of the West German system. And once Krenz, in a last desperate attempt to establish a *rapprochement* between regime and people, had opened the Wall, the GDR was rapidly pulled into the orbit of the Deutschmark. Most of the 'achievements' of state socialism paled into insignificance as East Germans were able to compare their way of life directly and regularly with that of their Western siblings.

Moreover, with the relaxation of censorship, the mass media abounded with stories of corruption among the political élite, environmental disaster, economic backwardness and repression by the Stasi's extensive apparatus of coercion and surveillance. West German Chancellor Helmut Kohl's proposal for a confederation of the two German states on 18 November 1989, and then his dramatic offer in early February 1990 of rapid economic and monetary union, were well designed to accord with and compound the popular bitterness and disenchantment not only with the leaders of the SED but with the GDR too. Devising a separate GDR path to socialism appeared to many as a waste of time and energy when the successful West German alternative appeared to be within reach.

Opposition Movements and Unification

The street demonstrations soon began to echo with cries of 'Wir sind ein Volk' once East Germans realized that unification was no longer an unrealistic prospect. In Leipzig, judging by the number of banners and flags, a slim majority were in favour of unification about one month after the opening of the Wall. Such was the momentum gathered by the unification bandwagon that, according to surveys conducted by Leipzig's Institute for Youth Research, the vast majority of East Germans were in favour of some form of unification by late January–early February (see Chapter 2). Until the beginning of February 1990, most supporters of unification, reflecting internal and external political realities, were in favour of a confederation. This changed as a result of Kohl's proposals for swift monetary and economic union, the greater involvement of West German parties in the GDR's domestic affairs and Gorbachev's acceptance, at the end of January, of the principle of unification.

The rapidly changing political situation required the citizens' movements as well as the established political parties to adjust their programmes and policies to the popular will and to reconsider their whole approach to power and governmental responsibility. Some movements and parties such as the newly founded German Social Union (DSU), the DA and a member of the SED-dominated Democratic Bloc, the East German CDU, adjusted relatively quickly to the changing circumstances, opting for unification and capitalism under the wing of Chancellor Kohl. From December 1989 onwards, the SDP drew closer to its West German counterpart, committed itself in mid-January to a united, federal Germany, and defected from its electoral pact with the other new opposition groups.

Of the many new parties and movements in the GDR, New Forum experienced the most serious problems of adjustment. The opening of the Berlin Wall set the alarm bells ringing among its leaders and supporters. Bärbel Bohley condemned it as a premature and arbitrary act on the part of the SED and feared that it would release forces incompatible with her own ideas on the country's future. In her opinion, both government and people, in the euphoria of the moment, had taken leave of their senses ('Die Taz', nd: 60). Bohley's concern was shared by one of her colleagues, Ingrid Köppe, for whom the breaching of the Wall meant that the time and patience required for nurturing a grass-roots democracy were no longer available as people wanted quick solutions to their problems (*Zur Person*, 1990: 90).

Fierce disputes broke out in New Forum over such central issues as the preservation of the GDR as a separate state, the status of New Forum as a citizens' movement, the protection of basic social rights in a united Germany, and participation in Modrow's government of national responsibility. The struggles reached a climax at the founding conference attended by 261 delegates in East Berlin at the end of January. Two factions emerged: the minority around the 'Berliners', Bohley, Köppe and Schult, was pitted against a second group of delegates, mainly recruited from the southern regions (Fink, 1990: 516). The 'Berliners' wish to preserve the GDR was swept aside by a majority vote for a Western-style market economy and a united Germany (albeit on the basis of existing borders), the demilitariz-ation of both German states, and withdrawal from NATO (Schulz, 1991: 55).

In the interest of New Forum's survival various compromises were reached. The politically unavoidable acceptance of German unity was qualified by the rejection of rapid unification and immediate monetary, economic and social union; the swift route would, it was feared, produce high unemployment, prosperity for a small minority and the legalization of extreme right-wing and neo-fascist organizations. Delegates preferred a slow drawing together on the basis of a referendum in the two states on the issue of unity, the democratization of the GDR, the stabilization and reform of the GDR economy, guarantees of the right to work, and restrictions on the operation of the market mechanism in such areas as education, health and culture (Krüger, 1990b: 8). This policy was encapsulated in the slogan 'As much market as necessary, as much social security as possible'. Yet even this compromise represented a watering-down of the radical elements in the original draft proposals of the working group on the economy. Whereas the draft programme had rejected a general privatization in favour of a comprehensive democratization of the economy, the revised version acknowledged the value of market mechanisms and removed the enterprise councils' right of veto over management decisions in key areas. Even the right to employment barely escaped deletion ('Die Taz', nd: 56; Schulz, 1991: 54).

Animated debates took place over whether New Forum should remain a citizens' movement or become a political party. Several basic groups favoured the latter course and broke away from the parent body to form the New Forum party at the end of January. Fundamental to the concept of a citizens' movement was the argument advanced by the committee of the national spokespersons' council that democracy requires, in the first in-stance, not political parties but mature and self-conscious citizens who can discuss and reach agreement on problems in a spirit of impartiality and tolerance. Politics, the committee insisted, begins not in Parliament but among people and their everyday problems. At the national congress in January, Jens Reich, in keeping with this concept, pleaded for more time for dialogue and for learning the process of democracy. Not every question, he argued, requires a simple answer; even politicians sometimes had doubts (Zimmerling and Zimmerling, 1990: 131). Although these were admirable sentiments they betrayed a certain political naivety. However, as the elec-tions to the People's Chamber approached and there was a possibility that only political *parties* would be allowed to participate in them, New Forum agreed at the delegates' conference in January that whilst it would remain a citizens' movement, it was prepared to contest the elections and to devise a political programme. And it was agreed that should the need arise, an extraordinary meeting would be called to review the question of the formation of a political party (Schulz, 1991: 39).

Democracy Now, the second largest citizens' movement was spared the fierce internal struggles of New Forum. On the other hand, it too had to abandon its original commitment to the notion of an independent GDR suffused with socialism. In mid-December a three-stage plan for national unity, largely the work of Konrad Weiss, was submitted to the first delegates' conference: reforms were to be implemented in both German states in the interest of social justice and environmental protection; Germany was to be demilitarized and a gradual unification process was to be preceded by a European peace treaty; finally, a plebisicite was to complete the process. Despite delegates' reservations about the slow pace of the envisaged unification process and their doubts about the willingness of West Germany to implement its own reforms, the plan was ultimately accepted (Wielgohs, 1991: 129–30).

The retreat from socialism can be illustrated by the main proposals in DJ's economic programme devised by a team under Hans-Jürgen Fischbeck. It envisaged a rapid transition to an ecologically-oriented social-market economy and the conclusion of a monetary and economic union with the FRG. All forms of ownership were to be allowed. Several modifications of the West German system were envisaged: both the election of managers and the ownership of shares by foreign investors should be decided by an enterprise ballot. Finally, DJ remained faithful to its recent past in that, whilst constituting itself formally as a political association, it continued to insist upon its role as a citizens' movement operating both inside and outside Parliament in order to ensure that the development of a new political culture was not monopolized by political parties (Zimmerling and Zimmerling, 1990: 97–9).

A major feature of GDR politics after the Wall came down was a second wave of party formations. The DSU, established *de facto* as a political party in January, articulated the socioeconomic and ecological grievances of East Germans in Saxony and Thuringia and acted as a springboard for the Bavarian CSU into the GDR. It soon emerged as a committed supporter of rapid unification and a determined adversary of any kind of socialism. A Green Party was established in late November 1989 as a response to genuine fears that ecological issues were being pushed too far down the agenda of other movements and parties. It was argued that a party-like formation would be an appropriate body for the pursuit of ecological matters at local level, as well as in Parliament.

The Green party's commitment to a higher representation of women in politics, including parity of office-holding within its own ranks, greatly facilitated the conclusion of an electoral pact with the Independent Women's Association (UFV) in February 1990. The official founding congress of the UFV was held on 17 February but the decision to form a political association had been taken two months earlier at a meeting of about 1,200 representatives in the *Volksbühne* in East Berlin. Many leading figures – Ina Merkel, Uta Roeth, Tatjana Böhm – had been involved in human rights, women's, ecological and peace groups during the 1980s and then, in the early days of the 'gentle revolution', in various women's initiative groups. Such groups as EWA (Erster weiblicher Aufruf and LILO (lila-offensiv)) sought to ensure that women's voice was heard in the process of change. At the *Volksbühne* meeting in December, opposition was expressed to German unification as it was feared that women would lose many of their social and legal rights – for example, the right to employment and to a place for children in kindergarten. A reformed socialist society, it was hoped, would enhance women's position by means of equal pay for equal work and through the introduction of job quotas (Hampele, 1991: 224–32, 234–41).

Although it was impossible to sustain the root-and-branch opposition to unification, the UFV attempted a holding operation. At the founding congress, and in its official programme, the League opted for gradual unification and a prominent role for the state in the running of the economy and in the protection of childcare facilities and jobs. The UFV pushed for training quotas in the belief that, as unemployment mounted, this would be one way of guaranteeing occupational parity with men. A proposal for a Ministry of Parity, on the model of the Office for the Parity of Women established by the Round Table, was envisaged as a major boost for a real transformation of gender roles (Funk *et al.*, 1991: 97–8, 101, 104).

The Round Table

The opposition groups' original concept of dialogue and the renewal of the GDR from below fitted in well with the proliferation of Round Tables at local, district, regional and central level as well as for special areas such as youth, the environment and sport. The most significant one was the Central Round Table, which had its first meeting in the Dietrich Bonhoeffer House in East Berlin on 7 December 1989 and its last on 12 March 1990. The Round Tables in the GDR, as elsewhere in Eastern Europe, constituted a forum for bringing together the old and the new forces and for facilitating the relatively peaceful, though difficult, transition from one political and social order to another.

The pace of events, however, dictated fundamental changes in the original self-conception and functions of the Central Round Table as well as in the political identity of its members. Even before the first meeting, the People's Chamber had deleted, on 1 December, the clause in the constitution which enshrined the SED as the leading force in society. And as the SED's authority waned, its traditionally loyal allies, notably the LDPD and the CDU, began to assert their independence and to seek a new political profile. Two of the so-called 'new' opposition forces, DA and the SDP (SPD) also underwent such significant political and ideological change that they eventually detached themselves from their original moorings in the alternative political culture.

A balance was struck on the composition of the membership of the Central Round Table between the 'new' opposition forces and those from the SED-dominated Democratic Bloc. The two groups received 15 votes each. On the opposition side, two votes were granted to DA, DJ, the Green party, the IFM, the SDP and the United Left and three to New Forum, whereas the old 'bloc' parties – SED, LDPD, CDU, NDPD, DBD – obtained three each. The principle of parity was maintained when the FDGB and the UFV were later granted the right of membership. Observer status was accorded to groups such as the DSU and the former communist youth organization, the FDJ (Thaysen, 1990: 31, 44, 46). Although the mandate of the members of the Round Table was inevitably a limited one as it had not been conferred through elections, New Forum and the other citizens' movements claimed that their public standing and vital contribution to the revolution legitimized their representation on the Round Table (see Mehlhorn, 1989: 14).

The controversy surrounding the Modrow government's attempt to reconstitute the state security apparatus led to a serious crisis of confidence between Modrow and the Round Table in early January. However, faced by threats of strikes, rumours of a Putsch, heavy losses of population to the West, a deteriorating economic situation and a weakening bargaining position vis-à-vis the FRG, Modrow not only abandoned the plan for an Office for National Security but, in order to stabilize the economic and political situation, invited members of the Round Table to join a government of national responsibility and to participate in the legislative process (Herles and Rose, 1990: 56; 80–3). The Round Table responded favourably to the latter proposal, agreeing, for example, to discussions by the appropriate committee of the People's Chamber on the Round Table draft on the Law on Parties and Association.

The citizens' movements and the embryonic political parties did not respond uniformly, however, to the offer of governmental posts, a clear indication of the splintering of the opposition under the new political circumstances. The Social Democrats, who reacted coolly to the idea, had one eye on the electoral advantages to be derived from distancing themselves from the SED–PDS. New Forum, the IFM and DJ were less concerned about scoring points in advance of the elections to the People's Chamber than with preventing further chaos in the GDR. This sense of co-responsibility was sufficiently powerful for them to overcome their reservations about their own political inexperience and the genuine fear of being muzzled by governmental office (*Der Spiegel*, 29 January 1990: 17, 19). After tough negotiations, it was agreed on 18 January that each of the 'new' opposition groups on the Round Table be granted a Ministry without Portfolio and on 5 February the People's Chamber confirmed eight members of the opposition as ministers: Tatjana Böhm (UFV), Rainer Eppelmann (DSA), Sebastian Pflugbeil (New Forum), Mathias Platzeck (Green party), Gerd Poppe (IFM), Walter Romberg (SPD), Klaus Schröter (Green League) and Wolfgang Ullmann (DJ).

The involvement of members of the opposition in Modrow's government and the enhancement of the Round Table's legislative function signified the transformation of the Round Table from a control and supervisory body into one with direct steering powers. In the process it had become *de facto* a co-government, although its powers were limited and even the members from the 'new' opposition did not speak with one voice. As the struggle for power unfolded, heated conflicts broke out among members. For example, the SPD proposed that a three-per-cent hurdle be erected for entry into the People's Chamber and that citizens' movements be debarred from the elections. Although this proposal was defeated, the SPD, DA and the CDU were able to ignore a majority vote debarring West German guest speakers from the election campaign. This proposal, submitted by the IFM, was backed by the other grass-roots movements (Herles and Rose, 1990: 107; Süss, 1991: 475).

A key aspect of the work of the Round Table, and one which was particularly dear to New Forum, DJ, the Green party and the UFV, was the protection of the vital socioeconomic and political interests of the citizens of the GDR. This became a matter of great urgency after Modrow's reluctant acceptance in early February of negotiations on German economic and monetary union. A Social Charter approved at the fifteenth session on 5 March, was designed by the Round Table to codify the GDR's fundamental interests and to provide the GDR government with a bargaining lever in its negotiations on economic, monetary and social union. The Charter spelled out a list of principles, including the right to work, the democratization and humanization of work, equality between the sexes, the right to a decent house and the right of women to decide on an abortion. It advocated as high a level of employment as possible, the retention of the extensive network of preschool institutions, state control over rents and a health care system independent of income and social status (Herles and Rose, 1990: 238–47).

One basic flaw lay in the failure to show how the Charter's recommend-ations could be sustained under fundamentally different political and econ-omic circumstances.

Much time and energy was devoted to the drafting of a new constitution. The draft constitution, which was not completed in time for debate at the Round Table's final session, combined elements of the West German Basic Law with principles of grass-roots democracy. Its authors intended it to provide the GDR with the constitutional foundation for gradual unification with the FRG. The plan was for the draft to be submitted by the People's Chamber to a plebiscite and for its subsequent incorporation into a debate on a new constitution for a united Germany. This course of action depended on the GDR's accession to the FRG by the slower route of article 146 of the Basic Law. In fact, in the stampede towards unification, the newly elected People's Chamber did not even refer the draft for discussion in committee (Süss, 1991: 476; Thaysen, 1990: 146–7).

The Opposition in the 1990 Elections

On 28 January 1990 the elections to the People's Chamber, originally due to be held on 6 May, were brought forward to 18 March. The campaign was essentially about the pace of unification and how GDR interests could best be safeguarded. The most cautious approach to unification was to be found among the citizens' movements New Forum, DJ and the IFM (linked together for the election campaign in Bündnis 90), the Nelken and the United Left in the Action Pact, the Green party and the UFV in the Elec-toral Pact, and the PDS. The Nelken accepted German unity in principle but were opposed to any annexation which would turn the GDR into the 'backyard' of Germany. Their pact partners, the United Left, could not swallow the idea of unification and continued to insist on the preservation of the GDR as a separate state and as a socialist alternative to the FRG. Both groups were anxious lest the GDR become a source of cheap, labour for the FRG and they insisted on protection for the potential victims of rapid economic and monetary union: pensioners, students, the handicapped, women, single parents and apprentices (*Wochenpost*, 1990: 4–5).

Whilst the groups in Bündnis 90 accepted the inevitability of German unification, they insisted, in their election programme, on protection for GDR interests through a gradual drawing together of the two states under-pinned by guarantees of the right to work and a dwelling, of the equality of the sexes and of a social minimum standard for everyone. In accordance with their perception of the need for grass-roots democracy, their pro-gramme advocated such forms of basic democracy as regional and national plebiscites, the direct election of the President and the active involvement of the public in important policy issues. Economic life would be democratized through the direct influence of trades unions, factory councils and supervisory boards on wage composition and environmental issues. Finally, both German states were to be demilitarized and to work for the transformation of NATO and the Warsaw Pact into political alliances ('DDR/ Programm-Synopse', 1990: 5, 7, 9). In short, Bündnis 90 made no easy promises to the electorate and desired unity through the exercise of democratic self-determination in the GDR. Or as Bärbel Bohley asserted: 'We will do it with our own strength' ('Interview', 1990: 96).

In an election campaign so deeply impregnated by West German political parties and money, it is not surprising that the underresourced and relatively inexperienced political actors like Bündnis 90 should have performed so badly. Even so, data on voting intentions since late November had not been encouraging. New Forum, according to Leipzig's Central Institute for Youth Research, peaked at 17 per cent in November but collapsed to 1 per cent in early March. Democracy Now, the Nelken, the United Left and the Green party all failed to score more than 3 per cent throughout this period (Förster and Roski, 1990: 134, 138, 142).

If the low vote for Bündnis 90 was a disappointment, it obviously did not come as a complete surprise to its leaders. But what was so demoralizing was the resounding success of the GDR-CDU and the ability of the PDS to mobilize so much support among that segment of the electorate which harboured fundamental doubts and fears about unification. Nationally, Bündnis 90 and the electoral pact of the Green party and the UFV scored a mere 2.91 per cent and 1.97 per cent of the vote respectively, giving them 12 and 8 seats in the new People's Chamber.

The representatives of the citizens' movements were deeply disturbed, Bohley describing herself as 'close to despair' on the evening of election day ('Interview', 1990: 95). The people, she felt, no longer had any confidence in their own strength. They had exchanged the tutelage of the old SED for that of the CDU in the hope that not the 'red' but the 'black' state would do everything for them (Bohley, 1990: 6). Ullmann, less acerbic in his criticism of the electorate, offered a more dispassionate analysis of the failure of Bündnis 90. The citizens' movements had, in his opinion, been too Berlin-oriented, too intellectual; the bulk of East Germans had opted for the party which offered them a swift and secure route to unity (Fink, 1990: 515). Impatient for unity and prosperity and sceptical of experiments in grass-roots democracy, the electorate had put their trust in the West German Chancellor and his GDR allies. In an election dominated by the socioeconomic aspects of unification and where the social structural variables associated with party affiliation in Western-style pluralistic systems had had no chance to develop, the victory went to the party which promised to implement a well tried and apparently successful system.

Bohley and her colleagues in Bündnis 90, Werner Fischer, Wolfgang Templin and Jens Reich, tried to console themselves with the thought that the results would not represent a long-term trend and that they could make a significant contribution outside Parliament to rebuilding democracy in East Germany. As the East German economy flounders and as unemployment rockets and xenophobic tendencies multiply, there is indeed much scope for grass-roots activities in the former GDR. However, the results of the three subsequent elections in 1990 – the local elections in May, those to the newly constituted *Länder* in October and then the first all-German elections in December – failed to reverse the electoral trend, although there were some minor gains for the citizens' movements in their various electoral pacts. For example, in the local elections the collective vote of New Forum, DJ, the United Left, the Green party, the Green League, the IFM and the UFV was slightly higher in all areas than it had been in March. The highest votes were recorded in Potsdam (16.9 per cent), Schwerin (9.1 per cent) and Jena (15.6 per cent) and the highest increases in Schwedt (9.4 per cent) and Wismar (8.9 per cent) (Müller-Enbergs *et al.*, 1991: 371). The same groups, except for the United Left as a composite group, campaigned for the Bundestag as the 'Electoral Pact: The Greens/Bündnis 90–citizens' movements'. Overall, the Pact obtained 6.0 per cent of the vote in the former GDR, which represented an increase of 1.1 per cent over that scored in the elections to the People's Chamber (Müller-Enbergs *el al.*, 1991: 380. The Pact members' collective vote had been slightly higher in the *Länder* elections).

Denouncement

In the 'romantic phase' of the East German revolution, hopes for a renewal of the GDR on the basis of democratic socialism did not appear unrealistic: the demonstrators' early demands focused on the introduction of social justice and democracy, not a capitalist market economy; the GDR incorporated the heartland of a strong left-wing tradition; the economy was believed to be in much better shape than in the other reforming states; the citizens' movements, anchored in a socialist tradition, enjoyed a legitimacy bonus from their activities in opposition circles before the *Wende*; and in October and November workers, intellectuals and fledgling opposition groups joined together in the dismantling of the SED citadel.

The rapid disintegration of this loose alliance and, with it, the vision of an independent, socialist GDR can be attributed in part to the massive interference of West German politicians and parties in the internal affairs of the GDR and to the rapid crumbling of Soviet-style socialism throughout Eastern Europe. Furthermore, contamination of the term 'socialism' by over 40 years of SED rule caused most East Germans to look askance at another socialist experiment. As for the citizens' movements, they lacked political experience, material resources, a well-oiled organization and a broad social base with firm roots in the working class. Having been marginalized in the alternative political culture and their ranks thinned out by Stasi repression, the citizens' movements were singularly ill-equipped for the struggle to fill the power vacuum created by the collapse of the SED. New Forum's agonizing conversion to German unity was too ambivalent and came too late for it to reap any political advantage and its stubborn refusal to adopt the status of a political party cost it dear in electoral terms.

In the final analysis, the attraction of the West German social market economy and political pluralism, as witnessed by the mass emigration before the Wall fell and the rapid entry of the GDR into the political and economic orbit of the FRG after 9–10 November, proved a much more powerful political force for the renewal of the GDR than the ill-defined concept of a 'third way'. Despite the correct diagnosis by New Forum and its allies of the social and economic problems inherent in rapid unification, they appeared to the bulk of the population as latter-day Canutes endeavouring to stop the national tide.

References

Bohley, B. (1990), *Süddentsche Zeitung*, 21 March, p. 6.
'DDR/Programm-Synopse' (1990), *Das Parlament*, (11), 9 March, pp. 4–9.
Dennis, M. (1988), *German Democratic Republic. Politics, Economy and Society*, London and New York: Pinter.
Dennis, M. (1991), 'Scientific–Technical Progress, Ideological Legitimation and Political Change in the German Democratic Republic' in M. Gerber (ed.), *Studies in GDR Culture and Society, 10*, Lanham and London: University Press of America, pp. 1–29.
Dennis, M. (1992), '"Perfecting" the Imperfect: the GDR Economy in the Honecker Era' in G-J. Glaessner, and I. Wallace (eds), *The German Revolution: Causes and Consequences*, Oxford and New York: Berg, pp. 57–83.
Donovan, B. (1989), 'Migration from the German Democratic Republic', *Radio Free Europe*, Report on Eastern Europe, Special Issue: The New Migrations, 1 December, pp. 9–12.
Fink, H-J. (1990), 'Bündnis 90, Die Revolutionäre der ersten Stunde verloren die Wahl', *Deutschland Archiv*, **23**, (4), pp. 515–17.

Forster, P. and Roski, G. (1990), *DDR zwischen Wende und Wahl Meinungsforscher analysieren den Umbruch*, Berlin: LinksDruck Verlag.

Funk, N. *et al.* (1991), 'Dossier on Women in Eastern Europe', *Social Text*, (27), pp. 88–122.

Hahn, A., Puchert, G., Schaller, H. and Scharich, L. (eds) (1990), *4. November '89. Der Protest. Die Menschen. Die Reden*, Berlin: Propyläen Verlag.

Hampele, A. (1991), 'Der Unabhängige Frauenverband' in H. Müller-Enbergs, M. Schulz, and J. Wielgohs (eds), *von der Illegalität ins Parlament Werdegang und konzept der Neuen Bürgerbewegung*, Berlin: Linsdruck Verlag, pp. 221–81.

Herles, H. and Rose, E. (eds) (1990), *Vom Runden Tisch zum Parlament*, Bonn: Bouvier Verlag.

Heym, S. (1991), 'Ash Wednesday in the GDR', *New German Critique*, (52), Winter, pp. 31–5.

Hilmer, R. and Köhler, A. (1989), 'Die DDR läuft die Zukunft davon. Die übersiedler–/Flüchtlingswelle im Sommer 1989', *Deutschland Archiv*, **22**, (12), pp. 1383–93.

'Interview with Bärbel Bohley conducted by Annette Dörfuss on 19 March 1990' (1990), *Politics and Society in Germany, Austria and Switzerland*, **2**, (3), pp. 95–8.

Kleines politisches Wörterbuch (1978), 3rd edn, Berlin: Dietz Verlag.

Knabe, H. (1990), 'Politische Opposition in der DDR. Ursprünge, Programmatik, Perspektiven', *Aus Politik und Zeitgeschichte*, (1-2), pp. 21–32.

Köhler, A. and Ronge, V. (1984), '"Einmal BRD – einfach". Die DDR-Ausreisewelle im Frühjahr 1984', *Deutschland Archiv*, **17**, (12), pp. 1260–86.

Krüger, P. T. (1990a), 'Bürgerbewegung Demokratie Jetzt, Mahner für Menschlichkeit, Mißtrauen gegenüber reiner Parteidemokratie', *Das Parlament*, 23 February–2 March, p. 17.

Krüger, P. T. (1990b), 'Programmatik der ersten Bürgerbewegung, Demokratie braucht Initiative und Phantasie', *Das Parlament*, 16 February, p. 8.

Kühnel, W. Wielgohs, J. and Schulz, M. (1990), 'Die neuen politischen Gruppierungen auf dem Wege vom politischen Protest zur parlamentarischen Interessenvertretung. Soziale Bewegungen im Umbruch der DDR-Gesellschaft', *Zeitschrift für Parlamentsfragen*, **21**, (1), pp. 22–37.

Lemke, C. (1986), 'New Issues in the Politics of the German Democratic Republic: A Question of Political Culture', *The Journal of Communist Studies*, **2**, (4), pp. 341–58.

Links, C. and Bahrmann, H. (1990), *Wir sind das Volk. Die DDR im Umbruch. Eine Chronik*, Berlin and Weimar: Aufbau Verlag and Wuppertal: Peter Hammer Verlag.

Maron, M. (1991), 'Writers and the People', *New German Critique*, (52), Winter, pp. 36–41.

Melhorn, L. (1989), in *Süddeutsche Zeitung*, 7 December, p. 14.

Mitter, A. and Wolle, S. (eds) (1990), *Ich liebe euch doch alle! Befehle und Lagerberichte des MfS Januar–November 1989*, Berlin: BasisDruck Verlag.

Opp, K-D. (1991), 'DDR '89, Zu den Ursachen einer spontanen Revolution', *Kölner Zeitschrift für Soziologie und Sozialpsychologie*, **43**, (2), pp. 302–21.

Pollack, D. (1990), 'Aussenseiter oder Repräsentanten? Zur Rolle der politisch alternativen Gruppen im gesellschaftlichen Umbruchspronzess der DDR', *Deutschland Archiv*, **23**, (8), pp. 1216–23.

Pond, E. (1990), 'A Wall Destroyed. The Dynamics of German Unification in the GDR', *International Security*, **15**, (2), pp. 35–66.

Poppe, U. (1990), 'Bürgerbewegung "Demokratie Jetzt" in H. Knabe (ed.), *Aufbruch in eine andere DDR. Reformer und oppositionelle zur Zukunft ihres Landes*. Reinbek bei Hamburg: Rowohlt Verlag, pp. 160–2.

Prins, G. (ed.) (1990), *Spring in Winter. The 1989 revolutions*, Manchester and New York: Manchester University Press.

Rein, G. (ed.) (1989), *Die Opposition in der DDR: Entwürfe für einen anderen Sozialismus*, Berlin: Wichern-Verlag.

Reissig, R. (1991), 'Vom Niedergang zum Untergang des "realen Sozialismus"', *Deutschland Archiv*, **24**, (4), pp. 395–402.

Rheinhold, O. (1989), Radio GDR talk reproduced in *Blätter für deutsche md internationale Politik*, (10), August, p. 1175.

Roth, D. (1990), 'Die Wahlen zur Volkskammer in der DDR. Der Versuch einer Erklärung', *Politische Vierteljahresschrift*, **31**, no. (3), pp. 369–93.

Schneider, R. (1990a), 'Die politische Moral ist dahin', *Der Spiegel*, 5 February, pp. 29, 31.

Schneider, R. (1990b), 'Tricks und nette Leute', *Der Spiegel*, 8 January, pp. 24–6.

Schult, R. (1990), Offen für alle: das 'Neue Forum' in Knabe (ed.), *Aufbruch in eine andere DDR. Reformer und Oppositionelle zur Zukunft ihres Landes*, Reinbek bei Hamburg: Rowohlt Verlag, pp. 163–70.

Schultz, M. (1991), 'Neues Forum' in H. Müller-Enbergs, M. Schulz and J. Wielgohs (eds.), *von der Illegalität ins Parlament. Werdegang und Konzept der neuen Bürgerbewegung*, Berlin: Linksdruck Verlag, pp. 11–104.

Sieren, F. and Koehne, L. (eds) (1990), *Günter Schabowski. Das Politbüro. Ende eines Mythos. Eine Befragung*, Reinbek bei Hamburg: Rowohlt Taschenbuch Verlag.

Spittmann, I. (1988), 'Der 17, Januar und die Folgen', *Deutschland Archiv*, 21, (3), pp. 227–32.

Süss, Walter (1990), 'Demokratischer Aufbruch, Auf der Suche nach Profil. Die Wandlungen einer jungen Partei', *Das Parlament*, 23 February–2 March, p. 17.

Süss, W. (1991), 'Mit Unwillen zur Macht. Der Runde Tisch in der übergangszeit', *Deutschland Archiv*, 24, (5), pp. 470–78.

'Die Taz' (nda), *DDR journal zur November Revolution. August bis Dezember 1989 Vom Ausreisen bis zum Einreissen der Mauer*, Frankfurt am Main: Tageszeitungsverlagsgesellschaft 'die taz'.

'Die Taz' (ndb), *DDR Journal Nr. 2. Die Wende der Wende. Januar bis März 1990. Von der öffnung des Brandenburger Tores zur öffnung der Wahlurnen*, Frankfurt am Main: Tageszeitungsverlagsgesellschaft 'die taz'.

Thaysen, U. (1990), *Der Runde Tisch. Oder: Wo blieb das Vokk?* Opladen: Westdeutscher Verlag.

Wendt, H. (1991), 'Die deutsch–deutschen Wanderungen – Bilanz einer 40 jährigen Geschichte von Flucht und Ausreise', *Deutschland Archiv*, **24**, (4), pp. 386–95.

Wielgohs, J. (1991), 'Die vereinigte Linke' in H. Muller-Enbergs, M. Schulz and J. Wielgohs (eds), *von der Illegalitat ins Parlament. Werdegang und Konzept der neuen Bürgerbewegungen*, Berlin: Linksdruck Verlag, pp. 283–306.

Wielgohs, J. and Schulz, M. (1990). 'Reformbewegung und Volksbewegung. Politische und soziale Aspekte im Umbruch der DDR-Gesellschaft', *Aus Politik und Zeitgeschichte*, (16–17), pp. 15–24, *Wochenpost* (1990), **37**, (11), pp. 4–5.

Zimmerling, Z. and Zimmerling, S. (eds) (1990), *Neue Chronik DDR. Berichte, Fotos, Dokumente, 4/5. Folge. 23. Dezember 1989–18. März 1990*, Berlin: Verlag Tribüne.

Zur Person. Friedrich Schorlemmer, Lothar de Maiziere, Gregor Gysi, Ingrid Köppe, Christoph Hein, Hans Modrow. Sechs Porträts in Frage und Antwort von Günter Gaus (1990), Berlin: Verlag Volk und Welt.

9   Concepts of Party Democracy in the East

Eva Kolinsky

The concept of party democracy has been developed to clarify how the linkage between people and state administration can be accomplished in mass societies. When democracy implied a limited franchise, informal networks may have sufficed. As the right of participation was extended to most or all adults, special organizational channels and formal procedures had to be instituted as the foundation of democracy. Political parties are such institutions. They emerged to pool and articulate the demands and expectations which inspired society or specific groups or classes within it. (von Beyme, 1985: 11 ff).

Party democracy refers, in the first instance, to the function which political parties fulfil as a link between society and policy-making at the state level. In government, they would shape policies; in opposition influence and monitor them; in parliament, they would contribute to political communication, policy-making and legislative action (Oberreuter, 1990; Sarcinelli, 1987). This broad meaning of party democracy is flanked by a second: the notion that parties should be constituted internally in a democratic manner in order to allow the transfer of popular demands to state policies, and invite the participation of those people or groups which they set out to represent (Oberreuter and Mintzel, 1987; Smith, 1990: 83 ff). Party democracy thus refers to party cultures, the recruitment and involvement of members, the function of party congresses, responsiveness to their electorate, and the impact of members or voters on the policy agendas (Greven, 1987).

Given their pivotal role in mass democracies, we might ask whether political parties meet the expectations invested in them – that they should be faithful and impartial mediators between people and state? From the outset, they have had a bad press. In the German state tradition, governments have always presented themselves as *überparteilich* (above-party). Parties tended to be vilified as distorters, rather than facilitators, of popular demands, as agents of quarrel and discord in a political process which was said to depend on consensus and shared responsibility for its success (Tempel, 1990: 32). Early in the twentieth century Robert Michels argued that the organizational structure of parties was intrinsically undemocratic and would always produce oligarchies and control by a few from the top down (Michels, 1954). Distrust of parties extended to parliaments which seemed mere talking-shops in a culture which disparaged talk and favoured executive government and strong action (Röhrich, 1983: 30 ff). In the Weimar Republic, the party democracy prescribed by the constitution turned into anti-party democracy: in recruiting for cabinet posts for instance, parliamentary membership or party involvement were deemed secondary to an executive track record or a special link with a powerful segment of society such as the military, the business community, or the big landowner interests in the East. While the organizational function of party remained, and even increased, its salience in the Weimar years, the function of party as a mainstay of parliamentary democracy and democratic government was rejected, or won only conditional acceptance.

The destruction of party democracy through the might of the National Socialist party organization – fortified by paramilitary formations and open hostility to the concept and institutional channels of democracy – smashed the parliamentary role of parties while leaving their organizational force and function intact as party and state merged and decreed to the people. Backed by police terror, manipulative propaganda and physical coercion, party and state organization became so closely intertwined that society was denied at voice. The core of party democracy, the dynamic and uncertain balance between interests, expectations, organizations, preferences and policies, between people's concerns and the state's agendas were eradicated in the National Socialist political system (Kershaw, 1990).

Concepts of Party Democracy: East and West

Recasting Germany after National Socialism meant recasting party democracy, rebuilding party organizations and re-establishing their role as intermediaries between society and state. On paper, the two Germanies on either side of the Iron Curtain claimed to abide by democratic principles, and to contain a plurality of parties to maintain the link between society and state; in short, each presented itself as a party democracy (Weidenfeld and Zimmermann, 1989). However, this semantic unison obscures both the rift between the two 'democracies' and the different function of political parties in each. Party democracy in the Federal Republic assumes interparty competition; it assumes that the party or coalition which wins the majority of votes in an election will command the majority of seats in the respective parliament and constitute the government. Party democracy also assumes a legitimate role for opposition both inside and outside parliaments (Smith *et al.*, 1989; Smith, 1986). It also implies that political opinion and political action can originate from groups, movements, media or individuals outside party organizations or parliaments (Dalton, 1988; Kolinsky, 1987).

The East German notion of democracy related quite differently to party. True to communist doctrine, the Socialist Unity Party, which was created in April 1946 through an enforced merger of the Communist party and the Social Democratic party in the Soviet Zone of Occupation, decreed that it represented the interests of the key segment of society – the working class – and was therefore entitled to maintain overall control in the polity (Weber, 1985; Sontheimer and Bleeck, 1975). However, strictly speaking, the GDR was neither a one-party state nor a party democracy in the Western mould. Although several political parties existed, there was no electoral competition between them, since the number of seats they were entitled to hold in the national parliament (*Volkskammer*) had been predetermined and the segment of the population that they were supposed to represent had been allocated to them. In effect they operated within the parameters defined for them by the state party (the SED). Within these parameters, they took in the permitted number of members, maintained an extensive, officially approved and funded network of party offices, and played the political role deemed appropriate for all political forces in the GDR: to acclaim the state leadership, and applaud the policies which originated in the SED and dominated the state (Lapp, 1988). Their political role was that of acquiescence within the National Front alongside the state trade unions (FDGB), the women's association (DFB), the state youth organization (FDJ) and other approved mass organizations. Each held a set number of seats in parliament.

The East German system purported to be democratic because it had institutionalized the representation of approved groups and sectors of society and guaranteed their official participation. Thus party democracy, in East German mode, referred to a pre-arranged division of political control: it was a political system in which one party monopolized the articulation of the presumed will of the people and the determination of matters of state, supplemented by block parties devoid of political power but entrusted with the task of integrating groups which, in the 1940s and early 1950s, had perhaps been reluctant to embrace state socialism and whose separate channels had since become an East German state tradition in their own right (Glaessner, 1990; Staritz, 1989).

Party Democracy and the New Participatory Agendas

Between the inception of the two German states in 1949 and their unification in 1990, one key dimension of party democracy changed dramatically: the balance between society and state and the presumed pivotal function of political parties in linking the two. In the West, party democracy initially replicated Weimar patterns in that party support was determined by such social factors as class, region, religious observance or trade union orientation (Padgett and Burkett, 1986; Rohe, 1990). However, since the mid-1960s the 'frozen party system' has been mobilized by the cross-pressures of dissatisfaction with the parties' responsiveness to citizens' expectations and West Germans' increased resourcefulness Germans in articulating their expectations, raising issues and also developing the confidence that individuals and their political activities could influence state agendas (Jesse, 1990). From 'democrats-by-the-book' who regarded democracy as a set of rules to be followed and procedures to be adhered to, West Germans of the post-war generations – the children of democracy and affluence – had turned into 'issue democrats', willing and eager to champion various causes and increasingly prepared to change their electoral preference towards the party perceived as most competent to deliver their desired policies (Kolinsky, 1991a).

In the 1970s and 1980s, environmentalism and equal opportunities for women emerged as issues which were capable of cutting across established party allegiances. No less relevant for electoral volatility have been conventional concerns about economic stability, unemployment and the personal quality of life. As traditional party loyalties have lost their prominence, electoral decisions have become individualized, compelling parties to fight for the electoral support which they may have taken for granted in the past. Party competition has intensified, as has the need for parties to remain flexible and responsive to the issues which move and mobilize society (Niedermayer and Stöss, forthcoming). Education has recast the West German electorate: not only has access to advanced secondary and higher education soared since the 1950s, it has also changed its political significance. In the past, the educated few tended to locate themselves on the right wing of the political spectrum; they were forces of conservatism or German nationalism in its various guises. Since the mid-1960s, access to advanced education has tended to correspond with political orientations towards the left of centre and a new emphasis on non-party participation in politics through action groups, initiatives and new social movements (Kolinsky, 1984; Rohe, 1990). The Green party, with its dual focus on participatory party styles, is both a product and beneficiary of these orientations.

At the threshold of unification, West German political parties were grappling to secure or create a foothold in society; none could ignore the themes of the others in case they were salient, and none could rely on voters, or even members, who would offer unqualified support and toe the party line without reservations or an eye to changing their preferences altogether. It has been suggested that political parties in general were at risk of being upstaged by social movement and non-parliamentary opposition, since these forces were poised to capitalize on both long-standing and new reservations about their overall relevance, usefulness and political trustworthiness (Dalton, 1989; Wasmuth 1989; Roth and Rucht, 1987). These developments have compelled political parties to be less complacent about their support base and to make special efforts to retain or extend their following. By the time unification brought the system of separate party democracies in a divided Germany to an end, the social basis of party politics in West Germany had become sufficiently assertive to leave its imprint on party actions and state agendas (Urwin and Paterson, 1990).

State-administered 'Democracy': the East German Model

In the East, the socialist version of party democracy failed to undergo a similar development of responding to demands emanating from society, and the SED continued to formulate policies from the top down until the very end of the GDR. Party congresses, public occasions, party-affiliated organizations, the *Volkskammer* and the media all combined to instruct the population in political direction and present their aims and results as positive and desirable (Voigt *et. al.*, 1987: 242 ff).

However, two further aspects of the GDR policy process need to be taken into account to complete the picture of the *vormundschaftlicher Staat*, the authoritarian and bureaucratic state administration which characterized the East German state (Henrich, 1989). The first concerns the state security system, the Stasi; the second the steady flow of refugees from the GDR since its inception.

The political system in the GDR depended, for its political survival, on the Iron Curtain between the Eastern and Western blocs and on the Soviet military presence and the ever-present threat that Soviet tanks would crush any forces of change as they had done in Berlin in 1953, in Hungary in 1956, and in Czechoslovakia in 1968. In addition, East Germany developed an internal system of surveillance, control and repression – the *Staatssicherheitsdienst* or Stasi. The organization and political importance of the Stasi has remained obscure. For some, the whole of the GDR can be compared to a concentration camp, and the whole of the East German state and party machinery seemed to be designed only to perform a hatchet job on freedom and human rights. Others attempted to detach themselves from anti-communist prejudice and regard the GDR as just another polity – indeed, in the field of women's equality or educational provisions, even as a model to its Western democratic neighbours (Backes and Jesse, 1985: 74 ff). The key role of the Stasi at the interface between state and society inside the GDR has been further obscured by the various spy scandals which seemed to indicate that the principal interest of East German state security had been to gather information and break the code of state secrecy in the West.

Unification, and the subsequent access to Stasi files, revealed that internal state security meant, in the first instance, the exercise of social and political control over the GDR population by recruiting about one in four citizens as informers, in return for real or presumed privileges (Fricke, 1989). The vast quantities of Stasi files may be seen as evidence of a proverbial German thoroughness but, more importantly, they are evidence of the fact that there was no dynamic balance in the GDR between state and society – the balance to which parties contribute in democratic settings. Rather, the state's uncertainties about the orientations, loyalties and pressures for change in society gave rise to a system of control and intimidation, a *Schnüffelgesellschaft* (spying society) designed to enforce compliance with the party line (Mitter and Wolle, 1990; Meier, 1990).

The second special feature of the GDR policy process which inhibited a dynamic link between society and the state concerns the flow of refugees. Since the foundation of their state, and throughout its existence, East Germans have looked towards the West as a refuge – an environment in which they could live the life they wanted to, hold views or engage in activities which were outlawed in the East and escape the intimidations and limitations imposed by the socialist party, state and their security apparatus. Exporting dissent – political, artistic, social or economic – has been a major feature of East German political life. Even before the mass exodus in 1989 which led to the collapse of the GDR, about one in four GDR citizens fled to the West (Baumann *et. al.*, 1990: 134; Ronge, 1990: 39 f). The construction of the Berlin Wall in 1961 and the hermetic closure of the German–German border had been intended to halt the flow of refugees which depleted the country's skilled workforce and human resources. Although the numbers of refugees declined in the face of the massive deployment of border guards with orders to shoot to kill, the official intent to generate a new GDR consciousness – a positive identification with the East German state and society which would induce people to stay – did not succeed as hoped. Forced to stay in the country, those who were dissatisfied with their living conditions, held dissenting views or were impatient to see changes now sought GDR-internal channels to articulate them – channels which the *vormundschaftliche Staat* could not and would not offer (Fricke, 1984; Knabe, 1989). Despite the risks, GDR citizens continued to escape from their state. Increasingly, however, the state took to exporting potential troublemakers to the West, and to legalizing emigration (Grundmann, 1990).

In the event, the state proved unable to impose socialist homogeneity or enforce the party monopoly of social activity and political orientation, and the 1970s and 1980s witnessed the emergence of a diversified opposition in the GDR (Woods, 1986). Sheltered from political interference by the Protestant Church which provided meeting places and venues for discussion, GDR citizens began to create and use a niche of unprecedented freedom from prescribed socialist practice (Bickhardt, 1988; Helwig and Urban, 1987: 93 ff). Where earlier generations acquiesced while making, as the German proverb goes, a fist in their pocket, the generations who had grown up in the GDR were little different from their Western counterparts – assertive in their expectations about the life they wished to lead and about the shortcomings of state administrations and policy-makers in meeting these expectations. The peace groups, prayer meetings and discussion circles which had perforated the prescribed version of party democracy in East Germany in the decade before unification can be seen as the equivalent of citizens' initiatives, new social movements and the new volatility of party preferences in the West.

The change in the political culture from corporate obedience to civil disobedience mirrors participatory pressures in West German party democracy. In the East, a specific set of social and political factors aided the political culture change which culminated in the collapse of the state. Access to Western television programmes and a relaxation of travel restrictions in the wake of *Ostpolitik* consolidated the positive image of Western lifestyles which had always filled popular beliefs in the GDR. No less important was the sense of relative deprivation. Compared to West Germans, citizens in the GDR had to endure long working hours, earned lower wages and lived in poor-standard housing. Aspirations to purchase consumer durables and luxury items could not be satisfied, since goods were either unavailable or of such poor quality that they fell too far short of Western models. In addition, the GDR economy, which had been hailed as the model economy of the Eastern bloc, had accumulated massive deficits since the 1970s and living standards, which seemed poised to rise in the early 1970s stagnated.

Rewarding political conformity with privileged access to consumer goods and affluent lifestyles remained one of the most effective devices of social control to the very end of the East German state. The opening-up of Wandlitz, the special housing complex for the political élite, revealed that GDR leaders had surrounded themselves with Western goods and created an enclave of luxury living within a shortage society. The Wandlitz revelations unleashed a popular wave of resentment and sense of betrayal. In essence, GDR citizens had known since the introduction of the Intershop system, where foreign currency would buy goods and services which were beyond the reach of ordinary GDR wage earners, that the material and personal limitations of GDR life did not apply to those who enjoyed positions of privilege (Voigt *et. al.*, 1987: 120 ff). Political élites and those prepared to toe the party or Stasi line were rewarded through access to consumer goods. Conversely, having to wait (and register on waiting lists) to obtain goods could be turned into a means of enforcing political compliance among ordinary citizens. In contrast to the 1950s and 1960s, when positions of privilege seemed to be reserved for members of the working class and East German society seemed to thrive on opening opportunities to the disadvantaged, élites have since engaged in the same cycle of self-recruitment so familiar in Western societies (Süss, 1990: 909–10). Education and qualifications which should have supported mobility, were increasingly blunted as means of change and used to underpin existing structures of political control and power. Contrary to the promise underlying the socialist state that opportunities to advance are open to all, the average citizen in the GDR perceived opportunities as restricted, both in terms of access to coveted positions of leadership or privilege, and in terms of rewarding efforts and commitment.

This sense of disappointment and lack of opportunity was decisive for the mass exodus from the GDR in 1989. The first signs of a rift between citizens and state had been visible in the mid-1980s when officially commissioned surveys of young people suggested that only those on the privileged track of higher education expressed the views expected of them. Indeed, young workers and apprentices were so hesitant to endorse the prescribed views that the survey results remained unpublished until after unification (Friedrich, 1990). The SED's determination to ignore the unexpected detachment of young workers highlights a major weakness in the East German version of party democracy: a rigid separation and state policy-making from the citizenry. This separation does not mean that the state did not aim to look after its people. Paternalistic acts of generosity included special legislation to assist working mothers to cope with housework or care for their sick children, and arranging special deliveries of Volkswagen Golf cars or bananas at Christmas time. These acts constituted the reverse side of the Stasi state. However, neither party, state administration or the Stasi could cope with the restiveness of a people who had lost confidence in the leadership's ability to meet their expectations of a better, more affluent and freer life – a lifestyle which seemed to blossom in the neighbouring countries to the West and to the East, and to which the GDR citizen seemed to be excluded (Friedrich, W-U., 1989: 13–27).

Party Democracy: Issues and Alternatives

The East German local elections of 17 May 1989, which should have been no more than a routine event in a state used to administering elections with near 100 per cent support for the National Front, brought an unexpected result: a public accusation of electoral fraud and an official complaint filed with the courts by the Protestant Church. These objections were the first rumblings of the 'gentle revolution' which later that year toppled the leadership of party and state, ended the political monopoly of the socialist party, introduced multi-partism and forced the SED to grapple for a new name (Party of Democratic Socialism) and a mellower profile. The step from the niche of dissent into the footlights of public protest in May 1989 marked the beginning of the end for the SED version of party democracy and the coming of age for the political forces which have been termed as the GDR opposition.

In 1988, an estimated 325 groups existed in the GDR, all articulating alternative concepts of social and political life (Klessmann, 1991: 62). Organizational structures and programmatic alternatives to official policies, which set opposition apart from dissent (Minnerup, 1989), began to emerge more clearly after the summer of 1989. By December the one-party state had collapsed, parliamentary democracy was revitalized and the GDR had several new parties and political movements eager to influence the course of politics. In June 1989, Democratic Awakening (DA) and Democracy Now (DJ) were founded, both rooted in Church-based opposition. In September 1989, the New Forum applied for (and repeatedly failed to win) official recognition as a political group. October 1989 saw the beginnings of a new Social Democratic Party, the SDP (later adjusted to SPD), and of a Vereinigte Linke. In November the Green party was founded as a prospective sister party of the West German Greens (Spittmann and Helwig, 1989). As the campaign got under way for the first free elections in East Germany, others followed: an Independent Women's Association (Unabhängiger Frauen Verband) in December 1989; the CSU partner, DSU, and the Deutsche Forumspartei (DFP) as a conservative alternative to the New Forum in January 1990, and especially the reorganization and reprofiling of the former bloc parties. By February 1990 the GDR could boast a multi-party system with over 40 separate groups and 23 competitors for parliamentary seats (Gibowski, 1990). The electoral developments since the change to multi-partyism confirmed what the undercurrent of discontent and detachment had signalled for decades: that the former one-party government could rely on little more than its clientele of officials, functionaries and members of the nomenclatura (that is, less than 15 per cent of the electorate).

Neither the concept of democracy nor the programmes of the new parties were decisive for the outcome of the elections of March 1990 and the drive towards monetary union and political unification which followed. The elections can be understood as a plebiscite for quick unification – a plebiscite against the very existence of the GDR. The major political parties which contested the elections and dominated the political process in the former GDR since the demise of SED–PDS control have been the main parties of West Germany, while the citizens' movements and opposition groups which emerged during the transformation of the GDR were unable to consolidate their position and sustain their initial promise that they might become innovative and decisive political forces. Even the East German SPD, which merged with its Western sister party in September 1990 and has secured a parliamentary role – albeit at a much reduced scale than had been expected – failed to consolidate its organization, let alone win new support.

The concepts of democracy which clinched the political mood in the GDR were those of the West or, to put it more accurately, concepts of democracy were less important than perceptions about the quickest way in which the difference between lifestyles and conditions in the two Germanies could be removed.

Yet the party programmes for March 1990 found a tone of their own. They called for 'solidarity' more emphatically than programmes in the Federal Republic; some even referred to the awkward past. The programme of the CDU-Ost contained an admission of 'our guilt in the deformations which we together with all citizens in our country are suffering' (*Das Parlament*, 11, 9 March, 1990) Generally speaking, the programmes of the new era avoided focusing on the GDR past of subservience to the SED and system support by the bloc parties, mass organizations and sizeable segments of the population (Klingemann and Volkens, 1991).

Common to all programmes – regardless of political orientation – was the issue of environmental protection. As a Green topic it could be regarded as unclaimed by traditional ideologies, not directly political and somewhat above-party. For the CDU (East) it constituted 'a human right' (*Das Parlament*, 11, 1990: 6); the DSU spoke of 'preservation and restoration of the natural bases of life' while Democratic Awaking, the third member of the conservative Alliance for Germany presented a detailed catalogue of measures from data protection to phasing out lignite use in industrial production and halting the construction of nuclear power plants (Weilemann *et al.*, 1990a). The Liberal parties (DFP, FDP and LDP) warned against environmental dangers to the lives of people now and in the future. The PDS, under whose control environmental considerations had been ignored, proclaimed bluntly: 'the quality of the environment is identical with the quality of life' (*Das Parlament*, 11, 1990: 6). For the NDPD, 'ecological security' rested on extensive legislation while the SPD, Greens, Women's Movement and the Bündnis 90 which inherited some of the political concerns of the New Forum demanded an economy dominated and inspired by environmental priorities. For the Greens, environmental destruction belonged to the same legacy of the GDR past as socialist economic incompetence:

> Hopeless economic mismanagement during the last decades severely disrupted the ecological balance and impeded the quality of life. It is of paramount importance to halt this detrimental development and to leave a naturally sound environment for our children. (*Das Parlament*, 11, 1990: 7)

The frequent reference to ecology may reflect a growing concern among citizens of the collapsing GDR about the environmental pollution in many parts of their country (Deutschland Archiv, 1985). There is little evidence that environmental protection has emerged as a major political concern among former East Germans since unification removed the obstacle of illegality. The new German *Länder* (that is, the former GDR) and the federal government in Bonn regard environmental protection as a priority and are poised to salvage the highly polluted areas in the East. As yet, there is no flourishing subculture of environmental action groups which would suggest that Green concerns were popular concerns. Although 92 per cent of former East Germans expected that unification would also bring improvements to the environment, they tend to look toward state actions and public measures, not to diverse activities and individual participation (Feist and Hoffmann, 1991: 11).

The emphasis on environmental protection in the early party programmes may be regarded as an attempt to focus on a topical theme which had been neglected by the SED, and which was a front-runner in the West. The environmental focus can also be understood as subterfuge: the call for an ecological future frees the caller from the necessity to spell out in detail which institutions might support it and which processes would put it into place. As a demand for a completely new format to conduct policies and make them relevant for the people, the environmental theme dovetails with the only concrete aspect to emerge from the party programmes: a condemnation of the old system, especially the breakdown of trust between state and society, government and people. The founding statement of New Forum put it forcefully:

In our country, communication between state and society has obviously been disrupted. Evidence for this are a widespread hopelessness, a withdrawal into a private niche or into mass exodus. ... The disrupted relationship between state and society paralyses the creative potential of society and makes it more difficult to tackle the pressing local and global tasks. We get bogged down in grumpy passivity while more urgent things would need to be done for our life, our country and mankind. (cited Schüddekopf, 1990: 29)

New Forum envisaged a change towards democracy which would stop short of the unrestricted competition and the cut-throat ethos of an achievement-based society by preserving communal dimensions of socialist life, and an atmosphere of solidarity.

We want room for economic initiatives but we do not want the denaturation into an elbow-society. We want to keep the good yet create room for innovation, in order to live more naturally and less in conflict with nature. We want orderly circumstances but no ordering about. We want to be free and self-confident people, yet act in a communal spirit. We want to be protected against violence without having to tolerate a state of lackeys and spies. (cited Schüddekopf, 1990: 29)

The September statement of the New Forum opened the floodgates for a stream of public pronouncements from actors, artists, trade unionists and individuals. With variations in the small print, they aimed at ridding East Germany of the bureaucratic government and party dominance. The political transformation which the declarations and pronouncements advocated was to result in the rebirth of the GDR as a socialist society:

Socialism has to find its own democratic format if it is to survive. ... We want that the socialist revolution which has stagnated in nationalization, is continued and made viable for the future. (Democracy Now cited Schüddekopf, 1990: 32–5; see also Müller–Enbergs, 1990)

'Socialism must be made newly attractive and motivate everyone into identifying with it' (Open letter to FDGB leadership; cited Schüddekopf, 1990: 46). Calling for a better socialism meant calling for a new scope for citizens to participate in their social and political environment.

Socialism, which also regards itself as an alternative concept to a bourgeois world order, is designed to serve the people, and the majority of the people have to take part in it and thus give it the necessary material, intellectual and moral vitality to succeed. (Praesidium of the GDR Academy of Culture; cited, Schüddekopf, 1990: 62)

The participation of citizens is a recurring theme – not only in contrast to established East German practices but as a corrective to presumed weaknesses of parliamentary government and party organizations. Politics, in the words of a local politician from New Forum, tends to be

> ... degenerated into party politics since the individual concerns of each citizen will be ignored as soon as party programmes take centre stage. We have experiences of this with the previously almighty party, but this danger exists with all parties. I believe ... a citizens' movement is essential to create a democracy. (Kleemann, 1990)

The focus on democracy in the East was characterized by a desire to improve rather than join the parliamentary democracy which had emerged in the West.

While the aversion against party organizations may be explained as an aversion against too much socialist party bureaucracy and added little to the ongoing debate about party cultures in West Germany, the focus on the nature of parliamentary democracy struck a more potent chord. Introducing elements of direct democracy in order to give citizens a regular say in representative democratic systems constituted a prominent feature of the demands for democracy which originated in the GDR. In February 1990, Democracy Now proclaimed:

> Parliamentary democracy does not reduce or even replace the responsibility of men and women in our society. This is why we wish to extend citizens participation and create a more effective right of petition. Within limits to be determined by legislation, a system of referenda [*Volksbegehren und Volksentscheid*] at local, regional and national level will complement and complete parliamentary decision making. (*Zeitung der Bürgerbewegung*, **13**, February 1990)

In a similar vein, the East German SPD distanced itself from the *Vertretungsdemokratie* – a democratic system of mere representation – and pledged to add elements of direct democracy (*Volksbegehren and Volksentscheide*). Uncertainty about the legitimacy of parliamentary majority decisions surfaced also in the national–conservative NDPD, a bloc party since 1948 with a strongly national profile, which argued that a new constitution would have to be approved by a referendum in order to reflect the will of the people (Weilemann *el al.*, 1990b). Since unification, the focus on direct democracy has inspired the debate over whether the Basic Law should be replaced and whether a new German constitution should follow the old *Länder* and make provisions for citizens' participation in politics through plebiscites, in addition to elections (Evers, 1991; Gebhardt, 1991).

Democracy as Dialogue

The agenda for public debate, political demands and for the SED government's rearguard actions in the final months of the GDR was accompanied, and also created, by the unprecedented number of public statements and appeals (Bahrmann and Links, 1990; Weber, 1990). The polyphony of views and the urge to take a public stand after decades of intimidation and criminalization of individual beliefs and opinions can be regarded as a form of civil disobedience and deliberate defiance of the official, prescribed views. Decisive, however, in raising demands, and in forcing the government to act, were the public demonstrations which dominated the political process in the GDR between October 1989 and March 1990 (Blanke and Erd, 1990). Discussions of political alternatives, which had previously taken place inside Church circles, now expanded into the public sphere. For the first time since the early 1950s, the people attempted to challenge the state and confront it with popular demands and expectations (*Gegenwartskunde*, 1991). The recent publication of Stasi documents has revealed how significant and persistent a drive for more democracy occurred in the early 1950s and how ruthlessly mass arrests and internal repression were employed to curb it (Mitter and Wolle, 1990; *Der Spiegel*, 22, 1991: 88–93). In the late 1980s the SED was foiled in its bid for Soviet military (and even political) support and was forced to find a political response of a kind which had hitherto been unnecessary: a response which would appeal to the population and would restore the credibility of the government. Detailed studies of the decision-making process in the SED and the sequence of the leadership change have revealed the inability of the party to grasp the force and the range of the pent-up resentments and demands which now began to surface.

From the vantage point of the people, democracy initially seemed to mean freedom to travel – ending the isolation from the outside world and allowing people mobility in Western, as well as Eastern, countries. Had *Reisefreiheit* meant no more than ease of travel, the government's promise of a new law – albeit in its usual bureaucratic language and fraught with trip-wire clauses – may have been welcomed as evidence that a new relationship, a dialogue between state and people, was under way. To establish such a dialogue was an early core demand: democracy was perceived as communication and cooperation between the two sides of a polity – a consensus between policy-makers on the one hand, and the people on the other. The call for dialogue had been intended as a device 'to reform this [GDR] system, to turn it into something which is really new and capable of becoming a new type of society, a community which might offer a future to mankind' (Kuby, 1990: 35). Based on dialogue, democracy seemed to promise a political environment in which all would be involved, and the emergence of a common ground as the foundation for political action. As Democracy Now put it:

> ... democratic argumentation is being eager to hear all differing views. It is not served by partial interests since putting them into practice would only cause problems in the long run if general agreement had not been forthcoming from all sides. Democratic argumentation is only interested in the truth. (Democracy Now publication, September 1989)

The urge for dialogue in the collapsing GDR generated two political 'institutions': first, the 'political public' (Süss, 1990), the protest culture of street demonstrations, chants and placards; and the second the so-called Round Table (Thaysen, 1990a; 1990b). Both these 'institutions' made a significant contribution to the collapse of the political system in the former GDR and the political reorientation which followed (see Chapter 8).

The People's Voice against their Masters

The use of the streets as a means to display the link between state and society, between government and people has been an integral part of the political culture in the GDR. Demonstrations used to be official show-piece acts, organized by the party and its affiliated associations, and used to underline how firmly rooted among the working people state and party were. The GDR population was accustomed to a political street culture, albeit ordered from above. They would be supplied with placards and approved slogans (permitted captions were published in the SED-controlled *Neues Deutschland* on the eve of such demonstrations) and would comply.

In the autumn of 1989, street demonstrations were able to build on this accepted form of political participation and become a numerically powerful and politically articulate platform, designed to show what demonstrations had always meant to show – the views of the people. Only this time, the views were not preformulated by the party functionaries but reflected discontent; the demonstrations served as a sounding-board for specific demands and as a means of expressing a breakaway from the East German state tradition. One of the hallmarks of this political street culture was the imaginative range and variety of the critical comment which could now be publicly directed against the government; it also suggested that the dislike of, and suspicions against, the aims and actions of the state leadership which hitherto had only found expression in the privacy of the

Nischengesellschaft were sufficiently intensive and consistent to be regarded as nascent opposition.

Unauthorized demonstrations began in the GDR on 7 October when tens of thousands called for freedom of speech and political reforms in several East German cities. Police and security forces used considerable force to crush the demonstration; many demonstrators were injured, and an estimated 1,000 people were arrested. Two days later, 70,000 extended the prayers for peace, which had become a regular event in Leipzig every Monday, and demonstrated in the streets. It was at this point that a flare-up into civil war might have occurred and was prevented by a joint appeal for calm and a promise of 'dialogue' agreed ad hoc between spokesmen for the people and Churches (particularly Kurt Masur, the director of the Gewandhaus orchestra, and the pastor, Peter Zimmermann) and the local SED administration. The following was broadcast on local radio, relayed through loudspeakers and read out from the pulpits as the demonstration got under way:

> We all need a free exchange of views about the continuation of socialism in our country. We therefore promise all citizens today that this dialogue will be conducted, not just in the district of Leipzig but with our government as well. (*Chronik*, 1989: 18–19)

The non-interference of the GDR security forces was an essential precondition for the articulation of public views which was to follow. Its importance in encouraging people to speak their minds, and quell the fears on which the GDR *Schnüffelgesellschaft* had been built, cannot be overestimated. Its importance, also, in radicalizing the political climate and leading from calls for reform to calls for an abolition of the East German state itself is equally great. It has been argued that the demands of GDR citizens focused on unification and on joining the West German political and economic system once they realized how corrupt their leadership had been and that improvements could not be expected from them (Knabe, 1990). However, a more pragmatic argument is that unification drowned the search for political reforms within the GDR once people realized that most of them were implicated by their socialist past and would have to account for their misdemeanours in a new GDR, while the *tabula rasa* of unification would bury the past with its state (Süss, 1990: 912).

The clearest concept of democracy to emerge from the demonstrations concerned the relationship between state and society. 'We are the people' – the slogan which dominated GDR demonstrations between October and December 1989 – challenged the legitimacy of party and state to speak for a people whose concerns they did not know. The fundamental message 'We are the people – and not the SED' was embellished and elaborated in many ways: 'SED alone – this must not be'; 'Cut down the functionaries – save the trees' or aimed at the leadership 'We are the people – you can go' are examples of a mass public rejection of the socialist party state. Power to the people meant demotion of those who abused that power for so long: 'My suggestions for the First of May – the leadership files past the people.' Christa Wolf spoke of 'literary abilities of the people' a 'state people which went onto the streets in order to recognize itself as a people' (Wolf, 1989). Helga Königsdorf raises an equally important point when she explains the powerful momentum of the search for change with the severity of the repression which preceded it:

> Perhaps one could say that the largest guilt of the past has been: to impose on the individual such a massive contempt and humiliation that people internalised them. Believing that the individual was worth nothing outside a higher, collective goal. How open to abuse is a human being who has been robbed in this way of his inner sovereignty! (cited Gotschlich, 1990: 7)

From December 1989 onwards, the demonstrating public chanted a different message: no longer aimed persuasively, or in a confrontational manner, at bringing those in power to their senses or instigating a change of leadership, the message now read: 'We are one people'. The surrounding statements had also changed: 'If the Deutschmark does not come to us, we shall go and join it'. The swing from GDR internal restructuring to unification came about one month after the opening of the Berlin Wall allowed millions of East Germans to visit West Germany and taste the freedom to travel which they had demanded for so long; it came as the mass exodus of people had been reduced but not halted, and it came after the changes in the SED and state leadership had failed to renew confidence and cooperation but rather had, with freedom of speech and a new investigative persistence of the media and the public, lifted the lid high enough for people to see the system of corruption and privilege, and to experience a sense of betrayal (Niethammer, 1990).

The sense of having been deceived by those in power was similar to that reported about the immediate post-war years after the defeat of National Socialism. The generations of those who had believed in National Socialism, who had served its presumed ideals and had given their best, felt sufficiently disillusioned to reject all political involvement in the founding years of the Federal Republic. In the GDR, the sceptical generation syndrome did not take root: it was the young who broke ranks with the subservience culture and began the exodus to the West. For those who were disillusioned and thought that their individual commitment and hard work had been squandered, unification offered a perspective (Ronge, 1990; Friedrich, 1990).

The sceptical generation now consisted of the original perpetrators of change: the critics, intellectuals or writers, the founders of citizens' movements or New Forum which continued to strive to improve socialism while the majority of the population had written it off and expected nothing from it for their future.

It would be erroneous to regard the public call for unification, which erupted in demonstrations in December 1989 and swiftly rewrote the political agendas of 1990 in both East and West, as a falsification of the political will in the GDR or as a plant by the Kohl government to capitalize on the issue of unity in the run-up to national elections (see, for example, Grass, 1990). The two-phased articulation of the relationship between people and state which emerged in the street culture of demonstrations in the GDR cannot be explained as people changing their minds. Rather, it was based on two different layers of political opinion: the corrective to the state implied in 'we are the people' emanated from intellectuals, writers, Church activists and young educated people eager to link the GDR with the most progressive developments in the Eastern bloc. The later 'we are one people' brought a different category of demonstrators into the streets – the parents of many who had left the GDR, the middle-aged, the working people whose standard of living had declined and who had no prospects of gaining access to the privileged track of consumerism and affluence. For them, a decent lifestyle, prospects, and a future for themselves, their families and children had been unobtainable in the GDR but seemed obtainable in the West where opportunities seemed to be more closely tied to individual commitment and effort. The image of the West moulded the political aims of GDR citizens and underlined the chasm which had opened not only with the government and top leadership but also within society itself, between a slim sector of the potentially privileged and the proverbial 'small man in the street'. For the latter, democracy meant, above all, opportunities to achieve a good standard of living and a fair society, something the West and its system seemed to offer more realistically than the East.

In the elections of 1990, the GDR population cast its vote in support of the CDU – that is, in support of the one party which seemed most competent to put unification into practice. In her essay on the shift from internal reform of the GDR to its abolition, the former East German writer Monika Maron highlights the complexities and uncertain consequences of the events which have become known as a 'revolution'

> The complaints about the wrong results of the revolution are based on the wrong assessment of what has been happening. It began with the call: 'Let's get out of the GDR' and ended – via the defiant sentence: we are staying – quite logically in the judgement: 'Let's get rid of the GDR.' ... Only this generated

the thesis that the revolution had already devoured its firstborn children. These firstborn were the children of those who later chanted; Germany, United Father-land! The firstborn children of the revolution were the refugees. A second error is needed to desire in all honesty a separate or relatively separate development of an East German state, and this error is guarded by the West German left like a treasure: the error that there ever existed something which could be called a GDR-specific identity. If something like this has come to the fore at all then in the guise of fear: fear of the market economy, fear of drugs and aids, fear of foreigners, for of the future and fear of the phantom of freedom. To stop this kind of fear, one would have to shut the gates of the Wall again. (Maron, 1990: 70)

Democracy in the Making: Institutional and Personal Dimensions

The hiatus between popular concerns and policy-making which gave rise to the dual culture of a private orientation to the West and a public compliance with the prescribed system and ideology, could only be bridged if a new linkage of democratic government and accountability could be forged be-tween the two. In the four months between the breaching of the Berlin Wall in November 1989 and the first democratic parliamentary elections in the collapsing GDR in March 1990, various futile attempts were made to recast the GDR from within. The most conspicuous of these occurred at the top leadership levels of the Socialist Unity Party, its affiliated mass organiz-ations, and the substitutions of government. In a similar effort at shedding its legacies, the *Volkskammer* turned itself, within weeks, into a real parlia-ment – a forum for debate and decision-making – after years of rubber-stamping decrees. Although many *Volkskammer* members resigned their seats and made room for new faces, these new faces came from the old parties – parties which had lost the confidence of the population. The failure to revitalize the *Volkskammer* by changing its composition and smashing the 'National Front' meant that the transformations of procedure, agenda and participation which did occur found no echo among the people anxious to see innovation and new beginnings. These, however, seemed to emanate from the so-called Round Table, a forum of parties and new oppositions which worked alongside, and in competition with, the *Volkskammer* and set itself a similar agenda of constitutional reform.

For a short time the GDR seemed to have created a democratic process of its own (see Chapter 8; also Thaysen, 1990a; 1990b: 257–308). By February 1990 the main groups of the Round Table had joined the Modrow government and were therefore less outspoken while the election campaign for March 1990 superimposed the West German model of party democracy on the East. The Round Table had been founded on the divide between the political forces of the old GDR and those of the new, and aimed to agree between them the image of the future GDR. However, the elections of March 1990 relocated that divide to run between those political groups and parties which found a West German equivalent and those who did not.

Even before the Round Table met for the last time in February 1990 to receive the draft constitution of a refurbished GDR, it had collapsed in substance. When spearheading the takeover of the Stasi buildings on 15 January 1990, the Round Table tried to respond to the people's desire to find and punish the guilty. The population's calls for revenge, retribution, punishment and show trials were hardly met by the Round Table's solution to set up a special committee to investigate the problem. It had lost touch with the current mood: the parties with Western partners had accepted that they would join the Federal Republic not upgrade the GDR; the groups which remained committed to upgrading the GDR were largely speaking for themselves with neither a base of political support nor an electoral following.

After unification, therefore, the institutions and processes to reshape political life and constitute a platform for political participation had not emerged from the period of system collapse, but had been imported and transplanted from the West. This applies to the organizational structures and policy priorities and, to a large extent also, to the new élites. Like the institutional frameworks in which they operated, many were drafted in from the old *Länder*, often on temporary secondment or as Western advisors to groom their Eastern counterparts for the new political and administrative roles. Social and political participation had to be relearned and adapted to the Western model.

The disintegration of the industrial base and the onset of labour market uncertainties and mass unemployment within months of unification extinguished the exuberance and hope which had inspired the street politics of 1989 and 1990. With everyday life unpredictable, with employment doubtful and dominated by new rules of achievement and efficiency, interest in local issues and in political participation faded. The year 1990 saw a decline in electoral participation even before the impact of unification on the fabric of society and people's lifestyles had become fully evident. The following year, 1991, brought the virtual collapse of party memberships, with all political parties losing members. Compared with mid-1990, the organizational strength of new ventures, such as the SPD and the CDU, had been reduced by half; the PDS had been reduced to a rump of staunch activists while New Forum was only kept alive by the last-ditch efforts of a small circle of increasingly isolated and embittered missionaries of a better GDR.[1] In the wake of the social and economic dislocations in the new

Länder the political involvement of the first hour did not last. In April 1990, for instance, the new women's movement in Leipzig could bring several thousand demonstrators into the streets to call for equality, abortion, rights and childcare facilities. Less than two months later, only a couple of hundred turned out to protest about the threatened closure of nurseries, and most of these were nursery nurses and other staff who worked there. In March 1991, the German Metalworkers Union tried to rekindle the mood of public protest: 25,000 followed the call 'Leipzig puts pressure on Bonn', but the original plan to revitalize the Monday demonstrations was quickly abandoned when a motley crowd of the old communist Left and the new extreme Right exploited the opportunity to voice their anti-democratic sentiments.[2]

Generally speaking, former citizens of the GDR are more doubtful than their Western counterparts about the future of democracy in a united Germany. In 1990, one in three believed that democracy might give way to a dictatorship (Schöppner, 1990: 24). Less content with their personal situation than West Germans, 37 per cent in the East compared with 65 per cent in the West thought their economic circumstances were good or very good (Schöppner 1990: 19). East Germans paint a bleak picture of the future: nearly 80 per cent rated the economic situation in their party of the country as bad or very bad; just 2 per cent of West Germans did so for their part of the country (Schöppner, 1990: 18).

Overwhelmed by everyday difficulties and thrust into a survival culture which is not dissimilar from that experienced in Germany in the immediate post-war years, Germans in the East are, above all, interested in their own personal situation. Since the collapse of the socialist political system failed to give rise to new institutional settings in which people participated during the transition and might continue to participate, the political agendas and the avenues for political participation are those which have been imported from the West. Continuities of involvement have no place in a political culture in which the implementation of prefabricated models of organization and purpose are the order of the day. This format seemed to work at first, when participation in the new structures also shielded activists from accusations that they might have been socialist functionaries and Stasi chattel in the past. As normalization swelled the economic and social uncertainties, East Germans reacted in the only way they have known: a cautious retreat into the private sphere.

With less fear of communicating than under socialist and Stasi rule, with better access to consumer goods, and endowed with the freedoms of mobility, creed, and choice on which democratic polities are founded, the citizens of the former GDR are exploring the meanings of democracy. In the first instance, it meant uncertainties for them: an end to the prescribed lifestyle, the administered grid in which each individual life would be contained. A sense of novel opportunities, of being able to break free from the shackles of collectivism, has begun to inspire the young generation, especially since work creation measures and retraining programmes have brightened personal prospects and promised an everyday culture where personal achievements would be rewarded. Like West Germans, East Germans believe in work and achievement as key dimensions of self-realization. Yet, among older generations a sense of demotion and hopelessness predominates. With few prospects of reintegration into the labour market and even fewer of regaining their former status at work and in their social environments, 40–55 year-old East Germans constitute a new sceptical generation for whom democracy may not be able to meet their expectations and who are likely to hanker for the life and political system they used to know.

At the other end of the generational spectrum, some young East Germans have opted out more forcefully: the skinheads and neo-Nazis defied the command culture for young people during the closing years of socialism and continue to defy the institutional settings and the political attitudes which underpin the new democracy in Germany (Kolinsky, 1992). Seizing on National Socialist ideas, actions and symbols, the young German Nazis espouse a past which both German states deemed untenable and which has been a focal point of protest for that very reason. Moreover, the young Nazis (and this applies to those from the new *Länder* as well as to the old) tend to be at the lower end of the socioeconomic spectrum with little education, few qualifications, outdated skills, and under threat of unemployment. In the new *Länder*, many of them did not even attempt to find a foothold in the new enterprise culture. Having left school early, they face a life without qualifications or secure employment. The mass housing of densely packed, cramped and poor-quality apartments which has been the hallmark of residential construction in urban areas of the GDR, has become a breeding-ground for despondency and social aggression. Among the young, it has taken on a neo-Nazi tinge and the foul taste of hostility against non-German residents or newcomers. Among the older generations, who had built their lives in the GDR and who seemed to have lost their personal future, the radicalism of the young has a strong, albeit more passive, echo.

The chance for democracy and the success of the West German model seems to rest on two legacies of the old GDR and their new political function: first, socialism conditioned the East German population to a certain degree of passivity, often laced with bouts of dissatisfaction, in exchange for a predictable living environment provided by the state. This legacy is likely to persuade the older generations to support the new political system, despite a sense of economic and social disappointment in the post-unification Germany.

The second legacy concerns the younger generations: their perceptions of the old GDR had increasingly been one of stagnation, of lack of opportunities and of stalemate (*Chancenlosigkeit*). For them, the social *Chancenlosigkeit* has given way to manifold opportunities, new careers and new challenges to fail or to succeed. When funds were released in mid-1991 for retraining and a professional new beginning, younger men and women were eager to grasp these opportunities. The new administrations are staffed by relearners from the young and middle generations. They perceive democracy as securing a living, building a career and shaping their own area of responsibility both at work and at home. The uncertainties about economic survival and personal well-being in the new Eastern regions need to be resolved before the social opportunities will sustain broader political participation and consolidate the democratic political culture which has been instituted there from the West.

Notes

1 Author's Interview with Bärbel Bohley, 5 October 1991; Steffen Wilsdorf, University of Leipzig, 21 August 1991.
2 Author's Interview with Ruth Stachura, Equalization Officer, City of Leipzig, 22 August 1991; Marion Ziegler, *Fraueninitiative* Leipzig, 21 August 1991.

References

Backes, U. and Jesse, E. (1985), *Totalitarismus, Extremismus und Terrorismus* (2nd edn), Opladen: Leske & Budrich.
Bahrmann, H. and Links, C. (1990), *Wir sind das Volk. Die DDR im Aufbruch-Eine Chronik*, Berlin: Aufbau Verlag and Wuppertal; Hammer Verlag.
Baumann, E. *et. al.* (1990), *Der Fischer Welt Almanach. Sonderband DDR*, Frankfurt/Main: Fischer.
Beyme, K. von (1985), *Political Parties in Western Democracies*, Aldershot: Gower.
Bickhardt, S. (ed.) (1988), *Recht ströme wie Wasser. Christen in der DDR für Absage an Praxis und Prinzip der Abgrenzung*, Berlin: Wichern Verlag.
Blanke, T. and Erd R. (eds) (1990), *DDR. Ein Staat vergeht*, Frankfurt am Main.
Chronik der Ereignisse in der DDR. Edition Deutschlandarchiv (1989), Cologne: Verlag Wissenschaft und Politik.
Dalton, R. J. (1988), *Citizens' Politics in Western Democracies*, New Jersey: Chatham House.
Dalton, R. J. (1989), *Politics in West Germany*, Boston: Little Brown.
Deutschland Archiv Redaktion (1985), *Umweltprobleme und Umweltbewusstsein in der DDR*, Cologne: Wissenschaft und Politik.

Evers, T. (1991), 'Volkssouveränität im Verfahren. Zur Verfassungsdiskussion über direkte Demokratie', *Aus Politik und Zeitgeschichte*, **B23**, May, pp. 30–45.

Feist U. and Hoffmann H. J. (1991), 'Landtagswahlen in der ehemaligen DDR am 14. Oktober 1990', *Zeitschrift für Parlamen fragen*, **1**.

Fricke, K. W. (1984), *Opposition und Widerstand in der DDR. Ein politischer Report*, Cologne: Wissenschaft und Politik.

Fricke, K. W. (1989), *Die DDR-Staatssicherheit. Entwicklung – Strukturen – Aktionsfelder* (2nd edn), Cologne: Wissenschaft und Politik.

Friedrich, W. (1990), 'Mentalitätswandlungen der Jugend in der DDR', *Aus Politik und Zeitgeschichte*, **B16–17**.

Friedrich, W-U. (1989), *DDR. Deutschland zwischen Elbe und Oder* (2nd edn), Stuttgart: Kohlhammer.

Gebhardt, J. (1991), 'Direkt-demokratische Institutionen und repräsentative Demokratie im Verfassungsstaat; *Aus Politik und Zeitgeschichte*, **B23**, May, pp. 16–30.

Gegenwartskunde. Sonderheft Revolution in der DDR, **1**, 1991.

Gibowski, W. (1990), 'Demokratischer (Neu-) Beginn in der DDR. Dokumentation und Analyse der Wahl vom 18. März 1990', *Zeitschrift für Parlamentsfragen*, **1**, pp. 5–21.

Glaessner, G-J. (1990), 'Vom "realen Sozialismus" zur Selbstbestimmung. Ursachen und Konsequenzen der Systemkrise in der DDR', *Aus Politik und Zeitgeschichte*, **B1–2**, pp. 3–20.

Grass, G. (1990), 'The Business Blitzkrieg', *Weekend Guardian*, **20–21** November, pp. 4–7.

Greven, M. T. (1987), *Parteimitglieder. Ein empirischer Essay über das Alltagsbewusstsein in Parteien*, Opladen: Westdeutscher Verlag.

Gotschlich, H. (1990), *Ausstieg aus der DDR. Junge Leute im Konflikt*, Berlin: Verlag der Nation.

Grundmann, S. (1990), 'Aussem- und Binnenmigration der DDR 1989: Versuch einer Bilanz', *Deutschlandarchiv*, pp. 1422–32.

Helwig, G. and Urban, D. (1987), *Kirchen und Gesellschaft in beiden deutschen Staaten*, Cologne: Wissenschaft und Politik.

Henrich, R. (1989), *Der vormundschaftliche Staat. Vom Versagen des real existierenden Sozialismus*, Reinbek: Rowohlt.

Jesse, E. (1990), *Elections. The Federal Republic of Germany in Comparison*, Oxford: Berg.

Kershaw, I. (ed.) (1990), *Weimar: Why did German Democracy Fail?*, London: Weidenfeld and Nicholson.

Kleemann, C. (1990), 'Die Chance für Demokratie in Rostock' *Platform. Freies Wochenblatt für Politik und Kultur*, (19), 22 May.

Klessmann, C. (1991), 'Opposition und Dissent in der Geschichte der DDR', *Aus Politik und Zeitgeschichte*, **B5**.

Klingemann, H-D. and Volkens, A. (1991), 'Die Programme der politischen Parteien: eine empirischer Vergleich.' Unpublished paper delivered at the ASGP Conference, Leicester, April.

Knabe, H. (ed.) (1989), *Aufbruch in eine andere DDR. Reformer und Oppositionelle zur Zukunft ihres Landes*, Reinbek: Rowohlt.

Knabe, H. (1990), 'Politische Opposition in der DDR. Ursprünge, Programmatik, Perspektiven', *Aus Politik und Zeitgeschichte*, **B1–2**, pp. 12–32.

Kolinsky, E. (1984), *Parties, Opposition and Society in West Germany*, London: Croom Helm.

Kolinsky, E. (ed.) (1987), *Opposition in Western Europe*, London: PSI and Croom Helm.

Kolinsky, E. (1991a), 'Socio-Economic Change and Political Culture in West Germany' in J. Gaffney and E. Kolinsky (eds), *Political Culture in France and Germany. A Contemporary Perspective*, London: Routledge, pp. 34–68.

Kolinsky, E. (1991b) 'The Euro-Germans. National Identity and European Integration in Germany' in J. Howorth and M. McLean (eds), *Europeans on Europe*, London: Macmillan

Kolinsky, E. (1992), 'A Future for Right Extremism in Germany?' in P. Hainsworth (ed.), *Right Extremism in Europe*, Brighton: Wheatsheaf.

Kuby, E. (1990), *Der Preis der Einheit. Ein deutsches Europa formt sein Gesicht*, Hamburg: Konkret Verlag.

Lapp, P. J. (1988), *Die 'befreundeten Parteien' der SED. DDR-Blockparteien heute*, Cologne: Verlag Wissenschaft und Politik.

Maron, M. (1990), 'Die Schriftsteller und das Volk', *Der Spiegel*, **1**.

Meier, A. (1990), 'Abschied von der sozialistischen Ständegesellschaft', *Aus Politik und Zeitgeschichte*, **B16–17**.

Michels, R. (1954), *Zur Soziologie des Parteiwesens in der modernen Demokratie. Untersuchungen über die oligarchischen Tendenzen des Gruppenlebens*, (2nd edn), Stuttgart: Deutsche Verlagsanstalt.

Minnerup, G. (1989), 'Politische Opposition in der DDR vor dem Hintergrund der Reformdiskussion in Osteuropa' in *Die DDR im 40 Jahr. Geschichte, Situation, Perspektiven. 22. Tagung zum Stand der DDR Forschung, Wissenschaft und Politik*, Cologne, pp. 66–74.

Mitter, A. and Wolle, S. (1990), *Ich liebe euch doch alle! Befehle und Lageberichte des Mfs*, Berlin.

Müller-Enbergs, H. (1990), *Demokratie Jetzt*, Berliner Arbeithefte und Berichte zur sozialwissenschaftlichen Forschung no. 19, January.

Niedermayer, O. and Stöss, R. (eds) (forthcoming), *Parteienforschung in der Deutschland*, Opladen: Westdeutscher Verlag.

Niethammer, L. (1990), *Die volkseigene Erfahrung. Eine Archäologie der Lebens in der Industrieprovinz der DDR*. vol. I, Reinbek: Rowohlt.

Oberreuter, H. and Mintzel A. (eds) (1987), *Parteien in der Bundesrepublik Deutschland*, Munich: Olzog.

Oberreuter, H. (1990), 'Politische Parteien: Stellung und Funktion im Verfassungssystem der Bundesrepublik', in H. Oberreuter and A. Mintzel, *Parteien in der Bundesrepublik*, Munich: Olzog, pp. 15–39.

Padgett, S. and Burkett, T. (1986), *Political Parties and Elections in West Germany. The Search for a New Stability*, London: Hurst & Co.

Rohe, K. (ed.) (1990), *Elections, Parties and Political Traditions. Social Foundations of German Parties and Party Systems*, 1867–1987, Oxford: Berg.

Röhrich, W. (1983), *Die verspätete Demokratie. Zur politischen Kultur der Bundesrepublik Deutschland*, Cologne: Diederichs.

Ronge, V. (1990), 'Die soziale Integration von DDR-Übersiedlern in der Bundesrepublik Deutschland', *Aus Politik und Zeitgeschichte*, **B1–2**.

Roth, R. and Rucht D. (eds) (1987), *Neue soziale Bewegungen in der Bundesrepublik Deutshland*, Bundeszentrale für politische Bildung.

Sarcinelli, U. (ed.) (1987), *Politikvermittlung. Beiträge zur politischen Kommunikationskultur*, Stuttgart: Bonn, Aktuell.

Schöppner, K-P. (1990), 'Mehr Macht, mehr vertrauen' in *Spiegel Spezial: 162 Tage Deutsche Geschichte; das halbe Jahr der Gewaltlosen Revolution*, Hamburg.

Schüddekopf, C. (ed.) (1990), *Wir sind das Volk*, Reinbek: Rowohlt.

Smith, G. (1986), *Democracy in Western Germany. Parties and Politics in the Federal Republic* (3rd edn), Aldershot: Gower.

Smith, G. (1990), *Politics in Western Europe* (5th edn), Aldershot: Dartmouth.

Smith, G., Paterson, W. E. and Merkl, P. H. (eds) (1989), *Developments in West German Politics*, Basingstoke: Macmillan.

Sontheimer, K. and Bleeck, W. (1975), *The Government and Politics of East Germany*, London: Hutchinson.

Spittmann, I. and Helwig, G. (1989), *Chronik der Ereignisse in der DDR, Edition Deutschland Archiv*, Cologne: Wissenschaft und Politik.

Staritz, D. (1989), 'DDR-Geschichte im deutsch-deutschen Wissenschaftsdialog', *Aus Politik und Zeitgeschichte*, **B34**, pp. 10–18.

Süss, W. (1990), '*Revolution und Öffentlichkeit in der DDR*', Deutschland Archiv, pp. 907–919.

Tempel, K. G. (1990), *Die Parteien in der Bundesrepublik Deutschland* (2nd rev. edn), Berlin: Landeszentrale für politische Bildungsarbeit.

Thaysen, U. (1990a), *Der Runde Tisch*, Opladen: Westdeutscher Verlag.

Thaysen, U. (1990b) 'Der Runde Tisch. Oder: Wer war das Volk?', part I, *Zeitschrift für Parlamentsfragen*, **1**, pp. 71–100; part II, *Zeitschrift für Parlamentsfragen*, **2**, pp. 257–308.

Urwin, D. W. and Paterson, W. E. (1990), *Politics in Western Europe Today*, Harlow: Longman.

Voigt, D., Voss, W. and Meck, S. (1987), *Sozialstruktur der DDR: eine Einführung*, Darmstadt: Wissenschaftliche Buchgesellschaft.

Wasmuth, U. C. (ed.) (1989), *Alternativen zur alten Politik? Neue soziale Bewegungen in der Diskussion*, Darmstadt: Wissenschaftliche Buchgesellschaft.

Weber, C. (1990), *Alltag einer friedlichen Revolution. Notizen aus der DDR*, Berlin: Quell Verlag.

Weber, H. (1985), *Geschichte der DDR*, Munich: Deutscher Taschenbuch Verlag.

Weidenfeld, W. and Zimmermann, H. (1989), *Deutschland Handbuch: Eine doppelte Bilans 1949–1987*, Munich: Hanser.

Weilemann, P. R. *et. al.* (1990a), *Nichtkommunistische Parteien und Gruppierungen in der DDR. Struktur und Zielvorstellungen*. Forschungsinstitut der Konrad

Adenauer Stiftung in Zusammenarbeit mit dem Institut für politische Bildung, Dokumentariche Übersicht: Sankt Augustin.

Weilemann, P. R. *et. al.* (1990b), *Parteien im Aufbruch: Nichtkommunistische Parteien und politische Vereinigungen in der DDR*, Deutschland-Report Nr.8, Melle; Knoth Verlag.

Wolf, C. (1989), 'Befreite Sprache und Gefühlswörter', *Tageszeitung* (taz), 9 November.

Woods, R. (1986), *Opposition in the GDR*, Basingstoke: Macmillan.

Index